The New
Southern-Latino Table

The University of North Carolina Press Chapel Hill

The New
Southern-Latino Table

Recipes That Bring Together the Bold and Beloved Flavors
of Latin America & the American South

Sandra A. Gutierrez

All rights reserved. Manufactured in the United States of America.
Designed by Courtney Leigh Baker with Tema Larter and set in
Odile and Gotham by Rebecca Evans. The paper in this book meets
the guidelines for permanence and durability of the Committee on
Production Guidelines for Book Longevity of the Council on Library
Resources. The University of North Carolina Press has been a
member of the Green Press Initiative since 2003.

Library of Congress Cataloging-in-Publication Data
Gutierrez, Sandra A.
The new southern-Latino table: recipes that bring together
the bold and beloved flavors of Latin America and the American
South / by Sandra A. Gutierrez.
p. cm.
Includes bibliographical references and index.
ISBN 978-0-8078-3494-7 (cloth: alk. paper)
1. Cooking, Latin American. 2. Cooking, American—Southern style.
3. Cookbooks. I. Title.
TX716.A1G885 2011   641.598—dc22   2011005516

cloth   15 14 13 12 11   5 4 3 2 1

To my beloved **Luis, Alessandra, & Niccolle** for being my inspiration and for encouraging me to do what I love

contents

acknowledgments ix

introduction 1

the basics 9

boquitas & southern starters 39

salads & cold dishes 79

main dishes 105

soups, stews, & braises 141

covered dishes & casseroles 165

vegetables & side dishes 193

desserts 219

glossary 253

navigating a latin tienda 257

sources for ingredients 263

selected reading 265

index 267

SIDEBARS

How to Make Proper Southern Biscuits 20 • Fearless Frying 25

The Flatbreads of Latin America 45 • A Dissertation on Mayonnaise 57

Cold Drinks and Other Libations 74 • Potatoes 93 • Chile Primer 98

The First Global Culinary Exchange 102 • Corn: The Gold of the

Americas 104 • All You Need to Know about Cooking with Chiles 116

The Cilantro Gene 121 • A Brief History of Pork in the Americas 126

Three Vegetables, Two Cultures 162 • Making Pastry by Hand 173

The Southern-Latino Garden 179 • Rice 200 • Tamales: The First

Southern-Latino Recipe Exchange 207 • The African Diaspora

and Food 216 • Southern Biscuits 226 • Buttermilk: Southerners'

Secret Ingredient 230 • A Brief History of Sugar and Candy in Latin

America 245 • The Love Apple of the Americas 250

Color photographs follow pages 68 and 164

Additional photographs may be viewed at sandraskitchenstudio.com

acknowledgments

To my partners at UNC Press, my heartfelt gratitude to Elaine Maisner, my editor, who upon first sight believed in this book as much as I did and nurtured it from its inception. To David Perry, who discovered potential in my sample chapter. Thanks to others in the editorial department, including Tema Larter and Mary Caviness. Special thanks to Gina Mahalek and Dino Battista and all the rest of the staff in the Press's marketing department, and thanks to the staff in the design and production department. Thanks to Vicky Wells, too, in the administration department.

Thank you, Lisa Ekus, my agent and friend, for embracing this book from infancy and for cradling it all the way into my publisher's arms, and thanks to Sally Ekus and your brilliant staff. Thank you, Jane Falla, for polishing my proposal until it shone.

It took a family to make this book; thanks to mine for unconditional support and for patiently waiting for me to shoot photos before every meal. To my beloved husband Luis: thank you for teaching me to see through the eyes of a camera. I owe infinite gratitude to our daughters, Alessandra and Niccolle, who inspire and move me, and who read every single recipe and helped me test and edit them.

Special thanks to my friend Nancie McDermott for opening the door and urging me to write this book. Thanks to dear friends: Fred Thompson, Belinda Ellis, Maria Baez-Kijac, Robin Asbell, and Jill O'Connor; and to Virginia Willis for your support and for liking my fried chicken. Thank you, Toni Allegra, for telling me I had an important message to share and for reminding me to embrace my ethnicity, and to Jean Anderson, who told me to write what I know. To Marilyn Markel, Jay White, Deborah Miller,

and my friends at A Southern Season in Chapel Hill, and to Kara Wurts at Williams-Sonoma in Durham: thanks for inviting me to break bread with amazing students, and special thanks to my cooking students. David and Dorothea Kelsey: many thanks for unforgettable evenings of cooking, testing, and tasting together.

Heartfelt thanks to the authors who taught me to love and respect Southern and Latin food. To all cooks who cross culinary borders, adapting and creating every day: let's not forget from whence we came and always strive to embrace where we are. I thank you, God, with humility, for blessings received.

The New
Southern-Latino Table

Born in the United States to Latin American parents, I moved at a young age with my family to Guatemala, my parents' homeland, and was instantly immersed in a world of melded cultures. My first words, I'm told, were in English, and I grew up as a student in an American school in the middle of Guatemala City. I learned the words to two national anthems, the pledges of allegiance to the U.S. flag and the Guatemalan flag, and the histories of two different cultures. Our school cafeteria was as likely to serve hamburgers and tuna salad one day as it was to offer milanesas and panes con frijol the next. Brownies and doughnuts shared the dessert counter with arroz con leche and buñuelos. Food at home was also a reflection of my fused reality: we ate tamales for special occasions, huevos rancheros for birthdays, and Carolina hot dogs every chance we got. We celebrated the Day of the Dead with fiambre, a salad composed of pickled vegetables, deli meats, pig's feet, sausages, cheeses, and olives, and Thanksgiving with a turkey dinner that included all the trimmings.

I spoke Spanish at home, English at school, and "Spanglish" with friends— and I still have a Latin accent today. I was lucky enough to travel widely throughout the world, but I regularly spent summer vacations in the United States. I embraced my American home and at the same time nurtured my ethnic roots. Taught to be proud of my birthplace, I learned at an early age that my U.S. citizenship was an honor and a responsibility. I was in my teens when civil war ravaged Guatemala, and I became aware that ownership of a U.S. passport meant hope for my entire family. "If ever things get desperately dangerous we could go back to the United States," my parents would tell me; and although at times it did become desperately dangerous, they remained in Guatemala. I, on the other hand, returned home to the United States. I had a wonderful college experience in the Northeast and then moved to the South, where I experienced the joy of starting a family.

I have a long personal history with food, beginning in the family kitchen in Guatemala. My culinary epiphany came at an early age, in the kitchens of my grandmother and my much-adored aunt, tía Maria. While my cousins busied themselves playing outdoors, I could always be found inside, working in the kitchen. My family was lucky enough to have hired cooks, and I was always an eager student of their craft. At first, I was given easy tasks, such as shelling fresh peas or removing the pebbles from mounds of beans. However, as I grew up, my culinary assignments advanced and I was put in charge of draping pastry over pies, wrapping tamales, frying kettle chips, or shaping empanadas side by side with the cooks. My grandmother oversaw the cooking activities, often abandoning her guests long enough to add the finishing touches to a meal. Nothing left the kitchen without her approval.

However, it's my tía Maria, who was both a writer (she wrote a society column way back when newspapers had one) and a famous caterer in Guatemala City, whom I most take after; it was an inevitable result of the countless hours she spent teaching me to cook in her kitchen or in mine, often inviting me to help her craft tiny appetizers or garnish sweet miniatures for her events. It's from her that I learned the knack for creating recipes out of whatever ingredients are on hand. She passed on to me a true passion for food and a deep respect for technique that has shaped the way I teach my classes today.

When I first moved to Durham, North Carolina, in the mid-1980s, I was a young bride eager to tackle cooking in my tiny, pink kitchen. While shopping, I would often encounter both familiar and unfamiliar ingredients, and each day brought forth the discovery of a new dish. "Hola y'all!" became my family's motto. As my husband, who also hails from Guatemala, spent his days in graduate school at nearby Duke University, I experimented with newfound ingredients, substituting what I could to re-create the flavors of our youth spent in Guatemala.

Combining flavors came naturally to me, more out of necessity than whim, because finding the ingredients I needed— such as fresh chiles, dried corn husks, and tomatillos—was a near impossible feat at that time. I recall field trips to Wellspring grocery (now a Whole Foods store) on Ninth Street—trekking across town just to purchase a bag of dried black beans. No one had heard of masa harina (nixtamalized cornmeal that has been dried and pulverized and that is used to make tortillas and other Latin dishes); fresh cilantro and tamales were faraway fantasies.

I would eagerly await care packages sent to me by my uncle who lived in Florida. These were usually filled with jars of annatto seeds to make my yellow rice concoctions and canned chipotles to add to my sauces. Dried chorizo, guava paste, and chile powders were always a welcome sight.

At first, I improvised with flavors, mixing ingredients until my foods resembled those I remembered from my childhood. I substituted finely ground cornmeal for masa and tinned chiles for fresh serranos. I became more ambitious and learned to make my own dulce de leche from scratch. After a few cans of boiling condensed milk blew up, I finally learned how to make it the safe way. My first tamales were wrapped in aluminum foil in lieu of corn husks; they were not like the ones we remembered, but they fed our nostalgia.

By now, I've spent most of my life in the South. I've cooked with many fellow Southerners, eaten in their homes, invited them to my family table, exchanged recipes, learned to cook in their kitchens, and taught them how to cook. To put it simply, Southern food found my soul. I learned to respect the ingredients and cooking techniques of my new home, and I mastered the skills of handling biscuits lightly—just enough to keep them tender and make them rise. I discovered grits, and fell in love with fried green tomatoes and pimiento cheese. As my two worlds melded, so did the food in those worlds. The Latina discovered her Southern belle within, and it was magic for me.

Today, my children are likely to ask for barbecue pulled pork with a side of guacamole, and hushpuppies slathered in tamarind butter. We say "y'all come back" and "adiós" in the same sentence and drink iced tea and coffee at the same meal. Mine is one of the millions of American families of diverse ethnic backgrounds whose food symbolizes the dichotomy of homes and the blending of cultures. We are some of the many Latinos—from all parts of the Americas—who call the South home. Throughout the years we have grown from a sprinkling of people here and there, to a gargantuan number of individuals who unexpectedly and by happenstance are effecting change in the culinary landscape of the South.

The culinary phenomenon occurring in the South is not taking place in a controlled manner; it's occurring serendipitously, through the merging of peoples over time, naturally. Latin and Southern cuisines are blending into new combinations that complement and build on existing dishes of both cultures.

As more Latinos enter the social, political, and economic worlds of the South, inevitable—though subtle—culinary revolutions are taking place. Latinos are finding it easy to become passionate about Southern food.

Likewise, Southerners are embracing all types of Latin cuisine. The new Latino influence in the South—stretching from Florida and Louisiana, Kentucky and Alabama, Tennessee and Mississippi, Arkansas and Georgia, and into the Carolinas and Virginia—can be easily detected in a visible explosion of tiendas (stores), taquerias (taco stands), and simple comedores (eateries) throughout the area. Schoolkids all across the South—and the rest of the country—are as likely to eat enchiladas and tacos in their school cafeterias as they are hamburgers and French fries. In fact, salsa and corn chips have long outsold potato chips and dip. However, other Latin dishes are also slowly but surely becoming part of the new Southern food scene—churros and burritos, for example, are a common sight at Southern fairs and festivals.

The early twenty-first century brought forth a new influx of Latinos into the South. This is a diverse and ambitious group that includes first-generation workers as well as second- and third-generation, English-speaking Latinos, many of whom are professionals in the medical, political, business, education, military, and technology sectors. All of us are proud of our heritage and hungry for the food of our ancestors—as were previous waves of immigrants to the United States. In recent years, Latinos have made homes in the South at some of the fastest national rates, and large populations have settled in such states as Georgia, North Carolina, South Carolina, Arkansas, and Tennessee. These Latinos have brought forth their own traditional ingredients, cooking techniques, and gastronomic history and are having a great time with them in the culinary context of their new homes.

What distinguishes this new American culinary movement is that dozens of different cultures thrive in Latin America. Latinos in North America don't share a single culinary voice because they don't share one within Latin America either. This is the elusive reality that prevents Latinos from being boxed together into a group. As Jorge Ramos, author of *The Latino Wave*, puts it: "There are no Latinos living outside the United States. By definition a Latino is someone who was born in Latin America (or is of Latin American descent) but currently lives in the United States. . . . A Latino is, by definition, a mix of cultures, languages, identities, possibilities and times, both past and future."

Outside of the United States you will not find "Latinos" but Mexicans, Argentineans, Guatemalans, and dozens of other nationalities, each with their own nationalistic pride. We come in all different colors and have very different food histories. The key implication here is that the Southern-Latino movement truly represents multiple cultures imparting changes and contributions to another. So, for example, the new Southern-Latino movement is not a Mexican movement alone—as is the case of Southwestern cuisine, in which Mexican elements do predominate. The Southern-Latino movement is, rather, catapulted by immigrants whose culinary contributions are as multicultural and multifaceted as they are. Up until very recently, the Southern-Latino movement has eluded the attention of the public and the food media, I think, because it's easier to detect a movement in which just two cultures intermingle than it is to detect one in which many more cuisines are involved.

Food tells the story of faraway places and of people long gone. From the beginning of time, peoples and civilizations have engaged in the kinds of cultural exchanges that have ultimately defined entire regional culinary landscapes. That is fascinating, but what is most exciting to me is that food is also a doorway into the future: a premonitory glimpse into the culinary revolutions to come. In my view, the real American melting pot is always changing, and it becomes most tangible within the context of the kitchen, where our cuisine has been shaped by a hodgepodge of flavors, an amalgamation of cultures, and an explosion of ethnic ingredients. The birth of new dishes continues today within the United States in our new millennium, and nowhere is this gastronomic revolution more apparent today than in the American South.

Both Latin American and Southern food developed through the intermingling of world cultures in one territory. The food of Latin America embraces a vast grouping of ingredients, techniques, and traditions of peoples from more than twenty countries, encompassing two continents and the Caribbean region. And, while for the purpose of this book I refer to "Latin cuisine," I highlight as much as possible the many individual traditions that comprise it. Both Southern and Latin food traditions have been shaped by numerous influences that have lent their flavors and histories to their dishes. Both cuisines have been influenced by people of three ethnicities: indigenous (Native Americans in the South and Aztecs, Mayans, Incas, and others in Latin America), African, and European. The two cuisines have in common a plethora of basic ingredients, such as tomatoes, corn, pork, beans, sugar, squash, potatoes, and nuts. They also share analogous cooking techniques such as barbecuing, braising, roasting, and deep frying. Of course, these similarities go only so far—it's equally fascinating to see how differently these common elements are interpreted in the South and in Latin America. But here lies the heart of this book: I'm not surprised but thrilled that, having finally met in the same territory, these culinary traditions correlate, intermingle, and evolve into one culinary movement. I call it the Southern-Latino movement.

Today, it's relatively easy to find a cornucopia of Latin ingredients in the United States; most cities and small towns boast at least one specialty store or tienda that carries them. Every time I teach a cooking class, my students want to know how to use these new ingredients. Their culinary inquisitiveness reflects the openness of the general public to exploring and enjoying new foods at an unprecedented rate. Great American chefs have been at the vanguard of the art of fusion in their state-of-the-art kitchens. In the 1980s, for example, Nuevo Latino cookery in Florida, which fuses Asian, Latin, and Caribbean cuisines, made its debut in restaurants. And Emeril Lagasse, well before he became the superstar he is today, showcased his New–New Orleans (NNO) Cuisine, in which Creole cookery met Asian, European, and New Mexican influences.

Great Southern food—and New Southern food trends—have been lovingly chronicled for decades by great Southern writers. In *The New Southern-Latino Table*, I'm writing about the culinary movement

in which grits are combined with roasted poblano peppers, chiles rellenos are stuffed with pimiento cheese, fried chicken is dipped into smoky ketchup, pulled pork is simmered in annatto and citrus broth, and sweet corn ice cream gets topped with hot praline sauce.

In this book you will find recipes with contemporary angles on both Southern and Latin classics, Latin twists on Southern favorites, and some of the original recipes that inspired them. You will find a chapter on basic recipes that make cameo appearances as building blocks for others. I've peppered the book's pages with historical background and fascinating facts in order to provide background for the recipes. And I've included many practical cooking tips that my cooking students have found helpful.

You will find recipes for appetizers, soups, salads, roasts, braises, fried treats, and desserts. I've also made sure to include plenty of dishes attractive to both children and adults, lots of vegetarian options, and recipes for those especially careful about eating in a healthy way.

These are my original recipes, my interpretation of the scope of flavors that have inspired me throughout my years in the South. Each dish came about in a random way, whenever creative muses were around to inspire me, and each is an answer to that burning question in my mind: "I wonder what would happen if I combined this with that?" It's my hope that when you try these recipes you'll wonder how something so different can taste so familiar to you.

I've created these recipes for your home kitchen. This is my interpretation of real home cooking, the types of meals you would find on any Southern or Latin table, but with a twist. There are no frills here, and very few bells and whistles. What I offer you instead are vibrant flavors and comforting dishes.

In addition to a list of sources for hard-to-find ingredients, at the end of the book you will find a chapter that will help you find your way around a Latin tienda, many of which are popping up all over the South. Although you are likely to find most ingredients in your local grocery stores, these guides will help you find any that they're lacking. I've also included a glossary of the culinary terms and ingredients that may be new to you.

With gratitude, respect, and pride, I wish to serve up a taste of how the culinary heritages of the Americas, in the widest sense, meet at the New Southern-Latino table, and prove, deliciously, that food brings people together. Here, there is something for everyone.

the basics

W henever I teach an introductory class on a new cuisine, I start with the basic recipes, or what I like to call the "building blocks." I find that my students feel much more confident about trying new dishes if they master the fundamentals of the cuisine, including understanding flavor bases, discovering key ingredients, and learning new cooking techniques. So consider this your guide and the chapter to refer to when you are looking for the practical tools that will make cooking from this book a simple undertaking.

Here you will find the recipes for items that appear several times in the book and play a supporting role to others, such as my Pimiento Sauce and my Classic Argentinean Chimichurri. Most of the others here can stand alone but also make great accompaniments to other dishes. But no matter how they're served, they provide you with all of the elements that make this new cuisine vibrant and exciting.

I believe that the difference between an average meal and an outstanding one is in the details, so I've included recipes for assorted breads, flavored butters, and exciting salsas that offer the finishing touches that make a meal exceptional. These are the ones that say: "You're special enough for me to go the extra step."

Because I recognize that we often look for easy ways to entertain, I've made sure that all of the recipes in this chapter are easy to follow. Some of them can be prepared well in advance and kept on hand to use whenever you want to cook from this book. Such is the case with the Achiote Oil and the Latin Pimiento Cheese, which will come in handy when you make other recipes such as Rice Fritters or my rendition of Shrimp 'n'

Grits. Likewise, my Basic Crepes can be prepared ahead of time, frozen, and thawed when ready to use.

Other recipes here can be made easily at the last minute, so they're perfect for impromptu entertaining: my Buttermilk and Pork Rind Biscuits come together so effortlessly that even if you don't have the time to prepare a New Southern-Latino meal every day, you can make them and present them as an accoutrement to any dish. The same is true for most of the recipes in this chapter.

This chapter features the basic ingredients that define Southern-Latino cuisine: explosive flavors with a dose of familiar comfort. All of these recipes offer an ideal complement to your everyday meals. The Brazilian-Style Cheese and Pimiento Buns, for instance, make a delectable substitute for any type of roll; and the Chiltepin Gremolata can be used instead of bottled hot sauce.

Spices and herbs are the most important elements in any cuisine. Thus I suggest you make space in your pantry for cumin, coriander (both seeds and ground), anise, annatto seeds (in paste, powder, and seed form), celery seed, Mexican cinnamon (canela), allspice, whole nutmeg, bay leaves, and assorted chile powders. Your refrigerator (or garden) should hold the fresh herbs you will be reaching for most often: cilantro, flat-leaf (Italian) parsley, sage, and thyme.

Latin American cuisine features all kinds of chiles, ranging from the fruity and mild to the fiery and hot, and my recipes reflect this. Be sure your pantry is stocked with a variety of chiles, including ancho, guajillo, chiles de árbol, and pasilla chiles. Stock up on canned chipotle chiles in adobo, assorted chile pastes, and preserved chiles, including chiltepines, ají panca, ají rocotó, and ají amarillo.

I also suggest you keep different types of flour in your pantry, among them all-purpose, self-rising, and yuca; stone-ground and finely ground cornmeal (both white and yellow); masa harina to make tamales; and arepa flour. All of them can be kept frozen for up to one year (let them come to room temperature before using). You can purchase grits in bulk and freeze them as well.

Be sure to have canned goods, like beans, low-sodium broth, hominy, dulce de leche, and cajeta on hand, as well as vegetable and olive oils, and jars of pimientos and guava jelly.

A word on cooking equipment: most of what you'll need you probably already own, like a blender (the most essential small appliance in Latin cuisine). A food processor isn't a necessity, but it can save you lots of time, as is the case with an electric mixer, and a few of my desserts require an ice cream maker. You'll also need an instant-read thermometer, casserole dishes in various sizes, baking sheets, assorted cake pans, and metal cooling racks. A deep fryer may prove helpful, although I prefer to use my enameled, cast-iron pans for this purpose. Keep your knives well sharpened and your basic ingredients at hand. Armed with this equipment, you'll be well on your way on a new culinary journey.

Simple ingredients must be of top quality to yield the best results. And cook with the seasons; fresh ingredients at their prime will always give you a great base to build upon.

Finally, when using the recipes in this book, keep in mind that unless specified to the contrary:

Eggs are large.

Heavy whipping cream is cream that contains at least 35 percent milk fat.

Butter is unsalted stick butter.

Lime, lemon, and orange juices are freshly squeezed.

Vanilla is always pure vanilla extract.

Preheat the oven for at least 20 minutes before baking.

A large skillet is 12 to 14 inches in diameter.

A medium skillet is 10 inches in diameter.

A small skillet is 8 to 9 inches in diameter.

A large sauté pan with high sides is 12 to 14 inches in diameter and
   3 to 4 inches tall.

A large Dutch oven is at least 5 to 6 quarts capacity.

achiote oil

Achiote (annatto seed) is a staple of Latin cuisine. Like saffron, achiote lends an exotic flavor to foods, but, unlike saffron, it is not expensive. It also is a natural food coloring that imparts yellow and vibrant orange hues to foods, from cheddar cheese to margarine. If you have ever had macaroni and cheese or a pimiento cheese sandwich made with orange cheddar, you've consumed annatto seeds. Annatto has different uses throughout Latin cuisine: as a color enhancer for rice dishes (in place of saffron), as a spice and colorant for sauces (such as *recados* for tamales), and as a flavoring for meats, chicken, or seafood wrapped in banana leaves. It is also used to color pastries, breads, and cake batters. Find jars of seeds or ready-to-use powder or paste in Latin tiendas and in some grocery stores. Here, seeds are steeped in warm oil to release their bright color.

1 cup of extra-virgin olive oil
¼ cup achiote seeds

NOTE: In order for rice to take on the color of achiote, it needs to be sautéed in the oil for several minutes before any liquid is added to it.

Place the oil and seeds in a small saucepan over medium heat. Heat the oil until small bubbles form on the sides of the pan, being careful not to burn the seeds, about 3–4 minutes. Remove from the heat promptly and steep the achiote until the oil has cooled completely, about 10 minutes. The seeds will turn a deep rust color, and the oil will take on a deep orange hue. (If the seeds turn black, they've burned, and you'll have to start over.) Strain the oil through a fine sieve and keep in a clean, glass jar for up to 1 month. *Makes 1 cup*

basic crepes

These thin, delicate pancakes are the base for South American canelones (cannelloni). Migration at the end of the nineteenth century and into the first half of the twentieth changed the culinary landscape of Latin America. Argentina was flooded by Europeans, among them Italian immigrants eager to find better fortune (*hacer la America*) in the New World. Similarly, German, British, and French immigrants arrived in Uruguay, Bolivia, and Chile. They brought along a tradition of cooking with these elegant pancakes. Crepes can be made ahead of time, wrapped in plastic wrap, and frozen for up to two months. Simply bring them to room temperature before using. If you're sure to let the batter rest so the flour can absorb the liquid fully, you'll be rewarded with tender, toothsome crepes.

1 cup whole milk
1 cup heavy whipping cream
4 eggs
1 cup all-purpose flour
¼ teaspoon salt
¼ teaspoon freshly ground nutmeg
2 tablespoons unsalted butter, melted

In a large bowl, whisk together the milk, cream, and eggs; slowly whisk in the flour. Whisk in the salt and nutmeg. Cover the bowl with plastic wrap and chill for 20 minutes (or up to 2 hours).

Heat a shallow, 9-inch nonstick pan over medium-high heat; brush lightly with melted butter. Ladle ¼ cup of the batter into the hot pan and tilt the pan in a circular motion so the batter covers the base of the pan. Cook for 1 minute on the first side, or until the edges of the crepe start to pull away from the side of the pan. To flip the crepe, tilt the pan so ½ inch of the crepe slides over the side of the pan; with your fingers, hold the edge and carefully turn the crepe over; cook for 10–15 seconds. Stack the completed crepes on a plate. *Makes 12–14 crepes*

NOTE: If your pan is larger or smaller than noted above, adjust the amount of batter accordingly. Crepes are thin and delicate, so if your pan is smaller, use less batter; if your pan is larger, more is required. The first crepe is almost always a throw away; you will quickly get the hang of these as you go on making them.

basic grits

Creamy, smooth grits epitomize the cuisine of the South. If you like corn, you will love this soft porridge made of hominy. Hominy is corn that has been alkalinized, that is, submerged in water with lye, in order to remove its coarse hull. It is then dried and ground finely into grits in the South and masa harina in Latin America. Grits need to be added slowly to boiling water, as they will clump if added too quickly. The tiny grains of hominy absorb liquid gradually, becoming perfectly plump after 20 minutes of constant, low-heat cooking. Instant grits are not a good substitute since they lack body and bite.

2 cups water
2 cups milk
1 cup stone-ground hominy grits
1 teaspoon salt, or to taste
¼ teaspoon freshly ground black pepper, or to taste
2 tablespoons unsalted butter

In a 2-quart saucepan, bring the water to a boil; add the milk and bring to a simmer. While whisking, add the grits in a thin stream; reduce the heat to medium-low. Cook, stirring, until they thicken, about 20 minutes. Remove from the heat; add the salt, pepper, and butter; stir until the butter is melted. *Serves 4-6*

béchamel sauce (salsa blanca)

This creamy, quintessentially French white sauce serves as the base of many recipes in this book. A thin version is used in recipes that require further cooking (for example, Kale Canelones with Country Ham and Mushrooms on page 185 and Macaroni con Queso on page 212). When it's used as a binder, as in my Crab Croquetas (page 55), béchamel needs to have a thicker consistency, much like mashed potatoes. Here I offer you both formulas. If you're not using the sauce right away, place a piece of waxed (or parchment) paper directly over the surface to prevent a skin from forming, which will make the batter lumpy. You can refrigerate béchamel for up to 24 hours, so feel free to make it ahead of time.

THIN BÉCHAMEL

4 tablespoons unsalted butter
¼ cup all-purpose flour
2 cups whole milk
¼ teaspoon freshly ground nutmeg
½ teaspoon salt

In a medium, heavy-bottomed saucepan, melt the butter over low heat. Add the flour and stir well to combine. Cook for 1–2 minutes, being careful not to let it turn golden or brown. Remove from the heat; add the milk, whisking vigorously until the mixture is smooth. Return to the heat; add the nutmeg and salt. Continue cooking and whisking until the mixture comes to a boil and thickens into a sauce of the consistency of heavy cream (about 10–12 minutes), being very careful not to let it scorch. Remove from the heat promptly. *Makes 2 cups*

THICK BÉCHAMEL

6 tablespoons unsalted butter
1 cup minced yellow onion
⅔ cup all-purpose flour
1 cup whole milk
¾ teaspoon salt
¼ teaspoon freshly ground nutmeg
⅛ teaspoon freshly ground
   white pepper

In a medium, heavy-bottomed saucepan, melt the butter over low heat; add the onions and cook for 3–4 minutes, or until soft but not browned. Add the flour and whisk well; cook for 1–2 minutes, being careful not to let it turn golden or brown. Remove from the heat; add the milk, whisking vigorously until the mixture is smooth. Return to the heat and continue cooking for 2 minutes, stirring constantly, being careful not to let the sauce burn. The sauce should be the consistency of thick mashed potatoes. Remove from the heat. Stir in the salt, nutmeg, and pepper; cool for a few minutes before using. *Makes 1¼ cups*

brazilian-style cheese and pimiento buns

These puffy, little buns are flavored with the essence of cheese. Breads made with yuca flour are typically prepared in South America. Bolivians call them *cuñapes* and Colombians make a larger version called *pandebono*. This recipe is inspired by the famous *pão de queijo*, or cheese bread, found in Brazil. Yuca flour has a texture similar to that of cornstarch and has a higher protein content than wheat flour, so these breads remain slightly sticky in the middle. They're simple to prepare using the food processor, a method I learned from my friend Maria Baez Kijac, author of *The South American Table*. I like to drop the dough into mini muffin tins using an ice cream scoop and enjoy watching them puff up in the oven. The addition of pimientos adds a Southern flair and imparts color. Serve these hot from the oven as a snack or in place of biscuits.

3 cups yuca or cassava flour
(found in Latin stores)
½ teaspoon salt
3 cups grated queso fresco
½ cup milk
½ cup vegetable oil
2 eggs
1 (2-ounce) jar diced
pimientos, drained

Preheat the oven to 425°F. Generously butter 48 mini muffin cups; set aside. In the bowl of a food processor fitted with a metal blade, combine the yuca flour and salt; pulse for 30 seconds. Add the cheese, milk, oil, eggs, and pimientos; process until smooth, 2–3 minutes. Transfer the batter to a bowl, cover with plastic wrap, and let it rest for 10 minutes. Use a 2-inch ice cream scoop to drop the batter into the prepared mini muffin cups. Bake for 15–20 minutes, or until buns have puffed up and are a light golden color. Serve hot. *Makes 48 buns, or 16 servings*

buttermilk and pork rind (chicharrón) biscuits

Slow-melting lard creates pockets of steam that separate layers of baked dough in these luscious biscuits. Buttermilk adds tang and tenderness; pork rinds add richness and a slight crunch. Put it all together, and you have luxurious, flavor-packed morsels that taste like a piece of hog heaven. These flaky biscuits are all about the pig. One of the many things Latinos and Southerners have in common is a love of pork—from the snout, all the way to the hooves—and an addiction to pork fat transformed into lard or rinds, called *chicharrones*. Lard is obtained from rendering the pig's fat slowly and gently. The rinds are made by frying the skin until it becomes crispy, crunchy, and utterly irresistible. I love to use these two forms of fat in combination. One taste and you will understand why these are favorites in my home, where we often slather them with Chipotle-Honey Butter (page 28).

2 cups self-rising flour
½ cup finely grated pork rinds
(about 3 ounces) (see note)
¼ cup chilled lard or bacon fat
(or shortening, if you must)
1 cup buttermilk
2 tablespoons heavy whipping cream

Preheat the oven to 450°F. In a large bowl, whisk together the flour and grated pork rinds. Using a pastry blender (or two knives), cut the lard into the flour mixture until the pieces of fat are the size of baby peas. Blend in the buttermilk with a wooden spoon (I use my hands) just until the dough comes together. Turn out the dough onto a lightly floured surface and knead it gently a couple of times. Pat it into an 8-inch circle (about ½ inch thick). Using a well-floured 2⅛-inch biscuit cutter, cut out 12 biscuits (you'll need to gather up the dough and pat it down again lightly after the first biscuits are cut to get all 12). Place the biscuits, with sides touching, in a 10-inch springform or cake pan. With your knuckle, make a small indentation in the center of each biscuit; brush the tops of the biscuits with the cream. Bake for 20–22 minutes, or until the tops are golden brown. Serve hot with butter or with Chipotle-Honey Butter. *Makes 1 dozen*

NOTE: Grate pork rinds using the smallest holes on a cheese grater or by pulsing in a food processor until they resemble bread crumbs. When cutting the biscuits, make up-and-down motions with the cutter so the biscuits don't stick.

COOK'S TIP: To make your own self-rising flour, add 1½ teaspoons baking powder and ½ teaspoon salt per cup of all-purpose flour required in the recipe.

how to make proper southern biscuits

When I moved to the South, I wanted to learn how to make the best biscuits possible. I took every opportunity to learn from my friends and their mothers, who took turns teaching me the right way to handle biscuits. One of my favorite memories is of watching my friend Belinda Ellis teaching master baker and friend Lionel Vatinet how to make biscuits in my kitchen. Here are the precious lessons I've learned throughout the years. First, use self-rising flour and measure it with a light touch—don't tap the measuring cup or pat the flour down, simply scoop and swipe a knife over the top to level. Second, use lard (or a mixture of shortening and butter, if you must), and be sure it's well chilled (I chill my flour and fat before I begin). Cut the fat into the flour by using the tips of your fingers (or, if you have warm hands like me, a pastry cutter) until the mixture resembles coarse sand. Incorporate the liquid (buttermilk, heavy cream, yogurt, or milk, but buttermilk is best) quickly with your hands with a minimal amount of mixing, just until a sticky dough is formed. Turn the dough out onto a lightly floured surface and knead it briefly and ever so gently, without a lot of pressure, then pat it down into the desired thickness. The trick is to handle the dough as little as possible (no longer than 30 seconds). With an up-and-down motion, cut out the biscuits with a tall, sharp metal biscuit cutter without twisting (twisting will pinch the sides of the biscuits and prevent them from rising properly when they bake). Place them on shiny (*not* nonstick) baking pans (sides touching for soft edges, not touching for crusty edges). Using your thumb, make a slight indentation in the top of each biscuit to help them rise. Brush the tops with melted butter or heavy cream (but don't let it drip over the sides of the biscuits or they won't rise properly) and bake them at between 450° and 500°F until the tops are golden. Finally, eat them fresh out of the oven, and never, ever, cut them with a knife; simply separate the layers with your hands. Eat them plain or slather them with fresh, creamy butter.

chile-cheese biscuits with avocado butter

Moist and light, these new-Southern morsels deliver just the right combination of spice and comforting goodness. Self-rising flour is made from Southern soft wheat flour to which baking powder and salt have been added; it has less protein and gluten than all-purpose flour. The addition of just a little bit of fat and liquid yields fluffy, tender biscuits. Poblano chiles add a mild heat (see sidebar, page 98). Queso seco is a Mexican dry-aged cheese that tastes similar to Parmesan; you can find it in most grocery stores. I learned to make biscuits from my Southern friends, who taught me to handle the dough with respect and loving hands. Serve these mildly spiced biscuits with this creamy avocado spread that melts in the mouth.

FOR THE BISCUITS

2 cups self-rising flour
1 cup grated queso seco (use Parmesan cheese in a bind)
1 teaspoon ancho (or pasilla) chile powder
¼ cup chilled lard, bacon fat, or shortening
1 poblano chile, roasted, peeled, seeded, deveined, and finely chopped (see page 116)
1-1¼ cups buttermilk
3 tablespoons heavy whipping cream

FOR THE AVOCADO BUTTER

2 Hass avocados
2 teaspoons lime juice
½ teaspoon salt, or to taste
Pinch freshly ground black pepper
Pinch dried Mexican oregano (optional)

Preheat the oven to 475°F. In a large bowl, whisk together the flour, cheese, and chile powder. Using a pastry blender (or two knives), cut the lard into the flour mixture until it resembles coarse sand. Stir in the chiles. Gradually add the buttermilk, mixing the dough with a wooden spoon or your hands just until it holds together (you may not need all of the buttermilk). Turn out the dough onto a lightly floured surface and knead it gently a couple of times. Pat it into an 8-inch circle (about ½ inch thick). Using a well-floured 2⅛-inch biscuit cutter, cut out 12 biscuits (you'll need to gather up the dough and pat it down again lightly after the first biscuits are cut to get all 12). Place the biscuits, with sides touching, in a 10-inch springform or cake pan. With your knuckle, make a small indentation in the center of each biscuit; brush the tops of the biscuits with the cream. Bake for 18–22 minutes, or until the tops are golden brown.

To make the avocado butter: Halve and pit the avocados; scoop out the flesh with a spoon into a medium bowl and mash into a smooth paste. Add the lime juice, salt, pepper, and oregano (if using) and stir until combined.

Serve the hot biscuits with avocado butter. *Makes 12 biscuits and 1½ cups avocado butter*

chile cornbread

Moist and spicy, this quick bread is easy to make and loaded with flavor. Buttermilk gives it acidity, and chiles add a touch of heat. Throughout the ages, cornbread has been a mainstay of the cuisine of the Americas. Native Americans mixed ground cornmeal and water to make simple bread. In the American South, cornbread is generally savory, unlike the kind made in the North, where sweeteners are added (which, incidentally, is blasphemous to Southerners!). The cornbread of the Aztecs and Mayas was the tortilla. South American cornbread, called *arepa*, is made with a precooked cornmeal mix. The addition of chiles is Mexican in origin. Here I take the marriage of cultures one step further by using a mixture of ground cornmeal and masa harina. The result is a tender crumb with deep corn flavor. Serve this at your next Fourth of July party or Thanksgiving dinner.

1 cup stone-ground yellow cornmeal
½ cup masa harina
½ cup all-purpose flour
1 tablespoon sugar
1 tablespoon baking powder
1 teaspoon baking soda
1 teaspoon salt
2 eggs
1½ cups buttermilk
2 tablespoons finely chopped jalapeños (seeded and deveined if less heat is desired)
1 teaspoon minced chipotle chiles in adobo
1 teaspoon adobo
1 cup corn kernels (fresh or frozen and thawed)
2 tablespoons melted lard (or vegetable oil)

Preheat the oven to 400°F. Brush a 9 ¼ × 5 ¼ × 2 ¾-inch loaf pan with the melted lard and set aside. In a large bowl, combine the cornmeal, masa harina, flour, sugar, baking powder, baking soda, and salt. In a separate, medium bowl, whisk together the eggs and buttermilk. Pour the liquid mixture into the dry ingredients and mix until just combined; stir in the jalapeños, chipotle, adobo, and corn, mixing just until evenly distributed (don't overmix). Pour the batter into the prepared pan and bake for 40–45 minutes, or until a toothpick inserted in the center comes out clean. Remove from the oven and place it on a cooling rack; cool in the pan for 5 minutes before unmolding and slicing. Serve warm with sweet butter.
Makes 1 loaf

NOTE: To make muffins, pour the batter into 12 well-greased muffin cups and bake for 20-25 minutes, or until a toothpick inserted in the center of a muffin comes out clean. Keep in mind that the darker the pan, the quicker the bread or muffins will bake, so plan accordingly. If using cast-iron pans, preheat according to the manufacturer's instructions.

chile hushpuppies

These sweet, puffy, and crispy fritters are filled with the flavor of corn and embellished with spicy, bright-green chiles. I instantly fell in love with hushpuppies the first time I tried them at a neighborhood pig-pickin' in Durham in the 1980s. They reminded me of the savory buñuelos I used to eat as a child. Jalapeños and corn are not strangers to one another; they've been a classic combination since pre-Columbian times when the indigenous peoples of ancient Mayan and Aztec civilizations flavored corn mush with spicy peppers. My hushpuppies have a distinct Latin twist. I like to make mine with stone-ground cornmeal because it provides more texture than finely ground cornmeal, but the latter works too. Either white or yellow cornmeal works here, although I love the color yellow cornmeal imparts. Serve these with Pimiento Cheese Butter (page 28).

2 cups stone-ground yellow cornmeal
2 tablespoons sugar
1 teaspoon baking soda
½ teaspoon baking powder
1½ teaspoons salt
½ teaspoon ancho chile powder
½ cup grated Vidalia onion
2 tablespoons minced jalapeños (seeded and deveined if less heat is desired)
1 egg
1¼ cups buttermilk
Vegetable oil for frying

Fit a large baking pan with a metal cooling rack. In a large bowl, whisk together the cornmeal, sugar, baking soda, baking powder, salt, and chile powder. In a medium bowl, whisk together the onions, jalapeño, egg, and buttermilk until well combined. Pour the wet ingredients into the dry ingredients and mix just until combined. In a large skillet with high sides, heat 2-3 inches of oil to 360°F (or use a deep fryer according to the manufacturer's directions); using a 2-inch ice cream scoop, carefully drop the batter into the oil. Fry the hushpuppies for 2-3 minutes, or until golden, turning them over halfway through. Using a slotted spoon, transfer them to the prepared rack to drain. Serve immediately or keep warm in a 250°F oven for up to 45 minutes. Makes about 24

chiltepín gremolata

This accoutrement adds a fiery kick and lemony accent to foods. The chiltepín pepper is a tiny, pea-size fruit that is slightly elongated at the bottom end. Also known as a bird's eye, it is the smallest pepper (and one of the hottest) in the world. I have not been able to find them fresh in the South, but pickled chiltepines are widely available in Latin tiendas. If you're lucky to find a plant, it is easy to grow in a pot. This salsa is a favorite throughout Central America, where chiltepines grow abundantly. Serve it on grilled meats, fish, or poultry or as a topping for stews, such as my Nuevo Red Beans and Rice (page 157). It is also great on eggs and mixed into guacamole. This is so deliciously addictive that I always keep a supply in my refrigerator.

1 cup chopped white onion
½ cup pickled chiltepines, rinsed, drained, and stems removed
Grated zest of 1 lemon
¼ cup lemon juice
1 garlic clove, chopped
1 cup cilantro (leaves and tender stems)
¼ teaspoon salt
⅛ teaspoon freshly ground black pepper

In the bowl of a food processor fitted with a metal blade, combine the onions, chiltepines, lemon zest, lemon juice, garlic, and cilantro; process until the mixture is finely minced (about 1–2 minutes), stopping once to scrape the sides of the bowl. Transfer the mixture to a medium bowl; stir in the salt and pepper. Cover and chill for 20 minutes to allow the flavors to blend. Covered and chilled, this keeps well for up to 2 weeks. *Makes ½ cup*

NOTE: The cilantro will be a vibrant green when the gremolata is fresh and will lose its vibrant color as it sits, but this will not affect the flavor. If you don't have a food processor, chop the onions, chiltepines, and cilantro as finely as you can with a knife (be sure to wear rubber gloves when handling the peppers) and then combine them with the lemon zest, lemon juice, salt, and pepper.

fearless frying

Southerners and Latinos share a love of fried foods. The indigenous peoples of the ancient American civilizations cooked their food over fire. When Spaniards introduced pork and beef, they also brought along with them lard, butter, and the techniques for frying foods. I love this cooking technique, which, when properly done, yields foods with crunchy and crispy crusts. From fish and chicken, to churros and buñuelos, Southern and Latin cuisines are full of examples of fried dishes. The idea behind frying is to cook food—sometimes breaded or coated with batter—quickly and at a very high temperature in order to produce a crispy exterior. Although you can use a deep fryer, I prefer to use my large, enameled, cast-iron pot. The optimum temperature for frying foods is between 360°F and 375°F. Only when the oil is heated to the right temperature can a crust form and prevent the oil from seeping into the food, making it greasy. Therefore, remember that temperature is crucial. For this reason, I suggest you use a deep frying thermometer or follow this simple trick: dip a dry wooden spoon in the oil, if it bubbles at contact, the oil is ready for frying. Most recipes call for draining fried foods on paper towels, but I find that when fried foods come into contact with paper towels, the towels cause the food to steam, turning crispy coatings into a soggy mess. My solution is to fit baking pans with oven-safe cooling racks and place the fried items directly onto them to allow excess fat to drain; then I transfer this setup to a preheated 250°F oven to keep the food warm. Fried foods can be kept warm for up to one hour without any loss of crispiness or moisture.

classic argentinean chimichurri

This pungent, gutsy Argentinean sauce is popular in Latin America and is making its way into North American kitchens. The origin of the name chimichurri is unclear, but, like the origin of many Latin dishes, it is surrounded by legend and lore. My favorite version claims that a Scot by the name of Jimmy Curry created a brand new concoction to serve with an Argentinean asado that was being prepared in his honor; unable to pronounce his name, Argentineans called his novel creation chimichurri. The term is most likely a derivative of the Basque word for mixture, tximitxurri. It is traditionally served as an accoutrement for grilled meats, poultry, and seafood. Chimichurri makes a great marinade and pairs nicely with pulled pork. Stir leftovers into butter or mayonnaise for a delicious sandwich spread.

1 cup flat-leaf parsley (leaves and tender stems), packed

1 cup cilantro (leaves and tender stems), packed

½ cup coarsely chopped onion

2 tablespoons grated lemon zest

¼ cup plus 1 tablespoon lemon juice

¼ cup red wine vinegar

5 large garlic cloves, minced

1 teaspoon freshly ground black pepper

1 teaspoon ground cumin

¼ teaspoon red pepper flakes

1 cup extra-virgin olive oil

In the bowl of a food processor fitted with a metal blade, combine the parsley, cilantro, onions, lemon zest, lemon juice, vinegar, garlic, black pepper, cumin, and red pepper flakes; pulse for 10–20 seconds, or until the mixture is finely chopped. With the motor running, add the oil slowly through the feed tube and process until the sauce is smooth. Transfer into a clean bowl or squirt bottle. The chimichurri will keep for 1 week in the refrigerator.

Makes 2 cups

coleslaw

No picnic or Southern barbecue would be complete without coleslaw. The Dutch introduced coleslaw (koolsla) to colonial America, and it has been a favorite ever since. Latin
countries have similar chopped salads called *curtidos* that are traditionally served
alongside fried foods to offer a refreshing contrast. Some recipes for coleslaw call only
for a vinegar-based dressing, but I prefer mine with a touch of mayonnaise and just a
smidgen of sugar to offset the acidity. Apple cider vinegar is traditional to Southern
cuisine in general, and here it adds enough tartness without masking the flavor of the
cabbage. Be sure to make this salad a couple of hours before you serve it so that the
cabbage can release its natural juices and loosen up the dressing. Try it with my Latin
Fried Chicken (page 125) or Mini Pibil Barbecue Sandwiches (page 62).

6 cups finely shredded green
    cabbage
2 cups shredded carrots
½ cup mayonnaise
¼ cup heavy whipping cream
¼ cup apple cider vinegar
1 tablespoon sugar
½ teaspoon salt
¼ teaspoon celery seeds
¼ teaspoon paprika
⅛ teaspoon freshly ground
    black pepper

In a large bowl, combine the cabbage and carrots. In a
small bowl, whisk together the mayonnaise, cream, vinegar, sugar, salt, celery seeds, paprika, and pepper until
well combined. Pour the dressing over the cabbage and
toss to coat well. Cover and chill (stirring occasionally)
for 2 hours. *Serves 6-8*

compound butters

These butters are flavor boosters, easy to reach for whenever you need to season dishes quickly. Compound butter is a mixture of softened butter, spices, herbs, and other seasonings that is blended together until a paste is formed. I like to shape these compounds into logs so I can slice them when needed. For longer storage, wrap them tightly in parchment or freezer paper and freeze them until solid. If frozen, they will keep for up to four months. Reach for one of these logs, cut off a slice or two, and return it to the freezer until the next time. Seasoned butters can be either sweet or savory and are delicious when slathered on warm breads fresh from the oven, like my Chicharrón Biscuits (page 18). For an elegant presentation, place slices of compound butter atop grilled meats, such as Rib Eyes with Pimiento Cheese Butter and Chimichurri (page 134), seafood, or poultry.

PIMIENTO CHEESE BUTTER

4 tablespoons unsalted butter, room temperature
¼ cup Classic Pimiento Cheese (page 35)
¼ cup minced cilantro (leaves and tender stems), packed
1 garlic clove, minced

In a small bowl, combine the softened butter, pimiento cheese, cilantro, and garlic. Mix with a fork until well blended. Place the mixture on a sheet of parchment paper and roll it up into the parchment to form a 5-inch-long cylinder; twist the ends of the paper (like a candy wrapper) and chill for 1 hour before slicing. *Makes about 1 cup*

CHIPOTLE-HONEY BUTTER

5 tablespoons unsalted butter, room temperature
2 tablespoons honey
1 teaspoon minced chipotle chiles in adobo
½ teaspoon adobo
Pinch salt

In a medium bowl, combine the butter, honey, chipotle, adobo, and salt. Mix with a fork until well blended. Place the mixture on a sheet of parchment paper and roll it up into the parchment to form a 5-inch-long cylinder; twist the ends of the paper (like a candy wrapper) and chill for 1 hour before slicing. *Makes about ½ cup*

fig preserves

Sweet figs meet gooey syrup in these delectable preserves. Figs are native to the Mediterranean. Brought to the New World by the Spaniards, figs appear extensively in the cuisines of Latin America, where they are candied, baked into pies, transformed into jellies, or used to top ice cream. Okracoke Island in North Carolina, where sandy soil and temperate climate have proven ideal for growing figs, is famous for its fig production. Preserving fruits is easy to do. Purchase perfectly ripened figs when they are in season—early fall—and clean them well. For the sweetener, I use piloncillo (raw sugarcane, also known as panela), but you can use dark brown sugar instead. Try these in Pecan Rum Cake with Figs (page 243) or to top Buttermilk Ice Cream (page 226).

3 pounds ripe figs (about 60), washed and dried (I prefer Black Mission figs, but any variety will work)

1 pound piloncillo or dark brown sugar

1 stick Mexican cinnamon (canela)

Using a small paring knife, cut a small X in the bottom of each fig; set aside. In a large, heavy-bottomed saucepan, combine the piloncillo, cinnamon, and 3 cups of water; cook over medium heat, breaking up the piloncillo as the mixture heats. When the piloncillo has melted (about 8–10 minutes), add the figs. Increase the heat to medium-high and bring the mixture to a boil. Reduce the heat to medium; cook, uncovered, for 18–20 minutes, or until the syrup registers 210°F on a candy thermometer (it will be bubbly and frothy). If the bubbles are rising too quickly, reduce the heat a bit. When the syrup reaches the proper temperature, reduce the heat and simmer until the syrup is thick, about 10–15 minutes; remove from the heat. When the figs are cool, remove them from the syrup, chop liberally (or process until almost smooth), and return to the syrup. Transfer the mixture to a clean container. Store well covered in the refrigerator for up to 1 month. *Makes 4 cups*

green tomato chutney

Pickles and relishes are a Southern tradition. Green tomatoes are summer's gift to Southerners. Their acidity serves as the perfect backdrop to the raisins and brown sugar featured here. The fruit and sugar combined offer a balance of sweet, spicy, and sour undertones. Pickled foods are popular in Latin America, where the Arab technique called escabeche was brought by the Spaniards. Similarly, the Indian technique for making chutney was introduced to the South by the British. Both involve cooking fruits and/or vegetables in a mixture of vinegar, sugar, and spices. Not as sweet as their Southern counterparts, escabeches are usually served as side dishes or appetizers, while chutneys and relishes serve as condiments. This particular chutney is simple to make, so don't be intimidated by the length of the ingredient list. It's great to have on hand to serve with cheese and crackers to unexpected guests.

1¼ cups apple cider vinegar
1 cup brown sugar, packed
5 cups peeled and chopped green tomatoes
2 cups chopped red onion
1½ cups peeled, cored, and chopped Granny Smith apples
2 tablespoons minced jalapeños
⅓ cup orange marmalade
2 teaspoons whole-grain or stone-ground mustard
6 whole cloves
1 teaspoon pasilla chile powder
½ teaspoon ground allspice
½ teaspoon salt
½ teaspoon ground cumin
¼ teaspoon freshly ground black pepper
1 stick Mexican cinnamon (canela)
1 cup raisins

In a large, nonreactive Dutch oven, stir together the vinegar and brown sugar until the sugar is dissolved; set it over medium-high heat and bring to a simmer. Simmer, stirring occasionally, for 10 minutes, or until it has thickened into a syrup. Stir in the tomatoes, onions, apples, jalapeño, marmalade, and mustard; simmer for 5 minutes. Add the cloves, chile powder, allspice, salt, cumin, pepper, and cinnamon; stir well and reduce the heat to medium. Cook for 10 minutes (the mixture will bubble madly, but be careful not to burn it; you may have to reduce the heat slightly). Stir in the raisins. Reduce the heat to low and simmer, uncovered, for 1 hour, or until the mixture has thickened (see note); cool completely and store in a clean jar for up to 2 months in the refrigerator. *Makes 3 cups*

NOTE: The juicier the green tomatoes are, the longer the chutney will need to cook.

latin tartar sauce

This creamy accoutrement for seafood is deliciously tart. One of my very first childhood memories involves a family vacation spent in El Salvador in the 1970s. The restaurant was called Siete Mares, and if memory serves me right, it was a white-tablecloth establishment renowned for its seafood. It was there that I first sampled the marriage of expertly breaded shrimp and tartar sauce. To this day, this is my favorite sauce to drape over the Calabash-style dishes of the Carolina coast. I find it equally delicious as a dipping sauce for simple, boiled shrimp or for my Crab Croquetas (page 55). The familiar remoulade serves as a reminder that culinary classics never go out of style. In my version, I use prepared relish for convenience and add chipotle chiles for heat and smokiness. Use a pastry cutter to chop hard-boiled eggs quickly.

1½ cups mayonnaise

¼ cup prepared pickle relish

2 tablespoons finely chopped flat-leaf parsley (leaves and tender stems)

2 tablespoons finely chopped cilantro (leaves and tender stems)

2 tablespoons minced capers

2 tablespoons white vinegar, or to taste

2 teaspoons minced chipotle chiles in adobo

1 teaspoon adobo

1 hard-boiled egg, finely chopped

Salt and freshly ground black pepper, to taste

In a medium bowl, combine the mayonnaise, relish, parsley, cilantro, capers, vinegar, chiles, adobo, and egg; stir until well blended. Season with salt and pepper and chill for 1 hour to allow the flavors to blend. Serve well chilled. Covered and refrigerated, tartar sauce keeps well for up to 2 days. *Makes 1¾ cups*

mango salsa

This gutsy salsa is luscious and refreshing. It features piquant flavors in combination with sweet embellishments and it is wonderful when paired with Catfish Soft Tacos (page 118). Native to India, mangoes are widely available throughout Latin America, where one can find them in all shapes and sizes. Green, unripe mangoes are as popular as the ripe ones. If you are able to find small, unripened mangoes, try them here; they are a bit sour, but the resulting salsa will still be delicious. The vibrant combination of mangoes, lemon juice, salt, and chiles is nothing new to Latinos; adding cilantro and red onion seemed like a tasty idea to me. Firm mangoes that are just ripe are easiest to chop.

3   cups peeled and diced mangoes
½   cup minced red onion
½   cup minced cilantro (leaves and
       tender stems)
¼   cup lime juice
¼   cup minced serrano chiles
       (seeded and deveined if
       less heat is desired)
    Salt and freshly ground pepper,
       to taste

In a medium bowl, combine mangoes, onions, cilantro, lime juice, and chiles. Stir until well blended and season with salt and pepper; chill until ready to use (for up to 48 hours). *Makes 4½ cups*

COOK'S TIP: Select mangoes that barely yield to the touch. If the mango is too ripe and soft, it will be difficult to handle and once chopped will not hold its shape. Peel the fruit with a serrated potato peeler or a sharp knife. To cut a mango, use a sharp knife. Slice off either tip of the mango so that it has a flat surface on which to stand easily on the cutting board. The seed of the mango is a flat oval pit that runs through the center of the fruit. Stand the mango on the cutting board and slice down one side of the mango, as close to the seed as possible. Do the same thing on the other side. Lay the seed flat on the cutting board and slice the pulp that remains on the sides of the seed. Chop the flesh of the mango as the recipe directs and discard the seed.

peach salsa

In this new spin on a classic, peaches replace tomatoes, and the result is a healthy, colorful, and refreshing salsa. Whether you choose to eat it with tortilla chips or use it to dress grilled fish, this peachy take on traditional pico de gallo will satisfy your cravings for sweet, sour, and spicy flavors. Select fresh peaches that are still firm, so their flesh will keep its shape when cubed. In the South, peaches are in season throughout the summer. I prefer free-stone varieties, which have loose pits that release easily from the flesh, making them much simpler to slice. Canned peaches in syrup will not work in this recipe (because of their mushy texture and overly sweet flavor). Frozen and thawed peaches may be used in lieu of fresh, but nothing beats the flavor of local, seasonal peaches. Make this salsa, and a kaleidoscope of colors will welcome you to taste.

2 cups peeled and cubed fresh
  peaches (about 3 large peaches)
¼ cup finely chopped red onion
¼ cup finely chopped cilantro (leaves
  and tender stems)
2 tablespoons minced jalapeños
  (seeded and deveined if less
  heat is desired)
1 (2-ounce) jar diced pimientos,
  drained
2 teaspoons grated lime zest
  Juice of 1 lime, or to taste
  Salt and freshly ground pepper,
  to taste

In a medium bowl, combine the peaches, onions, cilantro, jalapeños, pimientos, and lime zest. Add the lime juice and season with salt and pepper. Let the salsa sit at room temperature for 10 minutes before serving to allow the flavors to blend, or cover and chill until ready to use (for up to 24 hours). *Makes 2½ cups*

COOK'S TIP: Peel peaches easily by using a serrated vegetable peeler (available in cooking specialty shops) or by blanching them. To blanch them, bring a large pan of water to a boil; using a paring knife, cut a small X through the skin at the base of each peach. Drop the peaches into the boiling water for 30 seconds, then transfer them into a bowl of iced water for 2 minutes; peel the skin off starting at the base of the peach.

pico de gallo

In Spanish, all sauces (regardless of whether or not they're cooked) are called salsa. This refreshing, raw tomato sauce is without a doubt the most recognized of all Mexican accoutrements. Salsa began outselling ketchup in the United States in the 1980s. There are several theories as to the origin of the name pico de gallo, which, translated literally, means "rooster's beak." One is that "pico" comes from the Spanish verb *picar*, to chop, but I'm partial to the idea that the colors of this chopped mixture resemble those of a rooster's beak. I like to add mint to my version because it complements the flavor of tomatoes so nicely. If you dislike cilantro, replace it with flat-leaf (Italian) parsley and double the amount of mint. Traditionally paired with tortilla chips, pico de gallo is also quite delicious on grilled meats and fried eggs. This version is so easy to assemble that you might never purchase a jar of prepared salsa again.

10 plum tomatoes, seeded and finely chopped
1 cup finely chopped white onion
1 yellow bell pepper, finely chopped
4 finely chopped serrano chiles (or 2 large jalapeños) (seeded and deveined if less heat is desired)
1 cup finely chopped cilantro (leaves and tender stems)
¼ cup finely chopped mint
¼ cup lime juice, or to taste
   Salt and freshly ground black pepper, to taste
   Tortilla chips

In a large bowl, combine the tomatoes, onions, bell pepper, chiles, cilantro, and mint; stir well. Add the lime juice and season with salt and pepper. Let the salsa rest at room temperature for 20 minutes to allow the flavors to blend. Serve at room temperature or chill, well covered, until ready to use, for up to 12 hours. Serve with tortilla chips. *Serves 6-8*

NOTE: This tastes best when made just before serving.

pimiento cheese

I will never forget my first taste of pimiento cheese, this pungent, smooth, creamy perfection, sandwiched between slices of white bread. It was love at first bite! Pimiento is the Spanish term for all kinds of sweet bell peppers, but this classic cheese spread is 100 percent Southern. There are as many variations as there are Southern cooks. Some add grated onions, garlic, Worcestershire sauce, cream cheese, or pickle relish. I prefer using just a few ingredients that in combination provide a balance of zesty, spicy, salty, and tangy flavors in one bite. Pimiento cheese is featured in my Rib Eyes with Pimiento Cheese Butter and Chimichurri (page 134), Cocktail Chiles Rellenos (page 53), and Avocado and Pimiento Cheese Terrine (page 47). Here is the beloved classic version of pimiento cheese and one with a Latin twist.

CLASSIC PIMIENTO CHEESE

1 pound shredded sharp cheddar cheese (see note)
1 (4-ounce) jar diced pimientos, drained
1 cup mayonnaise
½ teaspoon freshly ground black pepper
½ teaspoon hot sauce (such as Tabasco)

In the bowl of a food processor fitted with a metal blade, place the cheese, pimientos, mayonnaise, black pepper, and hot sauce. Pulse just until combined. Makes 2¾ cups

NOTE: Many brands of pre-shredded cheese contain cornstarch to keep the cheese strands separate, which changes the texture and flavor of the cheese, so I suggest you grate it yourself.

LATIN PIMIENTO CHEESE

1 pound shredded sharp cheddar cheese (see note)
1 (4-ounce) jar diced pimientos, drained
1 cup mayonnaise
2 teaspoons minced chipotle chiles in adobo
1 teaspoon adobo
2 teaspoons grated red onion
½ teaspoon ancho chile powder
¼ teaspoon freshly ground black pepper

In the bowl of a food processor fitted with a metal blade, place the cheese, pimientos, mayonnaise, chipotle, adobo, onions, chile powder, and pepper. Pulse just until combined. Chill for at least 4 hours so that the flavors can blend; if your ingredients are fresh, it will keep, covered and chilled, for up to 2 weeks. Keeping with the New Southern-Latino way, try it in quesadillas. Makes 2¾ cups

pimiento sauce

This smooth, creamy, and delicately flavored sauce takes on a vibrantly coral hue from the colorful vegetables used to make it. This is my twist on the all-purpose to-mato sauce made throughout Latin America. The base of Latin tomato sauces is the ever-present sofrito—a combination of finely chopped garlic, onion, and tomatoes, but in this version, the flavor of red peppers rules over the rest. At home, I use this sauce interchangeably with classic tomato sauces as a base for other sauces, soups, and stews. You will have no trouble finding jars of these cooked, peeled, and pre-served sweet red peppers on your grocer's shelves. Use this sauce to dress Pimiento and Cheese Chilaquiles (page 187) or Collard Green Tamales (page 203); it is also great on fish, eggs, and vegetables.

2 tablespoons extra-virgin olive oil
2 cups roughly chopped yellow onion
1 cup peeled, seeded, and roughly chopped plum tomatoes
2 garlic cloves, roughly chopped
2 (7-ounce) jars diced pimientos, drained (juices reserved)
1 teaspoon ají panca paste or hot sauce (such as Tabasco)
½ cup water
1 teaspoon salt
¼ teaspoon freshly ground black pepper

In a medium saucepan, heat the oil over medium-high heat. Add the onions and sauté for 3–4 minutes, or until they begin to soften; add the tomatoes and garlic and cook, stirring, for 2 minutes. Add the pimientos, ají panca paste, water, reserved juices from the pimientos, salt, and pepper; bring to a simmer, cover, and cook for 10 minutes. Remove from the heat and cool slightly. Transfer the mixture to a blender or food processor and blend until smooth. Return it to the saucepan and keep warm until ready to serve. *Makes 2 cups*

sandra's ultimate guacamole

Buttery, with a light hint of lime and spices, this Mexican classic is a favorite in American homes. The Mayan word for avocado is *aguacatl*; in the Nahuatl language of the Aztecs, *moli* means mixture. Put them together and you have guacamole. I make mine in a molcajete (mortar and pestle)—chosen for me by my friend Diana Kennedy, cookbook author and authority on Mexican cuisine—but a bowl and a potato masher work just fine. My rendition is simple but scrumptious. Make sure you purchase unripe avocados a few days before you plan to make this; let them ripen at room temperature on your kitchen counter. Don't refrigerate avocados unless they are completely ripe—and only for a day—or they will turn brown and bitter. I grew up eating the small, black-skinned, Guatemalan avocados. In the South, I'm partial to the widely available Hass avocado, prized for its creaminess.

3 ripe Hass avocados
¼ cup minced white onion
2–3 minced serrano chiles
   (or jalapeños) (seeded and
   deveined if less heat is desired)
½ cup seeded and chopped
   plum tomato
¼ cup minced cilantro (leaves
   and tender stems)
Lime juice, to taste
Salt and freshly ground black
   pepper, to taste
Tortilla chips

Halve and pit the avocados; scoop out the flesh with a spoon into a large bowl; add a bit of lime juice to prevent browning. Mash the avocados with a fork or a potato masher. Add the onions, chiles, tomato, and cilantro, stirring to combine well; season with lime juice, salt, and pepper. Serve immediately with tortilla chips. *Serves 6-8*

boquitas & southern starters

t can be said that Southerners are known for their hospitality and Latinos are known for their conviviality. It's as common to stop by for tea on a neighbor's front porch in the South as it is to drop by for coffee and a visit in a friend's sitting room in Latin America. For centuries, these often serendipitous interactions have served as opportunities to exchange neighborhood news and trade niceties. More often than not, a little bite to eat follows.

It's often said that the only thing a Latino needs to organize a party is a good excuse. An unexpected visitor at my door is as good a reason as any to organize a fiesta; and yes, it's true: Southern hospitality is still alive and well. In my neck of the woods, neighbors waving from their front porch often signals an invitation to partake in a little conversation and sometimes a small libation—a glass of lemonade or some iced tea.

One of the first lessons I learned when I moved to the South was that when it comes to entertaining, simple, easy-to-make appetizers are the way to go. Spiced pecans, warm spreads, creamy dips, and fluffy biscuits, for example, can be put together quickly. Dainty sandwiches, tiny cakes, and complicated small plates are better left for fancier occasions such as weddings and christenings.

Latinos entertain a lot. This need to gather is an important part of Latin American culture and is due to a strong need for social network that, to this day, remains the easiest way to connect socially and professionally. In my opinion, the only thing as amazing as Southern hospitality is a Latino's penchant for partying.

Spanish is a rich and descriptive language, and each Latin American country has its own cooking vernacular. Latinos, therefore, have a wide spectrum of terms for appetizers: boquitas, botanas, pasapalos, aperitivos, and antojitos.

I adore appetizers. If, like me, you enjoy entertaining entirely around hors d'oeuvres, this chapter will become a favorite go-to guide. Here you'll find a wide variety of starter dishes that marry the best of both Southern and Latino cuisines. Some will require a bit more work than others; however, most are suited for informal get-togethers and im-promptu celebrations.

Let's face it: great hosts tend to be practical people. How else can they organize parties and make it seem effortless? For this reason, most of the recipes in this chapter can be prepared (in part or entirely) ahead of time. When applicable, I've given freezing instructions, in case you wish to have freezer-to-oven tidbits at the ready. These are particularly help-ful when you get the sudden urge to invite friends over on a whim. Such is the case with Ancho Chile-Cheese Wafers and Crab Croquetas with Latin Tartar Sauce.

Some, like my Arepitas with Goat Cheese and Green Tomato Chutney and my Warm Pimiento Logs, can be made ahead almost in their entirety and will only require last-minute finishing touches. All of the recipes in this chapter have been popular with my cooking students because they're delectable, convenient, and, above all, practical.

Some of these dishes have enough substance to hold you until meal time, such as my Jalapeño Deviled Eggs, Hamburger Sliders with Latin Pimiento Cheese and Pico de Gallo, and Mini Pibil Barbecue Sandwiches. Others are designed to whet your appetite and tease your palate, as is the case with my famous Leek and Mushroom Empanaditas (a favorite recipe among my students). Some recipes are comprised of subrecipes, but don't let this intimidate you; each part is simple to make and can often stand on its own.

There is a Spanish expression that says you eat with your eyes first. I agree: food should not only be scrumptious; it must also be beautiful to look at so that all the senses are engaged. This is even more the case when it comes to appetizers, which, offered alone or at the beginning of a meal, are meant to arouse the appetite and set the stage for what is to come. So make a good variety of hors d'oeuvres for your parties.

Try to mix and match different textures, colors, and ingredients. I suggest serving appetizers on white or crystal plates, so the serving platters don't detract from the visual impact of the food itself. I also like to keep each kind of appetizer on its own plate. Not only does this make for a more elegant presentation; it also prevents sauces, dressings, and dips from running into other tidbits and ruining the taste of all.

I've always said that entertaining should be enjoyable for the host first. So don't make yourself crazy trying to make too many recipes at the same time. Select a few you like best and make as many ahead of time as you can. The Avocado and Pimiento Cheese Terrine, the Pickled

Shrimp, and the Carrot Escabeche can all be made a day in advance. To complement these dishes, offer a crudités platter and slices of crusty artisan bread. A New Southern-Latino cheese tray could include a goat cheese, an artisan farmer's cheese, my fig preserves, and sliced guava paste. This is my way to entertain, and in my home, it's always fiesta time, y'all!

ancho chile-cheese wafers

Crispy and sinfully rich, these cheese crackers epitomize Southern hospitality and are ever-present at holiday parties and ladies' luncheons. They make quick and scrumptious hors d'oeuvres. Perhaps it's their ease of preparation that makes these so popular in the South; maybe it's the fact that no matter what you pair them with (whether it's a glass of champagne, cold beer, or iced tea), they always hit the spot. To me, these are the perfect example of how simple is sometimes better. As delicious as these are on their own, they also make a scrumptious base for chutneys, relishes, and salsas. Chile powder gives this version a subtle Latin kick. I love that these can be made by hand or easily whirred together in a food processor. Since they can be frozen for up to four months, I usually keep a box or two available for surprise visitors.

2½ cups shredded mild
    cheddar cheese
1½ cups grated queso seco or
    Parmesan cheese
1 cup (2 sticks) unsalted
    butter, softened
2¾ cups all-purpose flour
1 teaspoon salt
1 teaspoon ancho chile powder
¼ teaspoon ground cumin
2–4 tablespoons iced water

NOTE: You can use a round cutter instead; however, I like to use every last bit of dough and find it easier to cut it into squares or rectangles.

In a medium bowl, combine the cheddar cheese and queso seco and set aside. Place the softened butter in the bowl of a food processor fitted with a metal blade; pulse for 1 minute, or until the butter is fluffy (by hand, beat it well with a wooden spoon until fluffy). In a large bowl, whisk together the flour, salt, chile powder, and cumin until well combined. Add the cheese mixture to the dry ingredients and mix to combine. Add the flour mixture to the butter in the food processor and pulse for 30–40 seconds. Gradually add the iced water through the feed tube, pulsing briefly between additions, until the dough comes together and forms a ball. (If working by hand, combine all of the ingredients and add the water a bit at a time, kneading the dough until it holds together.) Turn the dough out onto a clean surface and divide it in half. Press each half into a disk and wrap tightly with plastic wrap; chill for 30 minutes.

Preheat the oven to 375°F. Line four large baking sheets with parchment paper. On a lightly floured surface, roll out the dough, 1 disk at a time, into a ⅛-inch-thick rectangle. Using a sharp knife or pastry wheel, cut the dough into 1½ × 1½-inch squares (see note). Place them on the prepared baking sheets and bake for 12–15 minutes, or until puffed and golden. Reroll the scraps and cut; continue with the remaining dough until all the wafers are baked. Transfer the wafers to metal cooling racks and cool completely before placing them in a food storage box or tin. *Makes 40–50 wafers*

the flatbreads of latin america

Most Latin American countries consume their own version of unleavened bread, or flatbread. The only countries that consume tortillas are Mexico and its Central American brethren. In Mexico, tortillas are made of nixtamalized corn masa or wheat flour; the corn tortilla is a bit thicker than the flour tortilla and tends to be smaller in circumference. When corn tortillas are fried, they become crunchy, whereas flour tortillas become flaky. The kinds of tortillas consumed in Central America vary by country. For instance, Guatemalans eat only corn tortillas, which are smaller, thicker (about ¼ inch thick), and meatier than those found in Mexico. The Honduran and El Salvadoran version is similar to the Guatemalan tortilla. The pupusa, made of masa, is a flatbread, also from El Salvador, that is about ⅓ inch thick and stuffed with beans, cheese, or pork mince, called chicharrón. In Nicaragua, tortillas can be as large as dinner plates. In South America "tortilla" refers to a frittata. In Venezuela and Colombia you'll find the arepa, a flatbread made with a precooked cornmeal that has a crispy exterior and a soft interior with a consistency akin to grits or polenta; arepas look a lot like the griddle cakes made in the South. In Brazil and Caribbean countries, the thin, crispy, and delicate crepe made with yuca or cassava flour (also popular in Colombia) is the flatbread of choice.

arepitas with goat cheese and green tomato chutney

Here, corn cakes are topped with tangy cheese and sweet chutney and explode with a combination of flavors that transcends culinary borders. Arepas are the national flat-breads of Venezuela and Colombia. Made with precooked cornmeal, called *harina pan*, they have crispy exteriors and soft centers with the consistency of grits. These are traditionally slathered with queso blanco, butter, or cream cheese. They can be grilled or baked, but I prefer to sauté them first in butter to create a crunchy crust that lends contrast to the smooth cheese. Corn, the common denominator of the food of the New World, is the perfect example of how the way one ingredient was used took on different characteristics depending on the region in which it was introduced; its many interpretations have fed the peoples of the Americas for centuries. It befits corn to join people together; this tantalizing recipe builds upon the similarities of the great cuisines of the Americas.

FOR THE GOAT CHEESE TOPPING

4 ounces goat cheese, at room temperature
4 tablespoons unsalted butter, at room temperature
¼ cup heavy whipping cream

FOR THE AREPITAS

2–2½ cups arepa flour
1 teaspoon salt
1 cup warm milk
2 cups warm water
⅓ cup (5⅓ tablespoons) unsalted butter, for sautéing
2 tablespoons vegetable oil
Green Tomato Chutney (page 30)
24 parsley leaves

NOTE: Arepa flour brands vary, so if the dough is too loose, add a bit more flour, 1 tablespoon at a time, until the dough can be formed into patties; if the dough is too thick, add a bit more water, 1 tablespoon at a time. Arepas must be served warm, so keep them (without the topping) in a 275°F oven (for up to 1 hour) before serving. They can also be reheated in the microwave.

In a medium bowl, mix the goat cheese, butter, and cream until smooth. Cover and refrigerate until ready to use.

Preheat the oven to 350°F. In a medium bowl, combine 2 cups of the arepa flour and the salt. Stir in the warm milk and water, mixing until the dough comes together (the texture should be like that of very thick mashed potatoes—see note). Cover the bowl with plastic wrap, and let the dough sit at room temperature for 10 minutes.

Melt the butter in a nonstick skillet over medium heat; add the oil (which will prevent the butter from browning). With moistened hands, shape 2 tablespoons of the dough into a patty 2 inches in diameter and $\frac{1}{2}$ inch thick and drop it into the skillet; repeat with the rest of the dough; sauté the arepitas for 2 minutes on one side, or until the bottoms begin to turn golden; flip them over and sauté for 2–3 minutes on the other side, or until golden. If the arepas are browning too quickly, reduce the heat. Transfer the arepas to an ungreased baking pan and bake for 10 minutes.

To assemble, place roughly 2 teaspoons of the goat cheese mixture on each arepa; top with a generous dollop of Green Tomato Chutney and a parsley leaf. *Makes 24 arepitas*

avocado and pimiento cheese terrine

Molded salads are a deeply rooted Southern tradition—from fruit concoctions to tomato aspic. Here, I combine two of my loves: pimiento cheese and guacamole. The addition of whipping cream offsets the pungency of the cheese, allowing it to meld seamlessly with the buttery taste of avocados. Impressive to look at, this bicolor loaf may look intimidating to make but is actually quite easy. Don't let the number of ingredients deter you; the ingredients for each layer are simply mixed together in the food processor (or a bowl) and spread into a loaf pan. Served with blue corn tortilla chips, this is the perfect appetizer for informal get-togethers. For fancier occasions, surround the loaf with toast points or sliced crusty bread. Make one large loaf or three smaller ones. Who knew that pairing avocado and pimiento cheese would result in a marriage made in culinary heaven?

FOR THE AVOCADO LAYER

¼ cup warm water
2 tablespoons unflavored gelatin
  (2 packages)
1 cup chicken broth
3 ripe Hass avocados, mashed
¼ cup mayonnaise
¼ cup finely minced white onion
¼ cup finely chopped cilantro
  (leaves and tender stems)
¼ cup finely chopped flat-leaf parsley
  (leaves and tender stems)
1½ tablespoons lemon juice
1 teaspoon Worcestershire sauce
½ teaspoon salt
⅛ teaspoon freshly ground black pepper
  Dash hot sauce (such as Tabasco), or
  to taste

FOR THE PIMIENTO CHEESE LAYER

1 tablespoon unflavored gelatin
  (1 package)
¼ cup warm water
¼ cup heavy whipping cream, warm
2 cups Classic Pimiento Cheese
  (page 35)
¼ teaspoon salt
¼ teaspoon freshly ground
  black pepper
  Dash hot sauce, or to taste

Line a 6-cup loaf pan with plastic wrap, leaving an over-hang; spray the plastic wrap well with cooking spray.

In a small bowl, sprinkle the gelatin over the warm water; let sit for 1 minute. In a microwave-safe bowl, heat the broth on high for 2 minutes (or heat it in a pan on the stove until it comes to a simmer). Stir the gela-tin into the broth; mix until the gelatin is dissolved; set aside. In the bowl of a food processor fitted with a metal blade, combine the avocados, mayonnaise, onions, cilan-tro, parsley, lemon juice, and Worcestershire sauce; pro-cess until smooth. (Alternatively, mash the avocados in a bowl using a potato masher until smooth and stir in the rest of the ingredients.) Transfer the mixture to a large bowl and stir in the salt, pepper, and hot sauce. Add the gelatin mixture and stir until smooth. Spread the avocado mixture evenly into the prepared loaf pan and chill for 30 minutes.

Sprinkle the gelatin over the warm water in a small bowl; let sit for 1 minute. In a microwave-safe bowl, heat the cream on high for 1 minute, or heat it in a pan on the stove until it comes to a simmer (don't let it boil). Remove from the heat; stir in the gelatin and allow the mixture to cool for 5 minutes. In a medium bowl, combine the pimiento cheese, salt, pepper, and hot sauce; add the cream and gelatin mixture and stir until smooth. Spread the mixture evenly over the chilled avocado layer. Cover the top well with the plastic wrap overhang and refrig-erate until set (at least 2 hours or overnight). To serve, uncover the top of the mold, unmold it onto a large plat-ter, and remove the plastic. *Makes 1 loaf*

black-eyed pea croquetas with chimichurri-benne mayonnaise

Hot and salty, these delicious croquetas have a golden crust that, when nibbled on, exposes a light and creamy interior. These are tasty by themselves but are particularly scrumptious when dipped into my tangy, smooth remoulade sauce. Black-eyed peas or cowpeas—known as *gandúles* in Puerto Rico—were brought to the New World by African slaves. Slave cooks were often in charge of preparing the food in homes in the antebellum South and colonial Brazil and the Caribbean. Their culinary influence was enormous and forever changed the foodways of the Americas. A closer look into Latin American and Southern cuisines demonstrates remarkable similarities in the use of certain ingredients and techniques that originated in Africa. Sesame seeds, known in the Low Country as benne seeds, were also introduced to the South in colonial times by African slaves. Here, I use prepared sesame seed paste, called tahini, for convenience. Fritters traditionally made in the South, like these, are similar to the delicious *acarajés* sold in the street stalls of Bahía. These freeze well and reheat easily in the oven.

FOR THE CROQUETAS

- 3 cups fresh (or frozen and thawed) black-eyed peas
- 2 cups fresh bread crumbs (about 4 slices of bread)
- 2 cups cilantro (leaves and tender stems), packed
- 1 cup minced yellow onion
- 4 large garlic cloves, minced
- 2 tablespoons minced jalapeños
- 1 tablespoon grated lemon zest
- 2 eggs
- 1 teaspoon ground cumin
- 1 teaspoon ground coriander
- 1 teaspoon cayenne pepper
- 1 teaspoon salt
- ½ teaspoon baking powder
- ½ cup flour for dredging
  Vegetable oil for frying

Fit a large baking pan with a metal cooling rack. In the bowl of a food processor fitted with a metal blade, combine the peas, bread crumbs, cilantro, onions, garlic, jalapeño, lemon zest, eggs, cumin, coriander, cayenne, salt, and baking powder; process until smooth (stopping to scrape the sides of the bowl once or twice). Let the mixture rest for 10 minutes. Shape the mixture into 2-inch balls and coat each lightly with flour.

In a large skillet with high sides, heat 2–3 inches of oil to 360°F (or use a deep fryer according to the manufacturer's instructions). Carefully drop the balls into the oil and fry for 2–3 minutes, or until golden brown, using two forks to turn them halfway through. Using a slotted spoon transfer the croquetas to the prepared cooling rack to drain. Sprinkle with salt. The croquetas can be kept warm in a 250°F oven for up to 1 hour before serving.

FOR THE MAYONNAISE

1   cup mayonnaise
2   tablespoons chimichurri
        (page 26)
1   tablespoon tahini
        Lime juice, to taste
        Salt and freshly ground black
            pepper, to taste

To make the mayonnaise. In a medium bowl, combine the mayonnaise, chimichurri, and tahini; season with lime juice, salt, and pepper. *Makes 2 dozen*

carrot escabeche

Sweet and meaty carrots cooked until just tender meet succulent vinaigrette in this most refreshing appetizer salad. A mixture of lively green herbs contrasts with the vibrant orange hue of this humble root vegetable, transforming it into an elegant victual with sublime, delicate taste, and indisputable wow factor. Escabeche is a pickling technique invented by the Arabs to preserve foods for longer storage. Brought to the New World by the Spaniards, this remains a popular way to prepare fish, poultry, meats, and vegetables in modern Latin American cuisine. This is exactly the kind of offering that can be put together quickly without fuss for impromptu guests. In the summertime, I make this often so I can always be ready to welcome friends dropping by for a quick drink by the lake. Carrots absorb vinaigrettes best when still warm. In order for the herbs to retain their luscious green hue, add them only when the carrots have cooled completely. Escabeches are best served at room temperature; pair this one with thinly sliced ham and a perfectly chilled glass of white wine.

2 pounds carrots, peeled and cut into
 ½-inch-thick slices
½ cup white wine vinegar
¾ cup extra-virgin olive oil
½ cup finely chopped cilantro (leaves
 and tender stems)
¼ cup finely chopped flat-leaf parsley
 (leaves and tender stems)
1 tablespoon minced fresh mint
1 teaspoon minced fresh rosemary
2 large garlic cloves, minced
½ teaspoon salt, or to taste
 Dash freshly ground black pepper

Place the carrots in a medium saucepan filled with cold water. Bring the carrots to a boil and cook over medium-high heat, uncovered, until fork-tender, about 15–20 minutes. While the carrots are cooking, in a small bowl, whisk together the vinegar and oil; set aside. Drain the carrots and place them in a bowl; pour the vinaigrette over the hot carrots and mix to combine. Allow the carrots to cool to room temperature. Add the cilantro, parsley, mint, rosemary, garlic, salt, and pepper; stir to combine. Serve slightly chilled or at room temperature. The escabeche will keep for up to 1 week in your refrigerator; bring it to room temperature before serving. *Serves 6–8*

cheese and fig thumbprints

Cheese and figs have always made a great pair, and these addictive shortbread cookies filled with fig preserves offer sweet and savory flavors in a single bite. Dainty, bejeweled beauties, these are fit for elegant entertaining. Fig trees grow abundantly in the South. When figs are in season, I recommend that you make a batch or two of my fig preserves (page 29) and keep them in your freezer so you can use them whenever you feel like making a batch of these. Otherwise, purchase an extra jar at your local gourmet store during the holiday season, when they seem to be most available. To save time, I use a food processor to make the shortbread base of this cookie, but it can also be prepared by hand using a pastry cutter. These are some of my favorite cookies to give away to friends and family during the Christmas season.

1 cup all-purpose flour
¼ teaspoon freshly ground
   black pepper
¼ teaspoon cayenne pepper
2 cups shredded Monterey
   Jack cheese
½ cup grated queso seco
½ cup (1 stick) unsalted butter,
   at room temperature
1 egg yolk
1½ cups finely chopped pecans
1 cup finely chopped fig preserves
   (or smooth fig jam) (page 29)

In a medium bowl, whisk together the flour, black pepper, and cayenne. In the bowl of a food processor fitted with a metal blade, combine the cheese and butter; process until smooth. Add the egg yolk and pulse until combined, scraping down the sides of the bowl occasionally. Add the flour mixture and pulse, just until a soft dough forms. Transfer the dough to a bowl; cover with plastic wrap and chill for 30 minutes.

To bake, preheat the oven to 350°F. Line 2 large baking sheets with parchment paper. Place the pecans on a plate. With hands (or a 1-inch ice cream scoop), roll scant tablespoons of the dough into 1-inch balls (it's easier to roll if hands are moistened or if scoop is dipped in water). Roll each ball into the pecans and place on the prepared baking sheets. With your thumb, make an indentation in the middle of each ball. Refrigerate the cookies for 20 minutes and then bake for 20–22 minutes, or until firm and lightly golden (don't overbake). Let them cool on the sheets for 5 minutes and then transfer to cooling racks. When they're cooled completely, fill the indentations with the fig preserves. (These can be frozen without the preserves for up to 4 months. Freeze on sheets, until solid, then transfer to airtight containers. They can be recrisped in a 350°F oven for 2–3 minutes, if needed.) When ready to serve, fill the indentations with the fig preserves.
Makes 36 cookies

cocktail chiles rellenos with latin pimiento cheese

If you like chiles rellenos, you'll love these. Who could resist the crispy coating, the creamy center, and the faint whisper of heat? Although poblano peppers are traditionally used in chiles rellenos, they're expensive and too large to serve as hors d'oeuvres. Jars or cans of roasted, peeled, and seeded piquillo peppers are sold in most grocery stores and gourmet shops. Not having to prepare the chiles saves a lot of effort, and these are just the right size to eat in one or two bites. Drain and dry them well in order to prevent messy splatters when you fry them. You should also fill and chill the peppers before you plan to batter and fry them; this helps the crust get crispy without causing the filling to ooze out while they fry. I will sometimes line small, crusty rolls with lettuce or shredded cabbage and make petite party sandwiches with these chiles.

24 whole piquillo peppers
    Latin Pimiento Cheese (page 35)
4   egg whites, at room temperature
3   whole eggs, at room temperature
¼   cup all-purpose flour
    More flour for dredging
    Vegetable oil for frying

Line a baking pan with paper towels. Place the pimiento cheese in a pastry bag fitted with a large round tip (a zip-top bag or disposable pastry bag cut at the tip works as well). Pipe about 2 tablespoons of the cheese into each pepper (start by placing the tip of the bag inside the pepper and squeeze as you pull the tip out). Place the filled peppers on the prepared baking pan and layer paper towels over them; wrap with plastic wrap and chill for at least 1 hour (preferably overnight) in order to solidify the cheese and remove excess moisture.

Line a large baking pan with parchment paper and fit with a metal cooling rack. In a large bowl, using a whisk or an electric mixer, beat the egg whites until they're frothy and have tripled in volume. In a separate bowl, beat the whole eggs for 3 minutes, or until they're a light, lemony color. Whisk the flour into the whole eggs, then fold in the egg whites, just until combined. Remove the chiles from the refrigerator and uncover.

In a large skillet with high sides, heat 2–3 inches of oil to 360°F (or use a deep fryer according to the manufacturer's instructions). Working with one pepper at a time, dredge the pepper in the flour; using a large spoon, slide the pepper into the egg batter and then lift it out with the spoon. Carefully slide the battered pepper into the oil. Fry the peppers for 3–4 minutes, or until the batter is golden brown, using two forks to turn them halfway through. Transfer the peppers to the prepared cooling rack; repeat until all peppers have been fried. You may fry 4 to 5 peppers at a time, but be careful not to crowd them; if you do, the oil temperature will drop and the peppers won't get crunchy. Using a slotted spoon, transfer the peppers to the prepared cooling rack. Cool for 5 minutes and serve. These can be kept warm in a 250°F oven for up to 1 hour.

Makes 24 chiles

crab croquetas with latin tartar sauce

Lighter than air, these addictive crabmeat hors d'oeuvres are paired with a bold and spicy dipping sauce. They rival any crab cake I've ever tried before. Croquetas, or fritters, are served in a variety of ways throughout Latin America, from soup garnishes to side dishes. They can be made with meat, fowl, seafood, or vegetables. Latinos inherited a taste for croquetas from the Old World, mainly from Portugal and Spain, where cod and ham fritters are still popular. In my version, the thick béchamel is the key to the croquetas' moist interior. After frying, these can be cooled, then frozen on a single layer and kept for up to 3 months in your freezer. To reheat, simply bake in a hot oven until heated through.

Thick Béchamel Sauce (page 17)
3½ cups lump crabmeat picked
      for shell fragments
1   (4-ounce) jar diced pimientos,
      drained
¼   cup minced capers
¼   cup minced chives
¼   cup finely chopped flat-leaf parsley
      (leaves and tender stems)
1   teaspoon salt
½   teaspoon freshly ground
      black pepper
¼   teaspoon smoked Spanish paprika
¼   teaspoon garlic powder
    Flour for dredging (about 1¾ cups)
3   eggs, beaten lightly
    Bread crumbs for coating
      (about 3 cups)
    Vegetable oil for frying
    Latin Tartar Sauce (page 31)

In a large bowl, combine the crabmeat, pimientos, capers, chives, parsley, salt, pepper, paprika, and garlic powder; mix well to combine. Stir the béchamel into the crab mixture, being careful not to break up the crabmeat too much; let the mixture chill for 10 minutes (or up to 1 hour).

Fit a large baking pan with a metal cooling rack. In a large skillet with high sides, heat 2–3 inches of oil to 360°F (or use a deep fryer according to the manufacturer's instructions). Using a 2-inch ice cream scoop, shape the crab mixture into balls and dredge them in the flour, coating them well; dip them in the eggs and into the bread crumbs to coat completely. Carefully drop the balls into the oil and fry for 2–3 minutes, or until golden brown, using two forks to turn them halfway through. Using a slotted spoon, transfer them to the prepared cooling rack to drain. Serve with Latin Tartar Sauce on the side for dipping. These can be frozen for up to 3 months. Freeze the cooled croquetas in a single layer on a baking sheet until solid, then transfer them to zip-top freezer bags. To reheat, simply bake in a 400°F oven until heated through. *Serves 8–10*

crab dip

Warm and bubbly, this rich dip tantalizes the palate with a combination of exciting flavors. There are many Southern renditions of this creamy spread, but mine takes a side trip through Latin America. Based loosely on traditional queso fundido (melted cheese), this hot, cheesy spread is both spicy and sweet. Lump crabmeat comes from the body of the crab, and I prefer it for its chunky consistency, which gives this dip a little bit of bite. Mayonnaise is a favorite ingredient in the South, and it's featured in myriad recipes—both savory and sweet. When baked, mayonnaise puffs up like a soufflé, creating a luscious, airy, and velvety texture. This easy dip can be prepared several hours ahead of time and baked when company arrives. Serve it with sliced baguette, tortilla chips, or plataninas (page 73).

2 cups lump crabmeat, picked for shell fragments

1½ cups grated Chihuahua or Monterey Jack cheese

2 poblano chiles, roasted, peeled, seeded, deveined, and chopped into ¼-inch pieces (see page 116)

½ cup sour cream

¼ cup mayonnaise

¼ cup thinly sliced green onion (white and light green parts only)

¼ cup finely chopped flat-leaf parsley (leaves and tender stems)

2 teaspoons minced chipotle chiles in adobo, or to taste

1 tablespoon adobo, or to taste

2 tablespoons lemon juice

½ teaspoon salt

¼ teaspoon freshly ground black pepper

Preheat the oven to 350°F. Butter a medium casserole dish. In a medium bowl, combine the crabmeat, cheese, poblanos, sour cream, mayonnaise, onions, parsley, chipotles, adobo, lemon juice, salt, and pepper, being careful not to break up the crabmeat too much. Transfer the mixture to the prepared dish and bake for 15–20 minutes, or until the dip is bubbly and the top is golden. Remove from oven and cool slightly, 4–5 minutes, before serving. *Serves 8-10*

a dissertation on mayonnaise

Mayonnaise, the creamy spread beloved by Southern and Latino cooks alike, is an emulsion of egg yolks and oil with either lemon juice or vinegar added for flavor. It has many culinary uses, not the least of which is adding twang to pimiento cheese, creaminess to ensalada Rusa, and moisture to chocolate cakes. And what would the classic Southern tomato sandwich be without mayonnaise? Homemade mayonnaise is very easy to make in a blender or food processor. Unfortunately, very few cooks make their own anymore because they either think it's too hard to make or don't want to risk salmonella poisoning associated with raw eggs.

The origins of mayonnaise are a bit unclear. Some claim the recipe was conceived in 1756 by the Duke of Richelieu's chef in the wake of the French victory over the British in the battle at Port Mahon. However, the medieval cookbook *Libre de Sent Soví*, written in Catalan in 1324, features several emulsions made with eggs and a garlic-infused sauce similar to aioli. What we do know for sure is that the French popularized mayonnaise (originally called *mahonese*) throughout Europe. Spaniards, in turn, brought it to Latin America. Mayonnaise is first mentioned in American cookbooks as early as the 1820s. Commercial mayonnaise began to be available in the early 1900s. In my opinion, Duke's mayonnaise, which was created in 1919 by Eugenia Duke of South Carolina is the closest to homemade as you can get. I find that most cooks are very particular when it comes to the brand of mayonnaise they like to cook with, however, so use your favorite brand for the recipes in this book.

hamburger sliders with latin pimiento cheese and pico de gallo

These tiny burgers are a great combination of texture and flavor: juicy, creamy, crunchy, and spicy. Hamburgers are the all-American meal, and from Charleston to New Orleans you'll find them topped with pimiento cheese. I'm partial to the versions served at Bill Smith's Crook's Corner in Chapel Hill, North Carolina. Down the road at The Carolina Inn, they're embellished with fried green tomatoes and fried eggs. Hamburgers are served all over Latin America, as well, a direct result of U.S. influence in the twentieth century. However, the use of ground beef for picadillos and tortas de carne (meat patties) has been part of the Latin culinary tradition since the Spanish conquest, when beef was first brought to the New World. For my get-togethers, I make the pimiento cheese several days in advance and shape the patties one day ahead, keeping them wrapped and chilled until ready to cook.

2 teaspoons vegetable oil
½ cup finely chopped yellow onion
1½ pounds ground chuck
2 finely chopped serrano chiles (seeded and deveined if less heat is desired)
1½ tablespoons Worcestershire sauce
1 teaspoon salt
½ teaspoon garlic powder
¼ teaspoon smoked Spanish paprika
¼ teaspoon freshly ground black pepper
24 mini party rolls or miniature hamburger buns
2 cups shredded iceberg lettuce
Pico de Gallo (page 34)
Latin Pimiento Cheese (page 35)

In a medium skillet, heat the oil over medium-high heat; add the onions and sauté for approximately 3–4 minutes, or until they begin to turn a golden color (caramelize); allow them to cool for 5 minutes. In a large bowl, combine the caramelized onions, ground chuck, chiles, Worcestershire sauce, salt, garlic powder, paprika, and black pepper; mix well. Divide the mixture into 24 equal portions to form into patties. The patties should be slightly larger than the buns; make an indentation at the center of each patty with the back of a spoon so that they cook evenly.

Heat an outdoor grill (or an indoor grill pan or a griddle) and cook burgers until done to your liking (2 minutes on each side for medium-rare).

To assemble the burgers, spread the pimiento cheese on both halves of the mini party rolls. Place some lettuce on the bottom halves; top with the beef patties and a spoonful of pico de gallo; top with the remaining bun halves. Serve immediately. *Serves 6–8*

jalapeño deviled eggs

These hearty morsels are rich, soft, and creamy. They offer just the right amount of crunch and a subtle kick from the chiles. Stuffed eggs, which are very popular in the South, are also common in Latin America, where they're usually filled with cold salads, such as Ensalada Rusa (page 90). They're easily made with everyday ingredients and can be made ahead of time. I often serve them at ladies' luncheons, picnics by the lake, or Sunday barbecues. Loved by adults and children alike, these are often the first to disappear from my table. I have a trick that makes peeling hard-boiled eggs a cinch: crack the bottom of the cooked eggs while they're still hot and then plunge them into iced water until they're cold. This scrumptious recipe can be doubled, tripled, or quadrupled, making it ideal for feeding large crowds. Easy to tote, consider taking these to your next potluck supper.

6 eggs
½ cup mayonnaise
2 teaspoons finely chopped yellow onion
2 teaspoons finely chopped jalapeños (seeded and deveined if less heat is desired)
2 teaspoons finely chopped cilantro (leaves and tender stems)
1 teaspoon finely chopped flat-leaf parsley (leaves and tender stems)
1 teaspoon yellow mustard
⅛ teaspoon salt
⅛ teaspoon freshly ground black pepper
Smoked Spanish paprika (optional, for garnish)
Curly or flat-leaf parsley (for garnish)

Place the eggs in a medium pan and cover with cold water. Set the pan over high heat and bring to a rolling boil. As soon as the water comes to a boil, cover the pan and turn off the heat. Let the eggs cook for 12 minutes. Plunge the eggs into iced water to stop the cooking process.

Once the eggs are chilled, peel off the shells. Halve each egg lengthwise; scoop out the yolk into a small bowl, and set the egg whites on a plate lined with paper towels. Using a fork, mash the egg yolks into a paste; add the mayonnaise, onions, jalapeños, cilantro, parsley, mustard, salt, and pepper and stir together well. (If not serving immediately, cover the egg whites and the filling separately with plastic wrap and store in the refrigerator for up to 6 hours.) Using a spoon (or a pastry bag), fill the egg white cavities with the egg yolk mixture (about 1 tablespoon). Chill them, loosely covered, until ready to serve (but no longer than 2 hours). When ready to serve, sprinkle the eggs with smoked paprika and garnish with parsley. *Serves 6*

masa-encrusted fried green tomatoes with cilantro crema

Fried foods are abundant in both Southern and Latino cuisines, but fried green tomatoes are a Southern specialty without compare. A crispy crust that tastes like seasoned corn chips envelopes tart slices of perfectly juicy tomatoes. When I first tasted fried green tomatoes, they reminded me of the tomatillos of my youth, so I decided to come up with my own version, what I'd call a reverse version of chips and salsa. Here, instead of dipping the chips into a tomato salsa, the tomato is hidden within the chip; and the cilantro crema adds a luxurious twist. This is a great way to use unripe tomatoes throughout the hot summer months. Although they're traditionally coated in cornmeal, I use masa harina instead. Green tomatoes have a sturdy flesh that helps them retain their texture; once fried, the crust stays crispy and the tomatoes keep their shape. Don't fry fully ripened tomatoes because they will fall apart. Topped with bacon and Latin Pimiento Cheese (page 35), leftovers make delicious sandwiches.

FOR THE TOMATOES

- 2 large green tomatoes
- 1 cup masa harina
- ½ teaspoon ground cumin
- ½ teaspoon ground coriander
- ½ teaspoon ancho chile powder
- 1 teaspoon salt
- ½ teaspoon freshly ground black pepper
- Egg wash made of 1 large egg beaten with 2 tablespoons water
- Vegetable oil for frying

FOR THE CILANTRO CREMA

- 1½ cups Mexican crema or sour cream
- ½ cup finely chopped cilantro (leaves and tender stems)
- 2 teaspoons lemon juice

Fit a large baking pan with a metal cooling rack. Cut each tomato into ½-inch-thick slices, then cut each slice into 4 wedges. In a small bowl, whisk together the masa harina, cumin, coriander, chile powder, salt, and pepper.

In a medium skillet with high sides, heat 2–3 inches of oil to 360°F (or use a deep fryer according to the manufacturer's instructions). Dip both sides of the tomato wedges in the egg mixture, then in the masa harina mixture and coat well; working in batches, carefully place the tomato wedges in the hot oil. Cook for 2–3 minutes, or until crispy and golden, on one side; flip them over and fry the second side until crispy and golden. Using a slotted spoon, transfer the tomatoes to the prepared cooling rack; immediately sprinkle with salt. Serve with the cilantro crema on the side.

To make the cilantro crema: In a medium bowl, combine the Mexican crema, cilantro, and lemon juice and stir until well blended. *Serves 6*

miami guava and cream cheese empanaditas

In these tasty empanaditas (mini versions of empanadas), a tender, flaky crust surrounds a creamy filling that juxtaposes the sweetness of tropical fruit with the tanginess of cheese. I grew up spending summer vacations in Key Biscayne, where I was introduced to this favorite Cuban-American combination. My husband, who lived in Florida as a student, ate his share of guava shells preserved in syrup with sliced cream cheese for dessert. Empanadas are like Southern hand pies and can be baked or fried. My pastry features a small amount of annatto powder, which infuses it with a golden color; a hefty addition of cream cheese adds silkiness. Guava jelly can be found in most grocery stores and Latin tiendas. Empanadas can be shaped and then frozen for several months. Freeze them in a single layer until solid and then store them in freezer bags. They can be baked to order without thawing.

FOR THE PASTRY

1½ cups all-purpose flour
1 tablespoon sugar
Pinch salt
1 teaspoon annatto powder
1 (8-ounce) package cream cheese, cubed and chilled
½ cup (1 stick) unsalted butter, cubed and chilled

In the bowl of a food processor fitted with a metal blade, combine the flour, sugar, salt, and annatto powder; pulse for 20 seconds. Add the cream cheese and butter and pulse until the mixture comes together to form a ball. Turn the dough out onto a clean surface and divide it in half. Press each half into a disk and wrap it tightly with plastic wrap; chill for at least 30 minutes or up to 24 hours. (You can freeze the dough for up to 2 months; thaw it in the refrigerator before proceeding with the recipe.)

FOR THE FILLING

6 ounces cream cheese,
   at room temperature

¾ cup guava jelly

   Egg wash made of 1 egg beaten
   with 1 teaspoon water

½ cup turbinado sugar

To make the filling: Place the cream cheese in a small bowl and fluff it up with a fork; add the guava jelly and combine well. Cover and chill for at least 20 minutes or up to 24 hours.

Preheat the oven to 400°F. Line 2 large baking sheets with parchment paper. On a lightly floured surface, roll out the pastry to about a ⅛-inch thickness. Using a 3-inch round cutter, cut out 36 rounds of pastry. Place 1 teaspoon of the filling in the center of each round; brush the edges of the rounds with the egg wash and fold the dough in half over the filling. Seal the joined edges well by pressing them together with the tines of a fork; use the tines of the fork to cut out vents on the top of each empanada. Transfer the empanadas to the prepared baking sheets; brush the tops with egg wash and sprinkle with sugar. Bake for 15–20 minutes, or until golden. *Makes 3 dozen*

mini pibil barbecue sandwiches

Slow-cooked pork in exotic citrus sauce meets creamy coleslaw in this, my twist on traditional Carolina pulled-pork sandwiches. Cochinita pibil is a richly spiced pork dish cooked in banana leaves from the Yucatán Peninsula. In my version, the pork is seasoned with a combination of orange and lime juices that mimics the flavor of the sour oranges found in Latin America and obtains its recognizable deep red hue from annatto paste. The Southern version is served as a meal with hushpuppies and coleslaw. Here, I transform it into bite-size sandwiches for appetizers. I've served these to my Southern friends to rave reviews. Until now, I had never revealed my secret to its deep flavor: lard. Annatto can stain your clothes; offer lots of napkins. Try this pork as filling for tacos.

- 1 (4–5 pound) pork butt or
shoulder, with bone
- 1 bar (3–4 ounces) achiote paste
- 1 cup orange juice
- 1 tablespoon grated lime zest
- ½ cup lime juice
- ¼ cup white vinegar
- 1 stick Mexican cinnamon (canela)
- 1 large bay leaf (or 2 small)
- 2 teaspoons salt
- 1½ teaspoons ground cumin
- 1 teaspoon freshly ground
black pepper
- ½ teaspoon dried oregano
(Mexican preferred)
- ¼ teaspoon ground cloves
- ¼ cup melted lard, bacon fat,
or vegetable oil
- 4 large banana leaves
(see note on page 64)
Coleslaw (page 27)
- 48 miniature party rolls
Hot sauce (such as Tabasco)

Place the pork in a large plastic bag (I use a 13-gallon garbage bag). In a medium, nonreactive bowl, place the achiote paste; add the orange juice, lime zest, lime juice, and vinegar and let it sit, at room temperature, for 30 minutes, to soften the paste. With a fork, stir the mixture until the achiote paste dissolves; add the cinnamon stick, bay leaf, salt, cumin, pepper, oregano, and cloves, stirring to combine. Pour the marinade over the pork in the bag; seal the bag and place it in a large bowl. Marinate the pork in the refrigerator for at least 8 hours (but preferably overnight), turning the bag occasionally to redistribute the marinade.

When ready to cook, line a large Dutch oven with banana leaves, making sure to leave a generous overhang. Remove the pork from the bag and place it in the prepared pan; pour the marinade over the pork. Pour the lard over the pork and cover it with the banana leaves. Set the pan over high heat, and bring the liquid to a boil; cover the pan with a tight-fitting lid, reduce the heat to low, and simmer for 2½–3 hours, or until the pork falls away from the bone and shreds easily with a fork. Remove from the heat; transfer the pork to a separate bowl (leaving the sauce in the pan) and cool slightly. Using two forks, shred the pork and return it to the sauce, stirring to coat.

To assemble the sandwiches, slice each roll in half horizontally. Place some coleslaw on the bottom half of each roll; top with a generous amount of pork and top this with the other half of the roll. Serve with hot sauce. *Makes 48 bite-size sandwiches, or 12 servings*

NOTE: The pork may be cooked, shredded, and frozen in the sauce for up to 4 months. If any pork is left over, it's great served on top of cooked white rice. Also, banana leaves, which are brittle and easily broken, need to be heated to become pliable. Using a gas stove, quickly move the banana leaves back and forth over a low flame; they will change color slightly as they soften. Using an electric stove, bring a large pan of water to a boil; add the banana leaves and boil for 2 minutes; the leaves will turn an olive green color as they soften. Remove the leaves from the water and rinse under cold running water to stop cooking. Proceed with the recipe. Fresh or frozen banana leaves can be found in Latin and Asian stores. If well wrapped, fresh banana leaves may be frozen for up to 1 year.

mushroom and leek empanaditas

Flaky pastry melts in the mouth and exposes an elegant filling in this fancy, daintier version of empanadas. This is one of my most popular recipes, often requested at parties and at my private cooking classes. This kind of vegetarian filling, a mixture of leeks and mushrooms, is similar to French duxelles but has gone through myriad transformations in the hands of Latin cooks, who have added condiments and spices to suit their taste. I love to entertain on a whim, so when I make a batch of these I freeze them. They can be frozen for up to four months and go directly from freezer to oven. Use any leftover filling in omelets and quesadillas.

FOR THE PASTRY

1½ cups all-purpose flour
 Pinch of salt
1 (8-ounce) package cream cheese, cubed and chilled
½ cup (1 stick) unsalted butter, cubed and chilled

In the bowl of a food processor fitted with the metal blade, combine the flour and salt; pulse for 20 seconds. Add the cream cheese and butter and pulse until the mixture comes together to form a ball. Turn the dough out onto a clean surface and divide it in half. Press each half into a disk and wrap tightly with plastic wrap; chill for 30 minutes or up to 24 hours (freeze for up to 2 months; thaw before proceeding).

FOR THE FILLING

2 tablespoons unsalted butter
¾ cup minced leeks (white and light green parts only), rinsed well (see cook's tip)
2½ cups finely minced white button mushrooms (caps and stems)
⅓ cup white wine
½ teaspoon ground cumin
½ teaspoon ground coriander
½ teaspoon salt, or to taste
¼ teaspoon freshly ground black pepper, or to taste
½ cup grated Parmesan cheese
    Egg wash made of 1 large egg beaten with 1 tablespoon water

COOK'S TIP: The best way to wash leeks is to slice them and then plunge the slices into a bowl of cold water, separating the rings and swishing them well. Let the leeks stand for a few minutes, so any sand falls to the bottom of the bowl; carefully lift the leeks from the water and transfer them to a kitchen towel; pat them dry.

To make the filling: In a large skillet, melt the butter over medium-high heat. Add the leeks, and sauté 2–3 minutes, or until soft. Add the mushrooms and sauté for 3 minutes. Stir in the wine, cumin, coriander, salt, and pepper. Lower the heat to medium and cook until all the liquid has evaporated, about 6 minutes. Remove from the heat; cool completely. Stir in the grated cheese.

Preheat the oven to 400°F. Line 2 large baking sheets with parchment paper. On a floured surface, roll out the pastry, 1 disk at a time, to about a ⅛-inch thickness. Using a 3-inch round cutter, cut out 18 rounds. Repeat with the other half of the dough. Place 1 teaspoon of filling in the center of each round. Brush the edges of each round with egg wash and fold the dough in half over the filling. Seal the joined edges well by pressing them together with the tines of a fork; use the tines of the fork to cut vents on the top of each empanada. Transfer the empanadas to the prepared baking sheets; brush the tops with egg wash. Bake for 15–20 minutes, or until golden. *Makes 3 dozen*

new year's collard green empanadas

Here, shredded greens, scented with smoked pork and enhanced with creamy good-ness, are enveloped in a crunchy layer of dough and transformed into delicate fried pies. *Empanizar* means "to encase in bread." In this case, I use conveniently prepackaged empanada dough cut into rounds, which can be found in the freezer section of most Latin tiendas. Egg roll wrappers will also work well; simply fold the wrappers into triangles instead of half moons. In the South, it's customary to eat collard greens on New Year's Day; they symbolize folded bills and are believed to bring good luck. I like to make these auspicious pastries ahead of time and freeze them before I fry them. They can go directly from freezer to fryer whenever I'm ready to serve them. Once fried, they can be kept in a 250°F oven for up to one hour.

2   tablespoons vegetable oil or
      bacon drippings
½   cup finely chopped yellow onion
4   large garlic cloves, finely chopped
10 cups thinly shredded collard
      greens or kale
½   cup cooked and finely chopped
      bacon (about 7 slices)
1   (8-ounce) package cream cheese
¼   teaspoon cayenne pepper
16 prepared empanada disks (thawed)
      Vegetable oil for frying

COOK'S TIP: An easy way to shred kale or collards is to remove the large thick stalks from the leaves and stack several leaves together, roll them up tightly, and slice the roll crosswise thinly with a sharp knife.

In a large skillet, heat the oil over medium-high heat; add the onions and cook, stirring often, for 2 minutes, or until they begin to caramelize (turn golden). Add the garlic and cook for 20 seconds. Working in batches, add the shred-ded collards, making sure to stir them quickly, so that the garlic doesn't burn. Reduce the heat to medium-low and cook the collards for 3 minutes, or until wilted; remove from heat and let cool for 10 minutes. In a medium bowl, combine the cooked collards with the bacon and cream cheese; add the cayenne and stir well to combine.

Working on a clean surface, separate the empanada disks (keep them covered with a clean towel as you work, to prevent drying). Place a heaping ¼ cup of the filling on one-half of each disk, making sure to leave a ½-inch rim. Fold the disk in half over the filling and press the edges firmly with the tines of a fork to seal.

Fit 2 large baking sheets with metal cooling racks. In a large skillet with high sides, heat 2–3 inches of oil to 360°F (or use a deep fryer according to the manufacturer's instructions). Working in batches, carefully slide the empa-nadas into the oil and fry them for 3–4 minutes, or until golden brown, turning them over halfway through. Using a slotted spoon, transfer the empanadas to the prepared cooling racks. Serve hot. *Serves 8*

pickled mushrooms

These meaty, juicy mushrooms offer a little bit of sweetness and a touch of vinegar in every bite. Pickled vegetables are a common feature in Latin and Southern repasts. The pickling technique used here, in which a vinaigrette is cooked along with the vegetables, pickling them as they cool, is known as escabeche. The beauty of this method is that it doesn't require a long period of time. Arab cooking techniques such as this one were introduced into Spain during the Ottoman Empire. Many of them made their way into Latin cuisine as a result of the European conquista. Modern Latin cuisine features myriad examples of this cultural amalgamation. Serve the mushrooms at room temperature with plenty of crusty bread to sop up the caldillo (juices).

½ cup white wine vinegar
¼ cup water
1 tablespoon sugar
⅔ cup extra-virgin olive oil
1 cup thinly sliced yellow onion
1 large red bell pepper, cored, seeded, and sliced into ¼-inch-thick strips
8 sprigs fresh thyme (or 1 teaspoon dried)
1 bay leaf
6 whole black peppercorns
1½ pounds whole white button mushrooms
4 large garlic cloves, sliced paper-thin
Salt and freshly ground black pepper, to taste

In a medium bowl, combine the vinegar, water, and sugar; set aside. In a medium stainless steel or enamel-coated saucepan with high sides, combine the oil, onions, bell pepper, thyme, bay leaf, and peppercorns; cook over medium heat, stirring gently, for 4–5 minutes (being careful not to brown the onions). Reduce the heat to medium-low and add the mushrooms; cook for 3–4 minutes, stirring often. Add the garlic and cook for 30–40 seconds. Add the vinegar mixture and increase the heat to medium. Simmer, uncovered, for 5 minutes. Remove from heat and bring to room temperature. Season with salt and pepper. Transfer the mushrooms to a nonreactive bowl; cover with plastic wrap and chill for at least 2 hours. Bring them back to room temperature when ready to serve. These keep, if properly chilled and covered, for up to 1 week. *Serves 6-8*

pickled shrimp

A mainstay of Southern entertaining, pickled shrimp is bathed in tantalizing brine that infuses each bite with flavor. The elegant onion vinaigrette featured in my version has enough acidity to preserve but not break down the shrimp's flesh or to overpower their delicate taste. The addition of chiles adds yet another dimension, offering a barely discernible heat that complements the other flavors. Since the fragile texture of shrimp can be destroyed when exposed to the acid in the vinaigrette, they're cooked just until they turn pink and chilled promptly to stop the cooking process. I like to boil shrimp with their shells still on and reserve the flavorful stock, often freezing it for later use in recipes like Crab Soup with Artichoke Fritters (page 153). Add fresh herbs last to preserve color; offer crusty bread to sop up the juices.

2 pounds large (16–20 count)
shrimp, unpeeled

½ cup apple cider vinegar

¼ cup water

2 tablespoons brown sugar, packed

2 teaspoons salt

1 cup extra-virgin olive oil

5 cups very thinly sliced
Vidalia onion

½ teaspoon minced chiles de árbol
or red pepper flakes

¼ teaspoon whole peppercorns

1 bay leaf

¼ cup finely chopped flat-leaf parsley
(leaves and tender stems)

¼ cup finely chopped cilantro
(leaves and tender stems)

Wash the shrimp under cold running water; set aside. Fill a bowl with iced water; set aside. Fill a large pan with 8 cups of water; season it with 1–2 tablespoons of salt (it should taste like the sea) and set it over medium-high heat. When the water comes to a boil, add the shrimp and cook for 2 minutes, or until pink. Immediately remove the shrimp from the boiling water with a slotted spoon and immerse it in the iced water (reserve the cooking liquid for other uses). Peel and devein the shrimp and set aside; discard the shells.

In a small bowl, combine the vinegar, water, brown sugar, and salt; set aside. In a large skillet, heat the oil over medium heat; add the onions, chiles, peppercorns, and bay leaf; sauté for 8–9 minutes, or until the onions are soft but have not browned. Add the vinegar mixture to the onions and cook for 3 minutes. Remove from the heat and stir into the shrimp. Let the mixture cool at room temperature for 15 minutes, stirring occasionally; cover and chill for 2 hours. Stir in the parsley and cilantro. Bring to room temperature before serving. These keep, if properly chilled and covered, for up to 1 week. *Serves 8–10*

Chile-Cheese Biscuits with Avocado Butter (page 21)
and Sweet Potato Soup (page 163)

Chilled Avocado-Buttermilk
Soup with Crab Salad Nacho
(page 150)

Green Mango Salad with Pepita and Benne–Dusted Shrimp (page 91)

Collard Green Tamales
with Pimiento Sauce
(page 203)

Layered Potato
and Egg Salad
(Causa Vegetariana)
(page 94)

Chile-Chocolate Brownies
(page 229)

Cajeta Bread Pudding
(page 228)

Pecan Rum Cake with Figs
(page 243)

Pimiento and
Cheese Chilaquiles
(page 187)

Albóndigas with Sweet Fire-Roasted
Tomato Chutney (page 110)

rolled ham salad cake (pionono)

Savory and sweet flavors join successfully in this dainty spiral cake, perfectly suited for an afternoon tea or ladies' luncheon. Both Southerners and Latinos often combine sweet and salty flavors (perfect examples are bacon with brown sugar or molasses glazed ham). Unassuming and elegant at the same time, jelly rolls and rolled cakes are extremely popular throughout Latin America. Sweet versions are known as *brazos gitanos* (gypsies' arms) and savory versions are called *piononos*. My spin on the traditional pionono features a quintessentially Southern filling and is reminiscent of the savory cakes found in Argentina, Bolivia, and Uruguay. These delectable cakes—the original sandwich wraps—are usually filled with cold cuts, sliced cheese, olives, hard-boiled eggs, and roasted vegetables. Piononos—so called after Pope Pius IX, who is said to have loved them—are usually served as a heavy snack or light lunch.

FOR THE CAKE

- ¾ cup plus 2 tablespoons all-purpose flour
- 1 tablespoon cornstarch
- 1½ teaspoons baking powder
- 4 eggs, separated, at room temperature
- ⅛ teaspoon salt
- ½ cup sugar, divided
- 1 tablespoon iced water
- Confectioners' sugar

Preheat the oven to 350°F. Line a 15½ × 10½ × 1-inch jelly roll pan (or baking sheet) with parchment paper; butter the paper and set aside. Sift the flour, cornstarch, and baking powder into a large bowl; set aside. Using an electric mixer or a whisk, beat the egg whites and salt until soft peaks form, about 2 minutes. Beat in 4 tablespoons of the sugar, 1 tablespoon at a time, and continue beating until stiff peaks form, about 1 minute. In another large bowl, beat the egg yolks until thick, about 1½ minutes; beat in the water. Continue beating until the yolks are pale yellow and thick, about 2–3 minutes. Gradually beat in the remaining sugar until the yolks thicken and form ribbons when the beater or whisk is lifted or they're dropped from a spoon, about 1 minute. Gently stir ¼ of the whites into the yolks; fold in the rest of the whites. Carefully, fold the flour mixture into the eggs, being careful not to deflate them. Spread the batter evenly in the prepared pan. Tap the pan lightly on a hard surface to remove air bubbles. Bake for 12–15 minutes, or until a toothpick inserted in the center comes out clean.

FOR THE HAM SALAD

3 cups finely chopped ham
(about ¾ pound)

1 cup mayonnaise

½ cup finely chopped celery

¼ cup finely chopped Vidalia onion

2 tablespoons finely chopped cilantro
(leaves and tender stems)

2 tablespoons finely chopped parsley
(leaves and tender stems)

2 teaspoons yellow mustard

Salt and freshly ground black pepper,
to taste

Lay a clean, damp towel on the counter; sprinkle liberally with confectioners' sugar. Quickly turn the cake upside down over the towel and remove the pan carefully; peel off the parchment paper (if it sticks, dampen the paper with a wet basting brush). Starting from the long side, roll the warm cake in the towel. Let it cool completely.

In the meantime, make the ham salad. In a large bowl, combine the ham, mayonnaise, celery, onions, cilantro, parsley, and mustard; season with salt and pepper. Unroll the cake and spread the ham salad evenly over the top and roll it back up again. Trim the edges and transfer it to a platter. The cake may be filled and rolled up to 3 hours before serving. Serve well chilled. *Serves 8*

shrimp and cilantro mousse

Creamy and tangy, this soft spread is packed with lively herbs and tender seafood. I spent my youth in the American School of Guatemala, immersed in an American way of life that included a cafeteria that served everything from hamburgers and milkshakes to chiles rellenos and churros. However, I never saw more gelatin-based salads than when I moved to the South. From molded fruit and marshmallow concoctions, to savory, creamy vegetable mélanges, gelatin molds are a Southern culinary tradition. In her book *The American Century Cookbook*, published in 1997, my friend Jean Anderson, consummate author and expert on Southern cuisine, writes, "Throughout the South and heartland, they are still a party staple." Indeed, at some parties, you'd swear the tables wiggle too. Here is my own rendition of a gelatin mold, tweaked with Latin flavors. Serve it as a first course or appetizer with elegant toast points.

1   package unflavored gelatin
¼   cup cold water
1   (8-ounce) package cream cheese
     (or Neufchatel cheese), at room
     temperature
1   cup heavy whipping cream
½   cup sour cream
½   cup lime juice
1   cup cooked shrimp, peeled, deveined,
     and finely chopped (about 10 large
     shrimp)
¾   cup finely chopped cilantro (leaves
     and tender stems)
2   tablespoons finely chopped chives
     Salt and freshly ground black pepper,
     to taste
10 cilantro leaves
     Lemon twists (optional, for garnish)

Oil a 3-cup, nonreactive gelatin mold or loaf pan. In a glass, heat-resistant measuring cup or bowl, combine the gelatin with the cold water; stir to dissolve and let sit at room temperature for 2 minutes. Place the gelatin mixture in the microwave and heat until the gelatin dissolves, about 15 seconds on high (or heat the mixture on the stove in a double boiler over medium-low heat for 2 minutes); set aside to cool slightly. Using an electric mixer, blend the cream cheese, whipping cream, sour cream, and lime juice until creamy and smooth. Add the gelatin mixture and combine well. Using a rubber spatula, fold in the shrimp, cilantro, and chives. Season with salt and pepper. Pour the mixture into the prepared mold; cover with plastic wrap and chill for at least 2 hours (up to 2 days) before unmolding. Garnish with cilantro leaves and lemon twists. Keep well chilled until ready to serve. Serve with toast points.

To make toast points, preheat the oven to 350°F. Using a serrated knife trim off the crusts of a loaf of sliced bread and then cut each slice on the diagonal into 4 triangles. Place the triangles on ungreased baking sheets and bake for 8–10 minutes, or until lightly toasted.

To make lemon twists: Using a lemon zester cut out strips of lemon zest with a potato peeler or lemon channeler and twist them into curls; keep well chilled until ready to use as garnish. *Serves 10-12*

shrimp ceviche with plataninas

A great point of departure, sweet and plump shrimp meet crunchy vegetables in this brightly flavored appetizer. A traditional dish of Peru and Ecuador, ceviche is one of the trendiest appetizers of the new millennium. It's low in fat and easy to make. Most ceviches are made by combining raw fish with citrus juices—usually lime or lemon, but orange and grapefruit also work—which "cook" the fish. If shellfish, such as shrimp and lobster, is used, it must be blanched briefly before marinating. Plataninas are thinly sliced plantain chips called *mariquitas* in Cuba (*chifles* and *patacones* in South America), not to be confused with the thicker, twice-fried tostones. Shrimp salads abound in the South, often stuffed into tomatoes or deviled eggs. You'll be hard-pressed to find a more refreshing appetizer than this one on a hot summer's day. Serve with icy cold beer.

FOR THE CEVICHE

1½ pounds shrimp, peeled and deveined
2 teaspoons salt
2 cups chopped tomatoes
1 cup chopped piquillo peppers
½ cup sliced green onion, white part only
½ cup chopped cilantro (leaves and tender stems)
1 teaspoon ají amarillo paste or hot sauce (such as Tabasco)
¾ cup lime juice

Fill a large bowl with iced water and set aside. Fill a large pan with water and set it over high heat. Bring the water to a boil; add the salt and bring the water back to a boil. Add the shrimp and cook for 2–3 minutes, or until barely pink and tender. Immediately remove the shrimp from the boiling water with a slotted spoon and immerse in the iced water to stop the cooking. Remove the tails and discard; chop the shrimp coarsely.

In a large bowl, combine the shrimp, tomatoes, piquillo peppers, green onions, and cilantro; stir well. In a small bowl, whisk together the ají amarillo paste, lime juice, and honey; add the mixture to the shrimp and stir well to coat. Season with salt and pepper; cover and chill for at least 1

2 teaspoons honey
   Salt and freshly ground black pepper,
      to taste
   Chopped cilantro for garnish

FOR THE PLATANINAS
3 green plantains (a little yellow on the
      skin is okay)
   Vegetable oil for frying
   Fine sea salt

hour (or up to 4 hours) to allow all flavors to blend before serving.

To make the plataninas: Fit 2 large baking pans with metal cooling racks. Peel the plantains (see note). Using a mandolin or a very sharp knife slice them lengthwise into thin strips ($\frac{1}{8}$ inch thick). In a large skillet with high sides, heat 2–3 inches of oil to 360°F (or use a deep fryer according to the manufacturer's instructions). Fry the plantains in batches for 2–3 minutes, or until golden and crisp. Using a slotted spoon, transfer the chips to the prepared cooling racks; immediately sprinkle with salt.

Before serving the ceviche, adjust the seasonings. Serve the ceviche in bowls with plenty of chips on the side. Garnish with cilantro just before serving. *Serves 6*

NOTE: To peel a green plantain, cut 1 inch off each end and slice the skin lengthwise with a sharp knife. Slide your thumb under the skin and loosen it before peeling it off.

COOK'S TIP: Always taste before you serve. Does a dish need a little more salt or an extra dash of hot sauce? You won't know until you try it!

cold drinks and other libations

The New Southern-Latino menu offers lots of wonderful, popular drinks. On hot days, nothing beats the heat better than sweetened iced tea, the quintessential beverage of the South. A popular tea in Latin America is one made with hibiscus flowers called *té de flor de Jamaica* (or *rosa de Jamaica*). It has a tart flavor reminiscent of cranberries and is always sweetened with either raw, unrefined brown sugar (panela or piloncillo) or sugar syrup. *Agua de canela*, a sweetened, cinnamon-infused water, is often served to children at birthday parties. Citrus-infused drinks, such as lemonade, limeade, and orangeade, which were introduced to the New World by the Europeans, are also very popular. My personal favorite Latin American beverage is *horchata*. There are many variations of this very refreshing sweetened drink. Some are made with rice; others are made with a tigernuts or morrito seeds (*Cresentia alata*). I prefer it made with rice, almonds, sugar, and cinnamon. *Batidos* are delicious fruit smoothies found all over Latin America. Beer is extremely well-liked in Latin America as well, and several Latin countries produce it. If served icy-cold, few drinks quench your thirst faster. Both Southern mint juleps and Cuban mojitos are made by muddling mint with sugar, adding alcohol (bourbon in mint juleps, rum in mojitos), and mixing with ice. A similar drink, minus the mint, is the Brazilian *capirinha*, made with *cachaça*, which, like rum, is made from fermented sugarcane. *Ponche*, a traditional Latin American holiday drink similar to mulled wine, is made with dried fruits, spices, and sometimes liquor. *Rompope*, a Latin eggnog (Puerto Ricans call theirs *coquito*), is enjoyed during the Christmas season.

spiced pepitas

These crunchy pumpkin seeds are lemony, salty, spicy, and zesty all at the same time. A handful of these toasted little tidbits makes a perfect nibble to whet the appetite. In the South, appetizers can be as simple as shelled pecans tossed together with spices. Here, I give the same easy treatment to pepitas, a classic Latin ingredient. When I shop at a tienda, I often purchase raw pumpkin seeds in bulk and store them in the freezer so I always have some on hand. You can find them in most grocery stores (usually in the organic section of supermarkets) and in specialty and health food shops. These take only minutes to make and will keep for a few weeks if stored in an air-tight container. Pair them with a cold beer.

2 cups raw pumpkin seeds
1 tablespoon grated lemon zest
1 tablespoon lemon juice
2 teaspoons salt
1 teaspoon ground cumin
½ teaspoon freshly ground black pepper
½ teaspoon ground coriander
½ teaspoon ancho chile powder
½ teaspoon cayenne pepper
¼ teaspoon garlic powder
¼ teaspoon sugar

Preheat the oven to 375°F. In a medium bowl, toss together the pumpkin seeds, lemon zest, lemon juice, salt, cumin, pepper, coriander, chile powder, cayenne, garlic powder, and sugar. Spread the mixture on a baking sheet. Bake for 5 minutes; remove the baking sheet and shake to redistribute the seeds. Return to the oven and bake for another 3 minutes; stop to shake the pan again. Finish baking for 1–2 minutes, or until the pumpkin seeds are crispy and golden, being careful not to burn them. Transfer to a cool baking sheet and cool completely before storing. *Makes 2 cups*

sweet potato chips with spicy honey

These mouthwatering wafers are crispy, crunchy, and absolutely addictive. Sweet potatoes (camotes, boniatos, or batatas, in Spanish) are native to South America, where they're as beloved as they are in the South. Southerners love them in casseroles, pies, biscuits, and soups, but this is one of my favorite ways to eat them. At The Soda Shop in Davidson, North Carolina, you'll find mouth-watering sweet potato fries with honey. Mine are reminiscent of papalinas, the kettle-fried potato chips I grew up eating in Central America. In order to make these chips as crispy as possible, they must be fried twice. The first fry is done at a slightly lower temperature; the second time, they're given a quick fry at a higher temperature. Serve them with bowls of sour cream and this sweet and spicy honey.

4 large sweet potatoes
Vegetable oil for frying
Salt
½ cup honey ·
½ teaspoon chipotle chile powder
Sour cream (optional)

COOK'S TIP: When you're deep frying food, you'll have to adjust the temperature occasionally. If foods are browning too quickly, reduce the heat, let the oil cool a bit, and then continue frying. The size of the frying vessel will also affect frying times.

Peel the sweet potatoes and slice them lengthwise, as thinly as possible (⅛ inch thick), with a mandolin or a very sharp knife. Fit 2 large baking pans with metal cooling racks. In a large skillet with high sides, heat 2–3 inches of oil to 350°F (or use a deep fryer according to the manufacturer's instructions). Working in batches, fry the potato slices for 3–4 minutes, or until they begin to turn light brown. Using a slotted spoon, transfer the potatoes to the prepared cooling racks. When all of the slices have been fried once, increase the temperature of the oil to 370°F. Working in batches again, fry the sweet potato slices for 1 minute—they will get darker, but be careful not to burn them. Using a slotted spoon, transfer the chips to the cooling racks; immediately sprinkle with salt. Cool to room temperature (they will continue to crisp as they cool).

In the meantime, make the spicy honey. In a small pan, combine the honey and chile powder. Heat the mixture over low heat for 3–4 minutes, or just until the honey is warm; transfer to a bowl. *Serves 6–8 (4 as a side dish)*

two-potato cakes with green butter

Crunchy potato patties are topped with creamy, luxurious, citrusy avocado spread. Jewish communities abound throughout Latin America, and I grew up living next to a Jewish family. On many Friday evenings we celebrated Shabbat dinner at their grandmother's house, and just as frequently we sang together in the choir at Sunday mass. Some of my happiest childhood memories were spent at their home, learning to cook in their kitchen. Although traditional latkes are made with white potatoes, I love the sweetness imparted by the South's favorite tuber—the sweet potato. For Latinos, avocados, or paltas (as they're known in South America), are often referred to as "green gold"; they're treated like butter, often spread on bread with just a few grains of coarse salt.

1½ cups peeled and grated
     Russet potatoes
1½ cups peeled and grated
     sweet potatoes
½   cup grated Vidalia onion
3   eggs, beaten
2   tablespoons all-purpose flour
1   teaspoon salt
½   teaspoon freshly ground
     black pepper
½   cup vegetable oil
1   Hass avocado
     Juice of ½ lime, or to taste
     Salt and freshly ground black
     pepper, to taste

NOTE: Avocados are very slippery. Protect yourself by layering a folded dishtowel over the hand that will hold the avocado before you cut into it.

Preheat the oven to 250°F. Fit a large baking pan with a metal cooling rack. Place the grated potatoes and onions in a large, clean kitchen towel; wring tightly over the sink, squeezing out as much liquid as possible. In a large bowl, combine the potato mixture with the eggs, flour, salt, and pepper; stir well. In a large skillet, heat the oil over medium-high heat; using a 2-inch ice cream scoop, drop scoopfuls of the potato batter into the oil, using the back of the scoop to flatten them into thin pancakes. Fry for 3–4 minutes, or until golden brown, turning them over halfway through. Using a slotted spoon, transfer the potato cakes to the prepared cooling rack; immediately sprinkle with salt and keep them warm in the oven while you make the avocado spread.

Halve and pit the avocados; scoop out the flesh with a spoon into a medium bowl. With a fork, mash the avocado until smooth; add the lime juice and season with salt and pepper. Remove the potato cakes from the oven and set on a platter and serve, topped with dollops of the avocado spread. *Serves 4-6*

warm pimiento cheese logs

Slightly toasted, these small canapés are stuffed with warm comfort. Each bite yields the creamy, melted goodness within. When my children were little, I would organize elegant tea parties and we would get dressed up. We'd ask their little friends and their moms to join us (sometimes dolls got an invitation too), and I'd serve these tasty snacks. When I was a kid in Latin America, Saturday afternoons where spent receiving company or dropping by to visit friends. Quick and easy snacks like these came in very handy then, as they do now. Armed with pimiento cheese and a loaf of bread, you'll always be ready to entertain. You can shape these logs ahead of time and store them in boxes. Freeze them for up to 2 months. Simply heat and serve.

2 cups Classic Pimiento Cheese (page 35)
20 slices white bread
¾ cup (1½ sticks) unsalted butter, melted
Smoked Spanish paprika (for garnish)
Curly parsley leaves (for garnish)

Line 2 large baking sheets with parchment paper. Using a rolling pin, flatten the bread slices. Spread an equal amount of the pimiento cheese (about 1½ tablespoons) on each slice. Roll up the bread slices, jelly-roll style. Using a serrated knife, trim off the crusts and discard; slice each roll in half. Place the rolls, seam side down, on the prepared baking sheets, brush with the melted butter, and sprinkle with paprika. Broil for 1–2 minutes, or until the tops are golden; transfer to a platter, garnish with parsley, and serve. Makes 40 bite-size logs

NOTE: Parchment or baking paper, which can be found in most grocery stores, prevents food from sticking to the baking sheets, making greasing unnecessary; best of all, it can be reused several times. Different from waxed paper, parchment is coated with silicone and resists high baking temperatures. Don't substitute waxed paper, which will ignite under the broiler.

salads & cold dishes

Christopher Columbus brought the first lettuce seeds from Spain into the West Indies. However, lettuce salads did not become popular in either the South or Latin America until the twentieth century. Unlike Europeans, who usually serve salads as their own course in the middle of a meal, Americans usually serve them alongside the entrée. As a matter of fact, the restaurant-style salad as we know it today—a fancy mixture of baby and multicolored lettuce leaves, topped with myriad ingredients, and tossed with vinaigrettes—is not the common fare on most Southern or Latino family tables. What you'll most likely find on a daily basis in both cultures is a simpler combination of lettuce, onions, and tomatoes tossed with an oil and vinegar-based dressing or with a creamy concoction, like buttermilk dressing. In Latin America, these salads are called *ensaladas mixtas*.

The variety of Southern salads is wide and includes gelatin-based molded creations that first appeared on the culinary scene in the 1800s. These are still very popular in the South and range from simple ones made with fruit and sweet gelatin to heftier versions filled with meats, mayonnaise, nuts, and/or vegetables. They make frequent appearances on Southern community buffet tables and family meals. Latin Americans make good use of gelatin as well, but they usually relegate these molds to the appetizer category (see my Shrimp and Cilantro Mousse on page 000 and my Avocado and Pimiento Cheese Terrine on page 47) and present them as elegant hors d'oeuvres; aspics rarely make appearances these days.

Salads in the South and throughout Latin America have similar characteristics, which is not surprising when we consider that our cuisines developed in pretty much the same manner, with the same prime ingredients and with similar cultural influences. We can draw a parallel between many of the styles of salads that are most popular in both regions today.

Let's start with potato salad. Potatoes are native to Peru and made it to North America only after traveling the world; once accepted in Europe, they were brought by the colonists. The first Europeans to adopt potatoes into their cuisine were the Germans, who favored warm potato salads and introduced them to the United States first and then later to the Latin American countries (Guatemala, Chile, and Brazil, among others) in which they settled in large numbers. Most potato salads made throughout the continent are dressed with mayonnaise (see sidebar, page 57). But the layered potato salads of Peru are usually dressed with citrus vinaigrette embellished with chiles. Called causas, these spud salads were created to fund the Peruvian war effort against Chile; easy to tote, they became an ideal street food that vendors could sell "for the cause."

In the South, a simple plate of sliced tomatoes or cucumbers constitutes a salad; the same is true in Latin America. My recipe for Tomato and Vidalia Salad with Mint Vinaigrette is a perfect example of this penchant for simplicity. The Broccoli Salad with Pepitas and Tamarind-Buttermilk Dressing offers a quick and easy option that packs loads of flavor. What matters most when making salads is not what's in them but rather that they're prepared with fresh, seasonal ingredients. My recipe for Two-Corn Summer Salad also illustrates how simple and unassuming elements can be transformed into vibrant dishes.

Southerners and Latinos also share a love for pickled vegetables. Thus, both cultures feature a good number of pickled foods, from okra, sun chokes, beets, mushrooms, and chiles to shrimp, pig's feet, and quail eggs. Try the Pickled Chiles, which feature my favorite escabeche technique and juxtapose sweet peppers with even sweeter Southern Vidalia onions.

Main course salads, made with beef, chicken, pork, or seafood and often mixed with mayonnaise, also have an important place throughout Latin America and the United States. In addition, Latin Americans make salpicones, which feature finely chopped vegetables and meats dressed with light vinaigrettes made with onions or shallots, herbs (cilantro, mint, and parsley are common), and vinegar or citrus juice.

Stuffed tomatoes are a popular Southern dish, as they are in Latin cuisine, in addition to stuffed avocados and peppers. Often served at ladies' luncheons and formal gatherings alike, they're particularly beautiful to look at and provide elegant individual portions. In Latin America, common fillings include everything from quinoa salads to crawfish salpicón, cold rice mélanges, chopped hearts of palm, and fresh corn. In the South, tomatoes are commonly stuffed with crab and shrimp salads. Here I offer you a Southern-Latino version: Tomatoes Stuffed with Quinoa Salad.

Most of these cold dishes come together almost effortlessly, like Cucumber Pico de Gallo Salad. Others require a bit more time, such as Crab Cakes Salad with Peaches and Tamarind Vinaigrette, but they're well worth the extra effort. The Black-Eyed Pea Salad and the Collard Greens, Oranges, and Pepita Salad with Buttermilk Dressing may even bring you luck. Regardless, all of the dishes in this chapter pack a load of flavor and feature tons of colorful elements that are sure to please.

For those times when all you want is a straightforward, green salad, I suggest you pick any of the vinaigrettes featured in the recipes in this chapter and use those; they're easy to make, can be made in bulk, and keep well for a few days in your refrigerator. Remember to keep it simple and fresh.

black-eyed pea salad

Spicy, sour, creamy, and crunchy all at the same time, this Southern classic is a must-have on New Year's Day. This easy and scrumptious rendition has been part of my holiday menu since the 1980s, when I first moved to North Carolina. Lore has it that during the Civil War, Confederate soldiers waved starvation off by eating black-eyed peas, which Union soldiers ignored during their rampage on the South. These legumes, also known as cowpeas, are native to Africa and are popular in Latin countries, where they're known by different names (gandúles in Puerto Rico, bolos in Cuba, and feijão-de-corda in Brazil, for example). Fresh peas cook the quickest, but you'll mostly find them sold dried, canned, or frozen. For a lucky combination, pair this with my crispy New Year's Collard Green Empanadas (page 66), or serve it alongside mouthwatering Latin Fried Chicken with Smoky Ketchup (page 125).

4 ½ cups cooked black-eyed peas, rinsed in cold water
1 cup finely chopped red bell pepper
1 cup seeded and finely chopped plum tomatoes
¾ cup finely chopped red onion
¼ cup finely chopped cilantro (leaves and tender stems)
2 tablespoons finely chopped jalapeños (seeded and deveined if less heat is desired)
1 large garlic clove, minced
½ cup lime juice
2 teaspoons Dijon mustard
1 ½ teaspoon salt
¼ teaspoon freshly ground black pepper
¼ teaspoon Worcestershire sauce
Pinch cayenne pepper, or to taste
¼ cup extra-virgin olive oil

In a large bowl, combine the black-eyed peas, bell peppers, tomatoes, onions, cilantro, jalapeños, and garlic; stir until well mixed. In a medium bowl, whisk together the lime juice, mustard, salt, pepper, Worcestershire sauce, and cayenne. While whisking, slowly add the oil in a thin stream; when the dressing is well combined, pour it onto the pea mixture and stir to combine. Chill the salad for 30 minutes before serving (or up to 24 hours), in order for flavors to blend. *Serves 8*

COOK'S TIP: Cold foods tend to require more seasoning than warm foods, so always taste bean, potato, or pasta salads just before you serve them. You'll likely have to add a little more salt, pepper, and vinegar or citrus juice. I always make an extra bit of dressing and set it aside, so I can add it right before serving.

broccoli salad with pepitas and tamarind-buttermilk dressing

Crunchy broccoli, crispy bacon, and toasted pumpkin seeds meet in this salad featuring sweet, sour, and salty flavors. I cannot tell you how many times since my move to the South I've encountered broccoli salad and many variations on the theme both at restaurants and at parties. I'm partial to my version, which calls for raw rather than cooked or blanched florets. Prepared in this manner, the broccoli stands up to the dressing without wilting and maintains its vibrant green color. When my daughters were little, I would serve the broccoli plain with the dressing on the side. They'd use the dressing as a dipping sauce, and I found it easy to get them to eat their vegetables. The addition of buttermilk to the traditional mayonnaise-based dressing lends the salad an additional twang that helps to balance the sweetness of the raisins and tamarind extract. Rediscover a classic with a slight twist.

6	cups raw broccoli florets
½	cup minced red onion
½	cup golden raisins
½	cup mayonnaise
¼	cup buttermilk
¼	cup apple cider vinegar
2	tablespoons tamarind concentrate (available in Latin tiendas or Indian grocery stores)
1½	teaspoons salt
¼	teaspoon pepper
½	cup cooked and crumbled bacon
¼	cup toasted pepitas (see note)

In a large salad bowl, toss together the broccoli, onions, and raisins. In a small bowl, whisk together the mayonnaise, buttermilk, vinegar, tamarind, salt, and pepper until smooth. Pour the dressing over the broccoli mixture and stir well; cover and chill for at least 2 hours (or up to 24 hours), stirring occasionally. When ready to serve, stir in the bacon and pepitas. *Serves 6*

NOTE: Toast pepitas on a dry skillet over medium-high heat; toss frequently until they're fragrant and start to puff up (anywhere from 1 to 5 minutes, depending on the amount of pepitas). They burn easily, so keep a close eye on them (¼ cup of pepitas can be toasted in 1–2 minutes). Transfer them to a plate to cool completely. Toasted pepitas can be frozen for up to 2 months or stored at room temperature for up to 14 days.

christmas wreath salad

If you enjoy refreshing, crunchy salads overflowing with colorful and interesting toppings, you'll flip over this one. The addition of a creamy dressing that combines Peruvian, Mexican, and Southern elements makes this is a salad of contrasts inspired by the Chino-Latino culinary movement taking place throughout Latin America. Here I combine chiles and citrus and blend them with soy sauce, a common ingredient in Peruvian cookery (in Peru, it's called sillao). I further enhance the dressing with a touch of Southern sweetness in molasses and emulsify it with velvety mayonnaise. The result is a smooth dressing with a balanced juxtaposition of sweet, sour, salty, and spicy flavors. Thin tortilla strips are cut to look like the dried leaves of the raffia palm tree, which grows wild in some Latin coastal areas. A striking presentation gives this salad a festive look.

6   corn tortillas
    Cooking spray
2   ears of corn, husks removed (or 1½
       cups frozen corn kernels, thawed)
2   teaspoons olive oil
1   cup mayonnaise
2   tablespoons soy sauce
2   tablespoons molasses
2–4 tablespoons lime juice, to taste
2   teaspoons minced chipotle
       chiles in adobo
½   teaspoon adobo
    Salt and freshly ground black
       pepper, to taste

Begin by making the tortilla raffia. Preheat the oven to 350°F. Stack the tortillas and, with a very sharp knife, slice them thinly into strips (about ¼ inch wide). Spray them with cooking spray and place them on an ungreased baking sheet; bake until crispy and golden (about 8 minutes), tossing occasionally. Remove from the oven and cool completely; set aside.

Heat an indoor grill pan (or an outdoor grill); brush the ears of corn with oil and grill, turning them occasionally, until the kernels have begun to char. Remove the corn from the grill and cool slightly; when cool enough to handle, scrape the kernels off with a sharp knife; set aside. If using frozen/thawed kernels, in a nonstick skillet, heat the oil over medium-high heat; add the corn and cook, stirring, just until it begins to brown (about 4–5 minutes); remove promptly.

In a medium bowl, whisk together the mayonnaise, soy sauce, molasses, lime juice, chipotle, and adobo until well blended. Season the dressing with salt and pepper and add more lime juice, if desired.

6 cups romaine lettuce, cut into
  bite-size pieces

4 cups red leaf lettuce, cut into
  bite-size pieces

3-4 cups seeded and cubed tomatoes

½ cup finely crumbled Cotija cheese,
  or to taste

On a large, round platter, arrange the lettuces in the shape of a wreath. Place alternate dollops of tomatoes and corn on the lettuce (to resemble Christmas lights on a wreath). Arrange the tortilla strips decoratively at the base of the wreath, to resemble a raffia bow. Drizzle the salad with the dressing and sprinkle with the cheese; serve immediately. *Serves 8-10*

collard greens, oranges, and pepita salad with buttermilk dressing

Tangy dressing counteracts the slightly bitter taste of greens while oranges lend traces of sweetness to this exquisite salad of contrasts. If you've never tasted raw greens before, you may be delightfully surprised to find that they have a crunchy, fresh, and vibrant flavor with a bit of a tang. Orange, chile, and pepita salads are very common in Central America, where they're often sold in little plastic bags from street cart vendors. Purchase already roasted and salted pepitas for this salad since they have more flavor than raw ones. I prefer just a hint of heat from the chiles so as not to overpower the flavor of the greens, so I remove the seeds. Buttermilk dressings are Southern specialties, and this one threads gutsy flavors together seamlessly.

6 cups thinly sliced collard greens,
  packed (see cook's tip, page 66)

2 oranges, peeled and sectioned

½ cup very thinly sliced red onion

½ cup buttermilk

½ cup lime juice

¼ cup seeded, deveined, and minced
  jalapeños

1 tablespoon extra-virgin olive oil

1½ teaspoons salt

¼ teaspoon freshly ground black pepper

⅓ cup roasted and salted pepitas

In a large bowl, toss together the greens, orange sections, and onions; set aside. In a medium bowl, whisk together the buttermilk, lime juice, jalapeños, oil, salt, and pepper; pour the dressing over the salad and toss well. Chill for at least 30 minutes (up to 3 hours), stirring occasionally, to allow flavors to blend. Sprinkle with pepitas and serve. *Serves 4-6*

crab cakes salad with peaches and tamarind vinaigrette

Hot, creamy crab cakes, sweet fruit, and refreshingly crunchy lettuce make this colorful main-dish salad a luxurious engagement of the senses. Blue crabs are abundant in the coastal areas of the South and are often used in stews, casseroles, and soups. Crab cakes, however, are among the most popular crab dishes made in Southern home kitchens and eateries. Here, Peruvian yellow pepper (ají amarillo) adds hefty spice to tender crab cakes. Tamarind, a fruit native to Africa and India, was introduced to the New World in the sixteenth century. Today, it's used in drinks and candy in Latin America; it's also a key ingredient in Worcestershire sauce. Here, I use its sweet and tart flavor to lend an interesting tang to this light vinaigrette, enhancing the sweetness of peaches and softening the peppery bite of leeks in a way that brings harmony to each bite.

FOR THE CRAB CAKES

- 1 pound lump crabmeat, picked for shell fragments
- 1 egg
- 1 egg yolk
- ¼ cup mayonnaise
- 1 tablespoon Dijon mustard
- ¼ cup finely chopped Vidalia onion
- ⅓ cup finely chopped red bell pepper
- 1 teaspoon ají amarillo paste or hot sauce (such as Tabasco)
- 1 tablespoon finely chopped flat-leaf parsley (leaves and tender stems)
- ½ teaspoon salt
- ¼ teaspoon freshly ground black pepper
- 1¾ cups fresh bread crumbs
- ¾ cup dried, unseasoned bread crumbs (you may not need all)
- 1 cup vegetable oil
- 2 tablespoons unsalted butter

Preheat the oven to 250°F. Fit a baking pan with a metal cooling rack; set aside. In a medium bowl, whisk together the egg, egg yolk, mayonnaise, mustard, onion, bell pepper, ají amarillo, parsley, salt, and pepper. In a large bowl, stir together the crabmeat and the dressing just until combined, being careful not to break up the crabmeat too much. Fold in enough of the fresh bread crumbs to hold the mixture together. Divide the crab mixture into 8 equal portions; pat each into a ¾-inch-thick cake. Place the dried bread crumbs in a shallow plate; coat both sides of the cakes with crumbs. In a large skillet, heat the oil and butter over medium-high heat; when the butter melts, add the cakes. Cook for 3–4 minutes per side, or until golden. Transfer the crab cakes to the prepared cooling rack; keep them warm in the oven (for up to 1 hour) while you make the salad.

FOR THE VINAIGRETTE

¼ cup apple cider vinegar

2 tablespoons tamarind concentrate

1 teaspoon Dijon mustard

½ teaspoon salt

¼ teaspoon freshly ground
black pepper

¼ cup vegetable oil

FOR THE SALAD

10 cups romaine lettuce, torn into
bite-size pieces

2 cups thinly sliced leeks (white and
light green parts only), rinsed
well (see cook's tip, page 65)

½ cup finely chopped red bell pepper

3 cups peeled and sliced peaches
(see cook's tip, page 33)

In a small bowl, whisk together the vinegar, tamarind, mustard, salt, and pepper. While whisking, slowly add the oil in a thin stream and then continue whisking until the mixture has emulsified.

On a large platter, arrange the lettuce, leeks, bell peppers, and peaches; drizzle liberally with the vinaigrette. Set the crab cakes atop the salad; serve immediately.

Serves 4-6

cucumber pico de gallo salad

This refreshing and crunchy salad is the kind I crave during a hot Southern summer. I love the succulence of cucumbers and often serve this salad—featuring the perfect balance of sour and spicy undertones—at my outdoor luncheons or lakeside meals. The fact that the dressing does not contain any ingredient that can spoil in hot weather makes it perfect for toting along, so it's ideal for picnics. Although I offer it as a salad, this is just as luscious when the vegetables are chopped into smaller pieces and served with tortilla chips or when draped over fried catfish instead of traditional salsa. English cucumbers contain fewer seeds than other varieties and have a much sweeter taste. Since they're not dipped in wax, you don't need to peel them, allowing their bright green color to come through. Salting them before they're added to the salad removes excess moisture.

2 English cucumbers, seeded
  and chopped
1½ teaspoons salt
1 cup minced Vidalia onion
1 cup minced cilantro (leaves and
  tender stems)
¼ cup minced, seeded, and deveined
  jalapeños (see note)
¼ cup extra-virgin olive oil
  Lime juice, to taste
  Salt and freshly ground black
  pepper, to taste

Place the chopped cucumbers in a strainer; sprinkle with salt and set the strainer over a bowl (or in the sink) for 15 minutes. Pat the cucumbers dry with paper towels.

In a large bowl, combine the cucumbers, onions, cilantro, jalapeños, and oil. Season with lime juice, salt, and pepper; chill for at least 30 minutes (or up to 8 hours). Serve well chilled. *Serves 6*

NOTE: Leave the seeds on a couple of the jalapeños for additional heat, if desired.

ensalada rusa (russian salad)

It's difficult to imagine church suppers in the South without at least one kind of potato salad. This is my interpretation of the ubiquitous potato salad of Latin America, made with creamy tubers that grab on to a citrusy mayonnaise-based dressing. The carrots and peas are classic additions to this dish. Here, I add pimientos to lend a touch of sweetness and additional color. It took more than a century for potatoes, which are native to Peru, to gain acceptance in Europe, where, along with tomatoes and eggplants, they were thought to be poisonous. However, once introduced to the South, potatoes became common fare. Today, you'll still find Latin American households preparing this salad with homemade mayonnaise. Ever since I moved to the South, however, only Duke's mayonnaise will do. Feel free to add other ingredients to this salad. Common additions include beets, capers, olives, tuna, shrimp, ham, or hard-boiled eggs.

6 cups cooked, peeled, and cubed Yukon
  Gold potatoes
¾ cup frozen peas, thawed
¾ cup diced carrots, cooked
¼ cup minced flat-leaf parsley (leaves
  and tender stems)
¼ cup minced Vidalia onion
1 (2-ounce) jar diced pimientos, drained
¾ cup mayonnaise
¼ cup sour cream
2 tablespoons lemon juice, or to taste
1 teaspoon Dijon mustard
1 teaspoon salt, or to taste
¼ teaspoon freshly ground black pepper,
  or to taste

In a large bowl, combine the potatoes, peas, carrots, parsley, onions, and pimientos. In a medium bowl, whisk together the mayonnaise, sour cream, lemon juice, mustard, salt, and pepper. Pour the dressing over the potato mixture and stir to combine. Chill salad for at least 1 hour (up to 8 hours) before serving. *Serves 6-8*

NOTE: You can use low-fat mayonnaise and light sour cream or Greek yogurt with good results. Make this an easy one-dish meal by adding a large can of drained tuna or salmon or cubed rotisserie chicken.

green mango salad with pepita and benne-dusted shrimp

Green mango salad with lime, salt, and dried chile is a very popular street food in Mexico and Central America. This citrusy salad, scented with cumin, coriander, and mint, is refreshing and strikingly colorful. Here, I coat plump shrimp with a ground mixture of nutty seeds. *Benne* is the African word for sesame seeds. Europeans introduced them to Latin America (where they're known as *ajonjolí*), and African slaves brought them to the South. The ingredient list is long here, but the steps are easy. Choose large, firm mangoes that are not too ripe; they should not give when pressed. The smaller, green mangoes sold in Asian stores will also work. Use a serrated potato peeler to remove their skins easily. This recipe doubles and triples perfectly, making it ideal for larger crowds. Pucker up!

4 cups firm, green mangoes, peeled,
   pitted, and sliced into ribbons
   with a vegetable peeler
2 cups carrots, peeled and grated into
   ribbons with a vegetable peeler
1 cup thinly sliced red onion
½ cup finely chopped cilantro (leaves
   and tender stems), packed
2 tablespoons minced jalapeño
   (seeded and deveined if less
   heat is desired)

FOR THE DRESSING
¼ cup lime juice
2 tablespoons extra-virgin olive oil
1 teaspoon salt
¼ teaspoon ground cumin
¼ teaspoon freshly ground
   black pepper
¼ teaspoon chipotle chile powder,
   or to taste
⅛ teaspoon ground coriander
4 large mint leaves, sliced thinly into
   ribbons (chiffonade)

FOR THE SHRIMP
½ cup raw, unsalted pepitas
1 tablespoon toasted sesame seeds
   (see note)
1 teaspoon salt
1 pound large (16–20 count) shrimp,
   peeled, deveined, and butterflied
   (leave tails on)
1 egg white, lightly beaten
¼ cup vegetable oil

In a large bowl, toss together the mango, carrots, onions, cilantro, and jalapeño; set aside. In a small bowl, whisk together the lime juice, oil, salt, cumin, pepper, chile powder, coriander, and mint. Toss the salad with the dressing; set aside for 20 minutes (or chill for up to 8 hours).

Grind the pumpkin and sesame seeds in a coffee grinder (or small food processor) until they're a fine powder, being careful not to form a paste; place in a small bowl and add the salt. In a large skillet, heat the oil over medium heat. Working in batches, dip the shrimp into the egg white and coat on both sides with the seed powder. Add to the skillet and sauté for 2 minutes on each side, or until golden and crispy. Arrange the salad on 4 plates. Top each with the shrimp and serve. *Serves 4*

NOTE: To toast sesame seeds, place them in a dry skillet over low heat, stirring until they're fragrant and have begun to turn golden. Watch them carefully so they don't burn. Toasted sesame seeds are available in bulk in most Latin tiendas.

potatoes

The humble potato has proud origins. Indigenous to South America, it was first domesticated by the Incas in Peru. After Pizarro's conquest of Peru in 1536, the potato—along with many treasures—made its way to Spain. It was catalogued as a member of the nightshade family, which includes a number of poisonous plants (belladonna, for example), so it was avoided. It's difficult to imagine that along with tomatoes and eggplants, potatoes were considered one of the most poisonous plants of the Americas until the Prussians began to harvest them for consumption. Tubers were brought to England via Poland and Russia. The French did not discover potatoes until much later, when French apothecary Antoine August Parmentier introduced the tuber. Parmentier, who had been fed potatoes in Prussia as a prisoner of war, returned home to find a famine-stricken France. He studied the nutritional benefits of potatoes and was the first to create soup kitchens so he could feed his people back to health. Chefs and avid foodies will no doubt recognize his name as one often given to potato dishes (à la Parmentier). The Irish embraced potatoes whole-heartedly, which first proved a blessing but led to disaster when entire harvests were lost to blight. Potatoes were introduced to North America in 1613 from the West Indies and later, after attempts to cultivate failed, from Ireland in 1719. Thomas Jefferson introduced French fries to the South, which he served to guests at the White House. Imagine a Southern table without potato salad, home fries, or chips! Likewise, the Latino table would not be complete without its causas (chile and citrus enhanced potato salads from Peru), locros (South American chowders and soups), or the Latin American classic ensaladas Rusas.

layered potato and egg salad (causa vegetariana)

Creamy mashed tubers envelop gutsy egg salad in my new-Southern rendition of a Peruvian classic, the layered potato salad called *causa*. Potatoes are native to the Incan territory; it's not surprising to find myriad dishes featuring them in Peruvian cuisine. Causas consist of mashed potatoes seasoned with ají amarillo, the spicy Peruvian yellow chile, and lime juice that are filled with mayonnaise-based salads. Popular fillings include tuna, chicken, and shrimp. Along with ceviches, causas are among Peru's most recognizable dishes. Versatile, these are always served cold, in casserole form or molded, like timbales. Here, I took traditional elements of a Southern classic potato salad and layered them in the Peruvian style. Potatoes get a brighter yellow hue from the gutsy chiles used here. Feel free to use purple or new potatoes, if you prefer. This salad pairs beautifully with Latin Fried Chicken with Smoky Ketchup (page 125).

FOR THE POTATO LAYER

- 4 pounds yellow potatoes (such as Yukon Gold), boiled, peeled, and mashed
- ½ cup minced white onion
- ⅓ cup key lime juice (see note)
- 1 teaspoon ají amarillo paste
- 2 teaspoons salt, or to taste
- ½ teaspoon freshly ground black pepper, or to taste
- ¼ cup extra-virgin olive oil

Spray a 9 × 13 × 2-inch casserole dish with cooking spray. Place the mashed potatoes in a large bowl; add the onions and stir to combine. In a medium bowl, whisk together the lime juice, ají amarillo, salt, and pepper until the ají paste is dissolved. Whisk in the oil and add the dressing to the potato mixture, stirring well to combine. In a medium bowl, combine the eggs, olives, capers, mayonnaise, mustard, pepper, and salt; stir to combine. Spread half of the potato mixture evenly in the prepared dish. Spread the egg salad evenly over the potato layer; top with the remaining potatoes. Garnish with the olives and chives. Chill for at least 1 hour (up to 24 hours) before serving. *Serves* 12

FOR THE EGG LAYER

9   hard-boiled eggs, finely chopped

½   cup finely chopped pimiento-stuffed
     green olives

2   tablespoons minced capers

⅓   cup mayonnaise

1   teaspoon yellow mustard

¼   teaspoon freshly ground black pepper
     Pinch salt

1   cup sliced pimiento-stuffed
     green olives

¼   cup finely chopped chives

NOTE: I prefer key limes, which are similar in flavor to Peruvian limes, but feel free to substitute Persian limes, the ones traditionally found in supermarkets.

mod-mex caesar salad with pecans

Refreshing and vibrant, this crunchy salad features a kaleidoscope of colors and a cornucopia of flavors that will take your palate by surprise. Spiciness, creaminess, sweetness, and sourness collide to produce the ultimate sensory experience. In 1924, Caesar Cardini created the first Caesar salad in his restaurant in Tijuana, Mexico, when he found himself with hungry patrons and only a few ingredients on hand. The original recipe called for romaine lettuce tossed with a rich dressing made with a velvety mixture of coddled eggs, lemon juice, and olive oil, which I've replaced with mayonnaise (an emulsion of the same ingredients). Anchovies may or may not have been part of the original recipe, but I include them in my version. I incorporate a touch of the South with sweet Florida oranges and meaty, Southern pecans. Top with grilled shrimp, chicken, or steak to transform this salad into a main course.

FOR THE CROUTONS

2   cups cubed, day-old crusty bread
     (such as baguette)

2   tablespoons extra-virgin olive oil

½   teaspoon chipotle chile powder

½   teaspoon garlic powder

¼   teaspoon ground cumin

Preheat the oven to 350°F. In a large bowl, toss together the bread, oil, chile powder, garlic powder, and cumin. Spread the bread cubes on a baking sheet and bake, tossing occasionally, for 12–15 minutes, or until golden and crisp.

FOR THE DRESSING

1 cup mayonnaise
½ cup sour cream
Grated zest of 2 lemons
2 teaspoons minced chipotle chiles in adobo
2 large garlic cloves, finely chopped
1 teaspoon anchovy paste
Lemon juice, to taste
Salt and freshly ground black pepper, to taste

FOR THE SALAD

1 head romaine lettuce, cut into ribbons
1 English cucumber, cored and sliced into rings
1 cup shredded carrots
1 cup thinly sliced red onion
2 oranges, peeled and sectioned
½ cup toasted pecan halves
½ cup freshly grated Romano cheese

In a small bowl, whisk together the mayonnaise, sour cream, lemon zest, chipotle, garlic, and anchovy paste until smooth. Season with lemon juice, salt, and pepper. In a large bowl, combine the lettuce, cucumber, carrots, onions, orange sections, and pecans; toss with the dressing. Add the croutons and Romano cheese and toss again; serve immediately. *Serves 6*

pickled chiles

Wonderfully garlicky, sweet, and sour marinade saturates soft, supple bell peppers and intoxicatingly sweet onions, imbuing them with succulence in this tasty dish. Escabeche is one of many great culinary techniques from the Arabs that made its way into the Latin repertoire via Spain. This method—a great way to preserve foods for longer storage—is still fashionable today. In the South, cooks pickle everything from watermelon rinds to okra and Jerusalem artichokes, and you'll find jars of these kinds of pickled items on the grocer's shelves. Here, the tang of vinegar is mellowed by a small amount of sugar, giving the escabeche the subtle *agridulce*—sweet and sour—taste so characteristic of the cuisines of Central and South America. As with any recipe that features only a few elements, only the best ingredients will do. This piquant salad is a great accompaniment to grilled meats and a delightful condiment for burgers.

½ cup apple cider vinegar

¼ cup water

2 tablespoons dark brown sugar, packed

1 teaspoon salt, or to taste

⅔ cup extra-virgin olive oil

6 cups thinly sliced red bell pepper

3 cups thinly sliced Vidalia onion

8 sprigs fresh thyme or 1 teaspoon dried

2 bay leaves

6 whole peppercorns

6 large garlic cloves, sliced paper-thin

Salt and freshly ground black pepper, to taste

In a small bowl, combine the vinegar, water, brown sugar, and salt and blend well; set aside. In a medium, stainless steel or enamel-coated skillet with high sides heat the oil over medium-high heat; add the bell pepper, onion, thyme, bay leaves, and peppercorns and cook, stirring occasionally, for 7–8 minutes, or until the peppers begin to soften. Add the garlic; cook, stirring, for 1 minute, or until fragrant. The vegetables should not brown. Add the vinegar mixture and stir well. Reduce the heat and cook, uncovered, for 8 minutes, or until the peppers are soft. Remove from the heat and cool to room temperature (about 30 minutes); discard the bay leaves and season with salt and pepper. Cover and chill for at least 30 minutes (or up to 5 days); bring to room temperature before serving. *Serves 8-10*

chile primer

Chiles are native to the Americas, dating back at least 8,000 years to the Maya, Inca, and Aztec civilizations. Their worldly propagation is credited to Spaniard and Portuguese traders, who took them back to Europe, from whence they made their way into the Far East, India, and Africa. Chiles are members of the *Capsicum* family. There are hundreds of varieties used in Latin cuisine—140 are grown in Mexico alone—ranging from sweet and mild, to fiery hot. The compound oil that produces the heat is called *capsaicin*. Found in the veins and seeds of the chiles, capsaicin withstands cooking at any length of time and survives subzero temperatures, which means that freezing chiles will not reduce their potency, as many believe. Remember the rule of thumb: the smaller the chile, the hotter it will be. In 1912, the American chemist Wilbur Scoville devised a test to measure the level of heat in chiles. The Scoville scale indicates the amount of capsaicin in a chile pepper. The milder the chiles, the lower the score (bell peppers, for instance, score a 0); the hotter the chile, the higher the score (habaneros score 500,000 units). The scores on some of the chiles I use in this book should give you an idea of their heat levels: pimiento, 100; poblano, 500; jalapeño and guajillo, 2,500; serrano, 15,000; Tabasco, ají amarillo, and cayenne, 30,000; chiltepín, 50,000; and rocotó, 100,000. Although removing the seeds and veins of the chiles ensures a much milder flavor, take care to select chiles according to your level of comfort. Always wear rubber gloves when handling chiles in case you're sensitive to the oils. When you're eating a dish that contains chiles, the worst thing you can do to counteract their fiery bite is to drink water, which will only spread the oil around your mouth. Go for a glass of milk or a dollop of sour cream instead.

romaine, orange, avocado, and pepita salad with creamy serrano vinaigrette

Lemony dressing coats crispy leaves while nutty pumpkin seeds add crunch to this refreshing salad. The dressing is invigorating and uncomplicated and features a spicy accent that complements without overwhelming. We can all thank Christopher Columbus for the dissemination of citrus and chiles throughout the globe. Arabs introduced citrus fruit into Spain, and Spanish conquerors brought it and the secrets of its cultivation into the Americas. Chiles may have been unknown to most of the world before the colonization of America, but the ancient Mayans had long believed in their aphrodisiac and medicinal powers. I cannot vouch for either power, but I can guarantee that this salad is both tasty and easy to make any day of the week. Make sure to cut the avocado just before serving so it doesn't turn brown. Turn this scrumptious salad into a complete meal by topping it with grilled flank steak, salmon, or shrimp.

8	cups romaine lettuce, torn into bite-size pieces
2	oranges, peeled and sectioned
½	cup toasted pepitas (see page 85)
½	cup thinly sliced red onion
1	teaspoon grated lime zest
½	cup lime juice
¼	cup heavy whipping cream
1	teaspoon Dijon mustard
2	garlic cloves, minced
2	finely chopped serrano chiles (seeded and deveined if less heat is desired)
½	teaspoon salt, or to taste
¼	teaspoon freshly ground black pepper, or to taste
½	cup extra-virgin olive oil
1	Hass avocado

On a large platter, toss together the lettuce, orange sections, pepitas, and onions; set aside. In a medium bowl, whisk together the lime zest, lime juice, cream, and mustard until the mustard is dissolved. Stir in the garlic, chiles, salt, and pepper. While whisking, slowly add the oil in a thin stream; continue whisking until the dressing is creamy. Adjust the salt and pepper. Cut the avocado in half lengthwise; remove the pit and peel. Dice the avocado and toss with the dressing; add the dressing to the salad and toss well. Serve immediately. *Serves 6*

tomato and vidalia salad with mint vinaigrette

Plump, juicy tomatoes and crunchy sweet onions are seductively bathed in silky and perfectly emulsified vinaigrette with hints of garlic in this simply delicious salad. Popular in the South, tomato salads, like this one, prepared with few embellishments are also made in home kitchens and served at restaurants throughout Latin America. From Cuba to Panama to Venezuela and Chile, cooks prepare various renditions of scantily dressed salads featuring this succulent fruit of the Americas. Mint is prevalent in Latin cuisine, where it's used in both sweet and savory recipes. Mint is particularly delicious when combined with tomatoes as it enhances their sweetness; here, it adds sparkle to an otherwise simple dressing. The skin on a tomato can be tough, so I like to peel the tomatoes for this recipe. When in a hurry, just throw all of the ingredients of the vinaigrette in a blender and whir until creamy. This summer salad would be equally appealing served on a Southern porch or on a South American *terraza*.

3 large beefsteak or heirloom
   tomatoes, peeled and sliced
   ¼ inch thick (see note)
¾ cup very thinly sliced Vidalia onion
¼ cup apple cider vinegar
2 tablespoons Dijon mustard
2 tablespoons finely chopped mint
2 teaspoons finely chopped cilantro
   (leaves and tender stems)
1 garlic clove, minced
¾ teaspoon salt, or to taste
¼ teaspoon freshly ground black
   pepper, or to taste
½ cup extra-virgin olive oil

Arrange the tomatoes on a platter and place the sliced onions decoratively on top of them. In a medium bowl, whisk together the vinegar, mustard, mint, cilantro, garlic, salt, and pepper until well combined. While whisking, slowly add the oil in a thin stream; continue whisking until the dressing becomes creamy. Serve the salad at room temperature, with vinaigrette on the side. *Serves 4*

NOTE: You can peel tomatoes using a serrated potato peeler (available in specialty cooking stores), or you can use the blanching method: bring a pot of water to a boil; fill a large bowl with iced water. Cut a small X into the bottom of each tomato with a sharp knife. Drop the tomatoes into the boiling water for 30 seconds and then transfer them with a slotted spoon to the iced water and let them sit for 1 minute. The skin should peel off easily.

tomatoes stuffed with quinoa salad

These edible vessels hold a hearty vegetarian filling studded with sweet elements. Quinoa, an ancient grain native to the Andes region of South America, means "mother grain" in Quechua. Lauded for its high protein content, it was introduced into this country in the late seventies but has just recently caught the interest of mainstream America because of its high nutritional value. Prepared in the same manner as rice, when quinoa is cooked, it becomes translucent and a ring, resembling a sprout, becomes visible around each grain. You'll need to rinse it well before cooking in order to remove the bitter compound (called saponin) that coats each grain. Find quinoa in most grocery stores, in health-food stores, and in specialty gourmet shops. For a striking presentation, plate the tomatoes individually before serving.

FOR THE SALAD

- 6 large beefsteak tomatoes
- 1 cup quinoa
- ½ cup raisins
- ¼ cup minced yellow onion
- ¼ cup finely chopped cilantro (leaves and tender stems), packed
- 2 tablespoons minced jalapeño (seeded and deveined if less heat is desired)
- 1 tablespoon grated lemon zest
- 1 teaspoon minced mint
- 1 medium garlic clove, minced

FOR THE DRESSING

- ⅓ cup lemon juice
- 2 tablespoons apple cider vinegar
- 2 tablespoons honey
- ¾ teaspoon salt, or to taste
- ¼ teaspoon freshly ground black pepper
- ¼ cup extra-virgin olive oil

Place the quinoa in a fine sieve and rinse under cold, running water, for 1 minute, or until the water runs clear. Place the quinoa in a small saucepan and cover with 2 cups of water; bring to a boil over medium-high heat. Reduce the heat to low, cover the pan, and simmer for 12–15 minutes, or until all of the water has been absorbed. Remove from the heat and transfer to a large bowl; cool completely. Add the raisins, onions, cilantro, jalapeño, lemon zest, mint, and garlic; stir to combine.

In a medium bowl, whisk together the lemon juice, vinegar, and honey until the honey is dissolved. Stir in the salt and pepper; while whisking, slowly add the oil in a thin stream until all is incorporated. Stir the dressing into the quinoa. Chill for 30 minutes in order for the flavors to blend.

Cut ⅛ inch off the top of each tomato; using a spoon or your fingers, remove all of the seeds and center pulp. Fill the tomatoes with the quinoa salad. Chill the tomatoes until ready to serve (up to 4 hours). *Serves 6*

the first global culinary exchange

Imagine how the first *conquistadores* felt upon first stepping into the New World. There were none of the animals they were used to eating—certainly no chickens, cattle, or pork. They would not have recognized any of the plants in their new environment, which meant that they had no idea where to begin to search for food. In order to survive, they would have had to learn what to eat from the indigenous peoples whom they had conquered. Thus the first culinary exchange took place between the Old World and the Americas, which ultimately changed the foodways of the entire globe. By the time Europeans reached the Americas, culinary connections had already been made between Europe and the continents of the Far East and Africa. Here are some of the ingredients that Europeans brought with them and their places of origin: chickens (Asia); pork (Asia and the Middle East); cows (Asia and Africa); rice (Asia); citrus (Asia); coffee (Africa); sugar (Africa); wheat (Turkey); spelt (Turkey); cilantro (Mediterranean region); saffron and sweet spices (Far East); bananas (Africa); yams (Africa); cowpeas or black-eyed peas (Africa); barley (Middle East); figs (Asia); onion, chives, leeks, and garlic (Europe and Middle East); mangos (Asia); and peaches (Asia). Some of the foods the Americas gave the world are chiles, bell peppers, cacao, squash, avocados, vanilla, turkey, potatoes, pumpkins, cranberries, blueberries, strawberries, pineapple, yuca (or cassava), peanuts, tomatoes, beans, quinoa, and corn. What would Italian food be like without tomatoes; Swiss food without chocolate; Asian food without chiles; Southern food without peaches or lard; Mexican food without cilantro; Cuban food without rice? Fusion cuisine is really nothing new; it's the perpetuation of the culinary exchange.

two-corn summer salad

Fresh corn and cooked hominy produce an explosion of contrasts when combined in this salad featuring a deliciously addictive dressing. Every single bite features an eruption of vibrant flavors: sweet and sour, crispy and creamy, fresh and earthy. Nothing compares to the taste of summer corn, buttery and sweet; it's scrumptious eaten directly from the cob or scraped into soups, puddings, relishes, and fritters. Fresh, in-season corn is particularly luscious when used raw in salads; its honeylike flavor is further enhanced by citrusy vinaigrettes. The nixtamalized corn of the Americas is the hominy of the South. When kernels are soaked in lye water to remove the outer germ, they puff up and soften; their texture changes from crunchy to chewy, and their sweetness is replaced by rustic and nutty flavors. The union of these two forms of corn yields a wonderfully refreshing and colorful salad. Behold summer in a bowl.

4   cups raw corn kernels, scraped
off fresh cobs
2 ½   cups cooked whole hominy
(or one 20-ounce can, drained
and rinsed) (see note)
2   cups quartered grape tomatoes
¼   cup minced, seeded, and deveined
jalapeños
¼   cup minced flat-leaf parsley
(leaves and tender stems)
      Grated zest of 1 lemon
¼   cup lemon juice
¼   cup red wine vinegar
⅓   cup extra-virgin olive oil
2   large garlic cloves, minced
      Salt and freshly ground black
pepper, to taste

In a large bowl, combine the corn, hominy, tomatoes, jalapeños, and parsley. In a medium bowl, whisk together the lemon zest, lemon juice, vinegar, oil, and garlic until well combined. Season with salt and pepper. Pour the dressing over the corn mixture and toss to coat. Let it sit at room temperature for 30 minutes (or refrigerate for up to 8 hours) before serving. Serve chilled or at room temperature. *Serves 4–6*

NOTE: Dried hominy can be found in Latin tiendas, where it's called *mote*. Find canned hominy in most supermarkets.

corn: the gold of the americas

"Thus was found the food that would become the flesh of the newly framed and shaped people."— from the Popol Vuh, the Mayan creation story.

Mayan legend has it that when God created men, he first made them with mud, then wood, and then flesh; but he was only pleased with the men he made out of corn. Corn, or maize (*maíz* in Spanish), was first domesticated by the Mayans over seven thousand years ago. By the time Europeans arrived in the New World, corn had also been domesticated in North America. When *conquistadores* took corn back with them to Europe, where it became a staple food, many people began to die from pellagra, which is caused by a lack of niacin in the diet and protein deficiency. Indigenous peoples didn't suffer from malnutrition, or from this disease in particular, because they had learned to soak corn in lye water, obtained from lime or ashes, to remove the outer hull of its kernels, a process known as nixtamalization, which frees niacin. Beans, which helped the body absorb corn's nutrients, were also a big part of their diet. Europeans so feared dying from this disease that for a long time corn was considered only fit for animal feed. By the seventeenth century, however, corn was a major crop in many European countries, including Italy, Spain, and Portugal. The oldest nixtamalized solids have been found in Guatemala and date back to 1500 B.C., giving credence to the theory that the Mayans first invented this technique. Had the indigenous peoples not developed this technique, the South wouldn't have hominy to make grits, cornbread, or hushpuppies, nor would Latin Americans have tortillas, posole, tamales, hayacas, or humitas.

main dishes

was moved to write this book by a desire to bring people together at the table by showcasing dishes that build upon similarities. What is striking about the cuisines of the American South and Latin America is not their differences but what they have in common. I've set out to present dishes that are familiar to both Southerners and Latinos so that when you try them for the first time you recognize them as something you've had before—but with a slight twist. Old favorites will become new again.

For instance, consider the love of pork in all its glory. Consider the fact that the indigenous peoples of the Americas had never seen a pig until Columbus brought Iberian hogs to the American continent. Pigs were as valuable a tool of conquest as the conquistadors' weapons themselves, for were it not for the food they brought, they would have starved. Records indicate that Hernán Cortés had pigs with him throughout his voyage through Mexico and Central America. When the Europeans introduced pigs to the South in the 1600s (Hernando de Soto brought one boar and three sows to the Jamestown settlement), they reproduced copiously, in such ridiculous numbers that many escaped into the wild. These hogs survived under difficult conditions and adapted to their new environment, ranging over the entire continent. It didn't take long for the indigenous peoples to discover their succulent taste (see sidebar, page 126).

Today, pork is the most popular meat in both Latin America and the South, and cooks make use of the entire pig—from skin to shin and head to toe. Pork stars in dishes such as Brazilian feiojada, Bolivian fritanga,

Mexican *carnitas*, Carolina barbecue, and Kentucky creamed ham. Both cultures share a love of pickled pig's feet and chitlins (pig intestines, or *menudo* in Spanish), crispy pork rinds, and lard. It should not be surprising that many of the New Southern-Latino recipes in this book make good use of lard and bacon, which add a distinct flavor to dishes like my Albóndigas with Sweet Fire-Roasted Tomato Chutney. Latinos tend to use pork ribs in braised dishes and stews, but my Whiskey and Tamarind-Glazed Baby Back Ribs reflect both the Latino and Southern styles.

Latinos love their beef. Columbus brought beef to the New World, but Hernán Cortés is responsible for introducing it into North America. Recipes made with cube steak are popular in both cultures but are interpreted differently. In Latin America, cube steaks are most likely marinated and then grilled; Southerners often bread and fry them. Here, I offer my interpretation, Country Fried Steaks with Cilantro-Lime Gravy. Hamburgers and grilled steaks are popular throughout Latin America. Steaks take on a new character in Rib Eyes with Pimiento Cheese Butter and Chimichurri and in Barbacoa de Carne with Vidalia Onion and Herb Salsa.

Poultry is perhaps the most accessible meat for Latinos and Southerners alike. Given that chicken is less expensive than beef, it makes a regular appearance in the daily menus of most households throughout America. In these pages you'll find my delicious Pecan Milanesas with Corn and Blueberry Salsa and, reminiscent of sweet barbecued chicken, my Caramelized Chicken. If you love Southern fried chicken, give my Latin Fried Chicken with Smoky Ketchup a try. Roast chicken is a comforting meal, and I offer you my simple and flavorful version featuring lime and chipotles.

In a letter to his daughter, Benjamin Franklin wrote, "For my own part I wish the Eagle had not been chosen the representative of our country . . . for the truth the Turkey is in comparison a much more respectable bird, and withal a true original native of America." This chapter would not be complete without a recipe featuring this bird, so I offer a New Southern-Latino Turkey that will be a welcome addition to a Thanksgiving table or to a repast for Nochebuena (Christmas Eve).

Seafood abounds in the waters of the Americas, and here I feature a new rendition for a Low Country favorite, Shrimp 'n' Grits. The French introduced the method of cooking food in paper packages—en papillote—and this healthy technique is used in my recipe for Yucatán Fish Cartuchos with Maque Choux, which incorporates flavors of both Mexico and Louisiana.

You'll find that most of the recipes in this chapter can be partially or totally made ahead of time; some of them taste even better a day after they're made, as is the case with my Drunken Chicken with Muscadine Grapes and White Wine. Some recipes require a solid investment of time but are easy to make. The Beef Carnitas Soft Tacos are a good example. In this case, the beef can be cooked a day in advance and the tacos assembled to order. These are also the dishes I often count on when I entertain because they can be reheated at the last minute without compromising flavor.

Best of all, my recipes don't require that you go out and get special cooking tools. Because the cooking techniques used in Southern and Latino cuisines are simple, you won't have to learn new cooking methods either. Grab an apron and join me in making these scrumptious dishes, one at a time.

albóndigas with sweet fire-roasted tomato chutney

Mexican sausage imparts accents of garlic, paprika, and oregano to these meatballs that simmer in sweet tomato relish spiked with spices and chiles. Each bite is filled with smoky, sweet, and spicy comfort. Throughout Latin America, albóndigas, or meatballs, are prepared in myriad ways. In Mexico they're bathed in chipotle sauce, and in South America they're laced with olives and raisins. Notice here the blending of cultures and taste a bit of the Arab influence in Latin cuisine. These albóndigas are quick to assemble and inexpensive to prepare, ideal for weekday meals when time is of the essence. Canned organic, fire-roasted tomatoes are available in most grocery stores. The chutney is a cinch to make: just stir and simmer. Cook the albóndigas ahead of time and freeze them; for a quick supper, simply heat them in the succulent sauce and serve them over steamed rice. To make this dish suitable for children, cut back on the chipotles.

FOR THE CHUTNEY

- 2 (14.5-ounce) cans crushed fire-roasted tomatoes
- 1 cup finely chopped Vidalia onion
- ¾ cup brown sugar, packed
- ¼ cup apple cider vinegar
  3-inch piece Mexican cinnamon stick (canela)
- 1 bay leaf
- 1 chipotle chile in adobo, minced
- 1 teaspoon adobo
- 1 medium garlic clove, minced
- 1 teaspoon salt
- ¼ teaspoon ground allspice
- ¼ teaspoon ground cumin

In a medium saucepan set over medium-high heat, combine the tomatoes, onions, brown sugar, vinegar, cinnamon, bay leaf, chipotle, adobo, garlic, salt, allspice, cumin, and ¼ cup of water. Bring the mixture to a boil, reduce the heat to medium-low, and simmer for 40–45 minutes, or until thickened, stirring occasionally. Remove from the heat and discard the cinnamon and bay leaf; set aside to cool.

FOR THE ALBÓNDIGAS

1¼ pounds ground chuck
½ pound Mexican chorizo
½ cup minced white onion
¼ cup finely chopped cilantro
    or parsley (leaves and
    tender stems)
2 tablespoons seeded, deveined,
    and finely chopped jalapeño
2 medium garlic cloves, minced
¼ cup masa harina (or ⅓ cup dried
    bread crumbs)
1 teaspoon salt
¼ teaspoon freshly ground
    black pepper
1 egg, lightly beaten
2 tablespoons vegetable oil

In a medium bowl, combine the chuck, chorizo, onions, cilantro, jalapeño, garlic, masa harina, salt, pepper, and egg; mix until well blended. Shape the mixture into 16 meatballs (about 4 tablespoons each). In a large skillet with high sides, heat the oil over medium-high heat. Add the meatballs and cook, turning, until all sides are nicely browned. Remove with a slotted spoon and set on a plate; discard all but 2 teaspoons of the oil left in the pan. Return the meatballs to the pan and cover with chutney. Bring to a boil over medium-high heat; cover, reduce the heat to low, and simmer gently for 20–25 minutes, or until cooked through. *Serves 4-6*

NOTE: The cooking time for the chutney will vary depending on how juicy the tomatoes are. Be sure to cook the chutney until the juices have reduced; continue cooking until it's thick enough to coat the meatballs. Alone, this chutney makes a delicious accoutrement for biscuits or crackers and cheese. If you don't have time to make meatballs, preheat the oven to 375°F. Coat a jelly roll or baking pan with cooking spray. Shape the beef mixture into an oval (about 9 inches long by 4 inches wide and 2 inches high) and bake until the surface of the loaf is browned and an instant-read thermometer inserted into the center registers 165°, about 50-55 minutes. Remove from the oven and let it rest for 10 minutes; serve sliced with chutney on the side.

COOK'S TIP: The flavor of rendered fat from beef, pork, and chicken is important in Latin American cuisines, but if you're concerned about the fat content of recipes, you can drain more of the fat.

bacon-wrapped pork tenderloin with guava and peanut sauce

Juicy, smoky, and tender pork topped with a peanut-laced sauce is ideal for occasions in which you need an elegant recipe that delivers great taste but takes only minutes to prepare. Both Americans and Latin Americans love pork. I love the sweet and smoky flavors so often fused in Southern cuisine, and I use them in this dish that merges the sweetness of fruit with the smokiness of bacon. Tenderloin can be dry, so wrapping it in a little bit of fat keeps it moist as it roasts. Creole mustard—made with distilled vinegar and salt—mellows as it cooks; here, it offers great balance and depth. Peanuts, native to South America, are widely used in Latin cuisine. They were brought to the South via South America by African slaves from the Congo. This sauce thickens as it sits; add more broth to thin it out.

FOR THE PORK

- 2 pork tenderloins (about 1½ pounds each)
- ¼ cup Creole mustard
- 1 tablespoon brown sugar, packed
- 2 large garlic cloves, minced
- ½ teaspoon dried sage
- 10 slices of bacon

FOR THE SAUCE

- 1 cup chunky peanut butter
- ¾-1 cup chicken broth (see note)
- ½ cup guava jelly
- 1½ teaspoons Worcestershire sauce
- ¼ teaspoon guajillo chile powder (or pinch cayenne)
- Salt and freshly ground black pepper, to taste
- ¼ cup very thinly sliced green onions, for garnish

Preheat the oven to 475°F. Pat the pork dry with paper towels; set aside. In a medium bowl, combine the mustard, brown sugar, garlic, and sage. Spread the mixture all over the pork loin; tuck the thin end of the pork under itself. Wrap the bacon slices around the pork, widthwise, using toothpicks to secure them into place, if needed. Set the pork on a roasting pan fitted with a rack (so the fat can render into the pan) and roast for 25–30 minutes, or until the bacon is golden and an instant-read thermometer inserted into the center of the tenderloin registers at least 155°F. Transfer the roast to a cutting board and let it rest for 10 minutes before slicing (see note).

In the meantime, make the sauce: In a medium saucepan set over medium-high heat, combine the peanut butter, ¾ cup of the broth, guava jelly, Worcestershire sauce, and chile powder. Bring the mixture to a boil and cook for 5 minutes, or until the sauce is thickened slightly (see note); season with salt and pepper. Serve the sliced pork on a platter with the sauce on the side; garnish with green onions. *Serves 6*

NOTE: I like this sauce on the thicker side, but if you prefer, thin it out by adding a little more broth. Also, larger pork tenderloins will take longer to cook; adjust cooking time accordingly. Finally, it's important to let meat and poultry rest before cutting into it so that the juices that have risen to the surface during cooking can be redistributed.

barbacoa de carne
with vidalia onion and herb salsa

Hearty beef meets lemony dressing in my favorite rendition of grilled steak. The word "barbecue" is derived from the term *barbacoa*, a cooking technique originating with the Taino people of the Caribbean in which meats are roasted over an open fire. The salsa, light and aromatic, complements the sturdy taste of the beef. Crunchy onion adds just the right amount of sweetness to the citrusy topping, while the sugar in the steak rub forms a caramelized crust, irresistible to the palate. Grass-fed beef is common in both Latin America and the United States, and it's available at many farmers' markets. I'm very partial to flat iron steak (also known as top blade) for its tenderness, and it's more affordable than beef tenderloin. For optimal flavor, serve it medium-rare. To preserve the color and vibrancy of the herbs in this salsa, it's best made just before serving.

FOR THE STEAK

- 1 flat iron or flank steak (about 2 pounds)
- 1 tablespoon vegetable oil
- 1 tablespoon lemon juice
- 1 teaspoon dark brown sugar, packed
- ½ teaspoon paprika
- ½ teaspoon ground cumin
- ½ teaspoon garlic powder
- ½ teaspoon dried oregano
- ½ teaspoon ancho chile powder
- ½ teaspoon salt
- ¼ teaspoon freshly ground black pepper

Rub the oil and lemon juice on both sides of the steak; set aside. In a small bowl, whisk together the brown sugar, paprika, cumin, garlic powder, oregano, chile powder, salt, and pepper. Rub the steak generously with the spice mixture; set aside at room temperature for 20–25 minutes (or refrigerate for up to 8 hours; let it come to room temperature before grilling).

FOR THE SALSA

1½ cups finely chopped Vidalia onion
½ cup finely chopped cilantro (leaves
   and tender stems)
¼ cup finely chopped chives
¼ cup finely chopped mint
1 tablespoon grated lemon zest
½ cup lemon juice
2 tablespoons finely chopped
   jalapeños (seeded and deveined
   if less heat is desired)
1 tablespoon extra-virgin olive oil
1 teaspoon salt
¼ teaspoon freshly ground black pepper

Make the salsa: In a medium bowl, combine the onion, cilantro, chives, mint, lemon zest, lemon juice, jalapeños, oil, salt, and pepper, stirring to blend; set aside for 10 minutes to allow the flavors to blend (or chill for up to 24 hours).

Heat the grill or grill pan to high (very hot coals) and place the steak on the grates over direct heat. Cover and cook for 3 minutes; rotate the steak a half turn to form searing marks and cook for 2 more minutes. Flip the steak over; for medium-rare, cook, covered, for 4 minutes, or until an instant-read thermometer inserted into the thickest part of the steak registers at least 140°F. Remove the steak to a cutting board; tent loosely with aluminum foil and let it rest for 10 minutes. Thinly slice the steak across the grain, on the bias; transfer to a serving platter. Serve the salsa on the side. *Serves 4*

beef carnitas soft tacos

Tender beef brisket in this recipe is wrapped in warm corn tortillas and dressed with lusciously creamy and pleasantly crunchy toppings to complement its bold taste. Taco trucks are now a permanent fixture in many Southern cities. They offer tacos with fillings that range from the typical ground beef to offal of all kinds for the more adventurous palates. Carnitas, or "little meats," are pieces of chopped meat (customarily pork) that are first braised in liquid and then cooked in lard until caramelized. In my version, beef simmers gently in beer—low and slow—until it falls apart; after chopping, it's left to cook until all of the liquid evaporates. This is the perfect party dish and tastes even better the day after it's made; plan to make it ahead of time and reheat it before serving.

1 (4-pound) beef brisket, trimmed
   of excess fat

¼ cup lard (or vegetable oil)

1 bottle (1½ cups) beer,
   preferably Mexican

1 small yellow onion, peeled
   and quartered

8 large garlic cloves, peeled
   and left whole

½ teaspoon dried thyme

2 bay leaves

1½ teaspoons salt

¼ teaspoon freshly ground
   black pepper

24 warm corn tortillas (see note)

2 cups sliced radishes

1 cup sour cream

1 cup finely chopped cilantro
   (leaves and tender stems)

Lime wedges

Pat the brisket dry with paper towels. Melt the lard in a large Dutch oven over medium-high heat; brown the brisket on both sides (about 3–4 minute per side, or until a brown crust forms). Add the beer, onions, garlic, thyme, bay leaves, salt, and pepper. Bring the liquid to a boil; cover with a tight-fitting lid, reduce the heat, and cook at a slow simmer for 2½–3 hours, or until the meat is tender enough to be shredded with a fork. Remove the beef from the pan and chop into bite-size pieces; strain the liquid left in the pan through a sieve to remove all of the solids. Return the beef and the cooking liquid to the pan and bring to a rolling boil over medium-high to high heat. Cook, stirring occasionally, for 10–15 minutes, or until all the liquid has been absorbed and only the beef and fat remain. Serve the carnitas with tortillas and all the trimmings on the side.

To assemble the tacos, wrap the beef, radishes, sour cream, cilantro, and a squirt of lime juice in the tortillas. *Serves 6–8*

NOTE: To heat tortillas, wrap them in a clean, damp kitchen towel; microwave at 1-minute intervals until warm. Alternatively, wrap them in foil and place them in a preheated 350°F oven for 10–15 minutes, or until warm. You can also heat them, one at a time, over the open flame of a gas stove (or outdoor grill) for about 1 minute on each side until warm. Keep the warm tortillas wrapped in a kitchen towel as you work. The longer you cook the beef in the remaining fat at the end of the recipe, the crispier the meat will be. Don't overcook.

COOK'S TIP: Brown meats very well before braising or stewing until they're golden all around. Deep flavor is produced through the caramelization of natural sugars in protein. Make sure not to overcrowd the pieces in the pot; rather, work in batches, turning the pieces only when a crust has formed on each side. This takes only minutes, and you'll be rewarded with plenty of flavorful brown bits in the bottom of the pan that will permeate the sauce.

all you need to know about cooking with chiles

The recipes in this book feature chiles in many different forms: fresh, dried, ground, roasted, and preserved. Always wear gloves when handling fresh or dried chiles. In general, my recipes for sauces and stews call for dried chiles; they contain pectin, which thickens liquids. To toast dried chiles, heat a dry skillet over medium-high heat and toast the chiles for 20 seconds on each side, or until they become pliable, being careful not to burn them. To seed a dried chile, using scissors, cut a slit in one side, from bottom to top, remove the stems, and shake out the seeds. To devein a dried chile, open up the slit chile like a book and pull the veins off. Dried chiles sometimes need to be reconstituted in liquid before being used in recipes. To do this, soak them in boiling water or stock for 10–20 minutes. Many of my recipes call for chile powder, which adds flavor and smokiness to dishes and blends quickly into sauces. In this book chile powders are used in recipes for sauces, stews, salad dressings, dips, and desserts. More than a few of the recipes here require roasted poblanos. To roast a poblano (or any other pepper or chile), hold it directly over the flame of a gas stove, rotating it until its skin has blackened (about 6 minutes). Place it in a bowl with a lid and let it steam for 10 minutes. Use a sharp knife to scrape off the skin. Alternatively, spread the poblanos in a single layer on a baking sheet and roast them in a 450°F oven for 4–5 minutes until they blister, or cook them over a very hot grill until their skins are charred. Proceed as instructed above. Preserved chiles can be used directly from the jar. Canned chipotles are preserved in a tomato, onion, and garlic sauce called adobo. If you've used only a few chiles from the can, you can freeze the leftovers; place each chile with a dollop of the sauce on a pan lined with parchment paper; freeze until solid and then transfer to freezer bags. Alternatively, puree the chipotles with the sauce and freeze the puree in ice cube trays. One teaspoon of the puree equals about half of a chile. Remember to use chiles cautiously—a small amount goes a long way. Start with a small amount first. You can always add more heat later, but you can't take it away!

caramelized chicken

Sweet, sour, sticky, and smoky, this delectable chicken is a favorite in my home. The basic ingredients in sofrito—onions, garlic, and tomatoes—and the sugar in orange juice and chiles produce a gravy with the consistency of barbecue sauce. Here is an example on how natural pectin found in dried chiles helps to thicken a sauce without making it spicy-hot. When I first arrived in the South, I was surprised to encounter myriad renditions of barbecued chicken smothered in sweet tomato sauce that reminded me of a favorite dish I grew up with in Guatemala called pollo *encebollado*. I make this recipe in a large skillet that has enough surface area to allow the sauce to reduce quickly as the chicken cooks; a splatter guard will keep your stovetop clean. Loved by kids and adults alike, this easy and quick entrée is perfect for everyday meals but elegant enough for company.

4 dried pasilla, guajillo, or ancho
  chiles (or a combination of
  all three)
1½ cups tomato ketchup
1¼ cups orange juice
1 teaspoon Worcestershire sauce
1 teaspoon salt
¼ teaspoon freshly ground
  black pepper
4 tablespoons vegetable oil, divided
2 cups sliced white onion
2 sprigs fresh thyme
  (or 1½ teaspoons dried)
2 bay leaves
2 garlic cloves, finely chopped
1 chicken (3½–4 pounds), cut into
  serving-size pieces

Place the dried chiles in a medium bowl; cover them with 2 cups of boiling water and weigh them down with a plate to keep them submerged. Soak the chiles for 10 minutes, or until soft (don't let them soak for too long or they'll lose flavor). Drain the chiles; remove the stems and seeds and cut the chiles into strips; set aside. In a medium bowl, combine the ketchup, orange juice, Worcestershire sauce, salt, and pepper; set aside.

In a large skillet with high sides, heat 2 tablespoons of the oil over medium-high heat; add the onions and cook for 5 minutes, or until soft. Add the thyme, bay leaves, and chiles. Cook over medium-high heat until the onions begin to caramelize, about 5 minutes. Add the garlic and cook for 1 minute; transfer the mixture to a plate and set aside. Add the remaining 2 tablespoons of oil to the skillet and brown the chicken pieces well on all sides (about 6–8 minutes total). Discard all but 1 tablespoon of the oil left in the pan. Place the reserved onion mixture over the chicken, distributing well. Cover the chicken with the ketchup sauce and bring it to a boil. Cover the

NOTE: If the chicken is cooked through and the sauce has yet to thicken, remove the chicken to a platter and continue reducing the sauce until it reaches the desired consistency. If the chicken is not fully cooked and the sauce has reduced too much, combine ¼ cup ketchup with ¼ cup orange juice and stir that into the chicken; simmer an additional 5 minutes, or until the chicken is cooked through.

skillet, reduce the heat to low, and simmer for 15 minutes. Remove the cover and simmer for an additional 20–25 minutes, or until the chicken is cooked through and the sauce has thickened to the consistency of barbecue sauce, turning the chicken pieces occasionally (see note). (The sauce will bubble quite a bit, so place a splatter guard or screen over the skillet to avoid a mess.)
Serves 4-6

catfish soft tacos with mango salsa

In this scrumptious dish, expertly seasoned, crunchy fish, crispy lettuce, creamy sauce, and vibrant salsa are all proficiently wrapped in a warm tortilla. An explosion of flavors and the perfect amalgamation of textures are captured in this exciting new version of soft tacos. As in the South, Latinos prepare catfish (called *bagre* in some Latin American countries) in many ways, including stewing, grilling, and baking it. My favorite way to prepare this strong-flavored fish is to coat it with earthy cornmeal in the Southern fashion and fry it. Some people complain that catfish has a heavy, sometimes "off" taste, which is why I prefer the fresh water over the salt water variety and soak it in buttermilk before cooking. You'll find nothing off-tasting about these tacos showcasing a sweet and spicy contrast to deliciously crispy fish.

3 pounds catfish fillets, cut into 24 strips

6 large garlic cloves, minced

¼ cup ancho chile powder

½ teaspoon chipotle chile powder

2 cups buttermilk

3 cups finely ground cornmeal

2 teaspoons salt

2 teaspoons ground cumin

1 teaspoon ground coriander

1 teaspoon freshly ground black pepper

1½–2 cups all-purpose flour

4 eggs, beaten

Vegetable oil for frying

1½ cups mayonnaise

2 teaspoons lemon juice

1 tablespoon minced chipotle chiles in adobo, or to taste

1 teaspoon adobo

2 cups shredded iceberg lettuce

12 warm corn tortillas (see note on page 115)

Mango Salsa (page 32)

Fit two large baking sheets with metal cooling racks; set aside. Rinse the fish and pat dry with paper towels. In a large, glass bowl, combine the garlic, chile powders, and buttermilk. Add the catfish strips and coat them well; chill for at least 1 hour (or overnight).

Preheat the oven to 275°F. In a large, shallow pan, combine the cornmeal, salt, cumin, coriander, and pepper. Place the flour in a plate and the eggs in a shallow pan. Dredge the catfish strips in the flour; dip them into the eggs and then dredge in the cornmeal mixture. In a large skillet with high sides, heat 2 inches of oil to 360°F. Working in batches, fry the fish for about 7 minutes per side, or until crispy. Transfer the fried fish to the prepared cooling racks. When you've filled one, place it in the oven while the rest of the fish is fried (the fish will stay crispy for up to 1 hour).

In a small bowl, combine the mayonnaise, lemon juice, chipotles, and adobo. To assemble the tacos, place 2 catfish strips on each tortilla and garnish with lettuce, chipotle mayonnaise, and mango salsa. *Serves 6*

country fried steaks with cilantro-lime gravy

Rich gravy, aromatized with cilantro and lime, envelops thin beef cutlets in this rendition of a Southern favorite. Instead of the thick gravy that is the customary accompaniment in the South, I dress these steaks with a sour cream sauce that gets a pleasant kick from jalapeños. Cube steaks are tenderized cuts of top round. In Cuba they're known as bistecs de palomilla. The machine used to tenderize them produces their signature dimpled imprints, which make flour coatings and marinades cling easily to the steaks. While Southerners often fry or braise cube steaks with onions, Cubans marinate them in a citrus and garlic mojo (sauce) instead. Masa harina and cornmeal join forces to produce a toothsome crust. Served with Three-Cheese Grits with Loroco (page 216) and a tomato salad, these are ideal for a casual Sunday supper.

FOR THE STEAKS

- 6 cube steaks (about 1½ pounds), pounded to ¼-inch thickness
- ¾ cup masa harina
- ⅓ cup stone-ground cornmeal
- 1 teaspoon salt
- 1 teaspoon ground cumin
- ½ teaspoon ground coriander
- ½ teaspoon chipotle chile powder (or cayenne pepper)
- 2 eggs, lightly beaten
  Vegetable oil for frying

FOR THE GRAVY

- ¼ cup (½ stick) unsalted butter
- ½ cup minced white onion
- 1 cup finely chopped cilantro (leaves and tender stems)
- ½ cup lime juice (or more, to taste)
- 1½ cups sour cream
- 1 tablespoon minced jalapeño (seeded and deveined if less heat is desired)
  Salt and white pepper, to taste

Preheat the oven to 250°F. Line a baking sheet with a metal cooling rack. In a large, shallow plate, combine the masa harina, cornmeal, salt, cumin, coriander, and chile powder; set aside. Working in batches, dip the steaks in the beaten eggs and coat both sides with the masa mixture, making sure to press down on the steaks so it adheres well. In a large skillet, heat 1½ inches of oil over medium to medium-high heat. Fry the steaks for 4–5 minutes on the first side and 3–4 minutes on the second side, or until the juices run clear and the crust is a golden brown (lower the heat if they're browning too quickly). Transfer the steaks to the prepared cooling rack and keep them warm in the oven while you make the gravy (or for up to 1 hour).

In a medium saucepan, melt the butter over medium heat; add the onions and sauté for 3–4 minutes, or until they're translucent (but don't let them brown). Add the cilantro and cook for 1 minute. Add the lime juice and bring the mixture to a simmer. As soon as it starts bubbling, remove the pan from the heat and stir in the sour cream and jalapeño; season with salt and pepper. Serve the steaks immediately with the gravy on the side.

Serves 4-6

NOTE: If you're using a dark pan such as anodized aluminum or cast-iron, which retain more heat than their lighter counterparts, the crust will brown more rapidly. If the outer crust is browning too quickly, you'll need to reduce the heat to give the steaks enough time to cook through. This gravy is meant to be sour; cut down on the lime if you prefer a less sour sauce. If you don't like cilantro, substitute equal parts of mint or parsley. You may also reduce the amount of cilantro in the recipe, to taste.

the cilantro gene

Cilantro is believed to be the most widely used herb in the world, and its culinary importance has been extolled for centuries. Native to Southern Europe, cilantro is often confused visually with Italian parsley. Both are members of the carrot family (*Umbellifearae*), but their similarity ends there. Whereas parsley is sometimes used in recipes just to add a bit of color, cilantro is always used for its flavor. The culinary love affair with this gutsy herb spans the globe: from Asia to Latin America. However, cilantro has only recently begun to figure prominently in America's mainstream cuisine. Also known as Chinese parsley, cilantro refers to the leaves of the coriander plant. If the coriander plant is allowed to flower, it produces a dry fruit known as coriander seed. Latin Americans also cook and eat the roots of the cilantro plant. The coriander plant is the only herb that produces three by-products with totally dissimilar tastes and culinary uses. While the flavor of coriander seeds can be described as a blend of anise and lemon, describing the flavor of cilantro proves an almost impossible task. I've heard it variously described as pungent, zesty, and even soapy, but the exact flavor of cilantro is best determined by the individual palate. One thing is certain: your first experience with cilantro is bound to be a memorable one. It will either seduce you into a life-long romance or turn you away like a scorned lover. Recent studies suggest that the strong negative reaction to cilantro may be genetic. Love it or hate it, though, cilantro is one of the most important herbs in Latin cuisine. If you don't like cilantro (and you're in good company: Julia Child herself expressed her dislike for this herb) I suggest substituting a combination of equal parts of parsley and mint. As with most fragile herbs, dry cilantro well before chopping to avoid bruising its leaves, and use the tender stems as well— they're as flavorful as the leaves.

drunken chicken with muscadine grapes and white wine

In this dish, plump chicken simmers gently in a light and fruity sauce that is slightly spicy. From Panamanian estofados to Cuban fricasées, most Latin countries feature recipes for chicken stewed in white wine. This one is reminiscent of those found in Chile—Latin America's wine country—where oregano is grown and used abundantly. Muscadine grapes are native to the American South and are in season from September to October. Of the many varieties, I'm partial to the green Scuppernongs and the purple Thomas. The grapes are stewed along with the chicken, adding sweetness to the sauce and developing a texture reminiscent of that of olives. If muscadines aren't available, use seedless grapes. The skins of muscadines have a lovely pectin content that thickens sauces. If you use regular grapes, you may have to simmer the stew a bit longer to reduce the liquid. Serve the chicken over rice and offer crusty bread to sop up the juices.

1 chicken (4 ½–5 pounds), cut into
    10 serving pieces
1½ teaspoons salt
½ teaspoon freshly ground
    black pepper
2 tablespoons extra-virgin olive oil
5 cups thinly sliced Vidalia onion
3 large garlic cloves, thinly sliced
2 tablespoons Dijon mustard
1 bay leaf
½ teaspoon red pepper flakes
1 cup white wine (such as a Chilean
    Chardonnay)
3 cups muscadine grapes, halved
    and seeded (along with any
    skins that slip off)
¼ cup chopped flat-leaf parsley
    (leaves and tender stems)

Pat the chicken dry with paper towels; season with the salt and pepper. In a large Dutch oven, heat the oil over medium-high heat; working in batches, brown the chicken pieces on all sides and transfer them to a platter; discard all but 1 tablespoon of the oil left in the pan. Add the onions to the pan and cook for 4–5 minutes, stirring occasionally, until soft. Add the garlic, mustard, bay leaf, and red pepper flakes; cook, stirring, for 30 seconds, or until the garlic is fragrant. Add the wine and deglaze by scraping the bottom of the pan; bring to a boil. Return the chicken (and all of the juices that have collected at the bottom of the platter) to the pan. Cover, reduce the heat to low, and simmer for 15 minutes. Add the grapes (and skins) and stir well; cover and simmer for 25 minutes, or until the chicken is cooked through (the juices will run clear when the chicken is pierced with a fork). Taste the sauce and adjust the salt and pepper. Transfer the stew to a serving platter and sprinkle with parsley; serve immediately.
Serves 6

garlic-studded pork

Sweet spices and red wine permeate this hearty pork roast with sumptuous, luxurious flavors. The result is moist, garlicky, and sweet meat that melts in your mouth. You'll want to use bone-in shoulder or butt (known in the South as picnic roast). The bone helps to keep the flesh moist, adds flavor, and makes for a beautiful presentation. Make sure you get a cut that still has skin attached to it so that the roast will stay juicy; when the roast is cooked, the skin will crisp beautifully, giving you a little extra something to nosh on. Although I call for marinating the pork overnight to allow the meat to soak up more flavor, you can skip this step altogether and still get incredibly flavorful results. For my parties, I like to slice it thinly and serve it cold on miniature brioche rolls with a dollop of chipotle-enhanced mayonnaise and shredded cabbage.

1 bone-in pork shoulder or butt or picnic roast (10-12 pounds)

15 garlic cloves, slivered (they should look like slivered almonds)

30 pitted prunes

1 tablespoon dried thyme

1 teaspoon dried rosemary

6 bay leaves

2 sticks Mexican cinnamon (canela), broken into pieces

Pat the roast dry with paper towels. With the tip of a very sharp knife, make 30 deep incisions into the pork—don't slice but simply pierce it and then insert your index finger into the hole and wiggle it to expand each incision. Insert a garlic sliver into each prune. Carefully, insert a prune into each incision in the pork. In a large plastic bag (I use a 13-gallon garbage bag), combine the remaining garlic, thyme, rosemary, bay leaves, cinnamon, oil, and wine. Place the pork in the marinade and seal the bag closed; marinate the pork in the refrigerator for 12-24 hours, turning occasionally to redistribute the marinade. (If you don't have the time to marinate, skip this step: just mix the ingredients for the marinade in a bowl and pour them over the roast in the roasting pan.)

¼ cup extra-virgin olive oil

8 cups red wine (such as Merlot)

4–6 cups chicken broth

2 teaspoons salt

½ teaspoon freshly ground black pepper

Preheat the oven to 400°F. Remove the roast from the marinade and place it in a large, deep roasting pan; pour the marinade around the bottom of the pan and add the chicken broth. Sprinkle the roast with the salt and pepper and roast, uncovered, for 1 hour. Remove the roast from the oven and baste with marinade; cover the pan with foil and seal it well; roast for another 3–3 ½ hours, or until an instant-read thermometer inserted into the center of the roast registers at least 160°F, basting every half hour. Uncover and continue cooking until the skin is crispy (30–35 minutes). Transfer the roast to a platter; let it rest for 30 minutes before slicing thinly on the bias.

In the meantime, strain the juices left in the pan to remove all solids; degrease the sauce. Season the roast liberally with salt and pepper and keep warm until ready to serve. Serve with the sauce on the side. *Serves 10-12*

herb-encrusted pork tenderloin

When I want a quick meal to put on the table, pork tenderloin always fits the bill. In this instance, it's assembled in advance and left to marinate, absorbing the vibrant flavors of garlic and herbs; then it's cooked briefly at a high temperature. While it's a terrific simple meal, it's also elegant, making it perfect for fancier occasions. Most Latin and Southern recipes for pork call for cooking it until it's well done, but I like to cook mine so that it's slightly pink in the center—safe to eat but still moist and succulent. It's delicious either way. I love to round out this simple meal with lots of side dishes, for example, Maduros (page 213), Coconut Rice (page 202), and Tomato and Vidalia Salad with Mint Vinaigrette (page 100).

2 pork tenderloins (about
1½ pounds total)

½ teaspoon salt

¼ teaspoon freshly ground
black pepper

4 large garlic cloves, minced

1 cup minced cilantro (leaves
and tender stems), packed

2 tablespoons minced
flat-leaf parsley (leaves
and tender stems)

3 tablespoons extra-virgin
olive oil, divided

Using a sharp knife, remove all of the silverskin from the tenderloins; season them on all sides with the salt and pepper. Fold the tail of the roasts over to the center and tie with kitchen twine (to make the tenderloins the same width throughout for even cooking); set aside. In a small bowl, combine the garlic, cilantro, parsley, and 2 tablespoons of the oil and blend well. Rub the herb mixture on all sides of the tenderloins. Place the tenderloins in a nonreactive pan and cover with plastic wrap (or place in a zip-top bag) and refrigerate for at least 6 hours (or overnight).

Preheat the oven to 400°F. In a large, oven-safe skillet, heat the remaining tablespoon of oil over medium-high heat. Sear the tenderloins on each side for 2 minutes. Transfer the skillet to the oven. For medium doneness, roast the tenderloins for 15 minutes, or until an instant-read thermometer inserted into the center of the roast registers 150°F (see note). *Serves 4 to 6*

NOTE: Pork should always be cooked to at least 140°F, the temperature at which trichinosis is killed. If the tenderloins weigh more than 1½ pounds, adjust the cooking time accordingly.

latin fried chicken with smoky ketchup

Nothing says "South" more than fried chicken. Crispy, juicy, spicy, and moist, my version takes a bath in spiced-up buttermilk before it's cooked. This is one of the most requested recipes in my cooking classes. Chicken is first fried, then blasted in a hot oven to finish cooking, creating a crunchy exterior. This cooking method prevents the spices and flour from burning and allows excess fat to render out. The result is chicken that is moist but not greasy. Made this way, chicken can be kept in a warm oven for a full hour before serving without becoming soggy. No more burnt coatings and undercooked chicken! My secret to a crunchy crust is to use self-rising instead of all-purpose flour. You can find bottled Latin ketchup with various levels of heat at Latin grocery stores; my rendition delivers a gutsy kick. Pair this with iced tea or ice-cold cerveza.

FOR THE CHICKEN

- 1 chicken (5–5 ½ pounds), cut into 10 serving pieces
- 1½ cups buttermilk
- ¼ cup minced cilantro (leaves and tender stems)
- 2 tablespoons minced chipotle chiles in adobo
- 1 teaspoon adobo
- ½ teaspoon garlic powder
- 1 teaspoon salt
- Pinch freshly ground black pepper

In a large glass bowl, combine the buttermilk, cilantro, chipotle, adobo, garlic powder, salt, and pepper. Add the chicken and toss to coat; cover and chill for at least 6 hours (or up to 24).

Preheat the oven to 325°F. Fit two baking pans with metal cooling racks. In a large bowl, combine the flour, paprika, salt, coriander, garlic powder, cayenne, chile powder, and pepper. Dredge the chicken in the flour mixture and set on one of the prepared racks. Let the chicken air dry for 5 minutes.

a brief history of pork in the americas

Pork is so prevalent in the cuisines of Latin America and in the Southern United States that it's hard to believe that there was once a time when pigs did not exist on our continents. In fact, when Christopher Columbus arrived in the New World, he was surprised not to find most of the animals Europeans were accustomed to, including cattle, sheep, goats, chickens, and horses. On his second voyage to the New World, Columbus brought several animals, among them eight Iberian pigs, which adapted quickly to their new environment and multiplied exponentially. The Spanish *conquistador* Hernán Cortés stopped in Cuba (before setting sail to conquer the Aztecs), where he purchased pigs to take along on his journey. Once in Aztec territory, many escaped to the wild and

3 cups self-rising flour
2 teaspoons paprika
1½ teaspoons salt
1 teaspoon ground coriander
1 teaspoon garlic powder
1 teaspoon cayenne pepper
1 teaspoon ancho chile powder
½ teaspoon freshly ground
   black pepper
   Vegetable oil for deep frying
   (about 4–5 cups)

FOR THE KETCHUP
1½ cups ketchup
2 tablespoons minced chipotle
   chiles in adobo
1 teaspoon adobo
2 teaspoons ancho chile powder

In a large Dutch oven, heat 3½ inches of oil to 360°F. Working in batches, dredge the chicken in the flour mixture a second time; fry the white meat for 8 minutes and the dark meat for 10 minutes, or until the crust is crispy and reddish-brown. Transfer the fried chicken to the other prepared rack. Bake for 20–25 minutes, or until an instant-read thermometer inserted into the thigh of the chicken registers between 180°F and 185°F (the juices will run clear when the chicken is pierced with a fork). To keep the chicken warm (up to 1 hour), reduce the oven to 250°F.

In a small bowl, combine the ketchup, chipotle, adobo, and chile powder; chill until ready to use. The ketchup will keep, covered tightly, for up to 1 week in the refrigerator.
Serves 4-6

eventually ranged throughout Mesoamerica. Historical accounts of the colonization of Latin America describe the herds of pigs Europeans brought to breed for later consumption. From Hernán Cortés in Mexico to the Pizzaro brothers in Peru, the *conquistadores* knew that in order to succeed in their missions they needed to secure sources of food. They also brought with them cooking techniques, in particular how to make hams. In exchange, natives taught them *barbacoa*, a culinary technique in which meats were cooked on spits over an open fire. In 1593, Hernando de Soto arrived in Florida and brought thirteen pigs, and it wasn't long before they began to procreate in the wild and multiply throughout the Southern United States. The rest, as they say, is history.

lime and chipotle roast chicken

Moist, spicy, and succulent, this roast chicken tastes of homemade goodness. Family traditions are very important to both Southerners and Latinos. Sunday suppers in the South are often informal affairs where comfort food is shared family-style. Likewise, Latinos often meet at abuela's (grandmother's) house and celebrate meals with simple but flavorful dishes that are passed around the dinner table. This roast, with its beautiful, crispy, caramel-colored skin makes a perfect centerpiece to any table. Its tender flesh is infused with a richly spiced compound butter that melts slowly, basting the chicken from within as it roasts. Every flavor element joins seamlessly in this recipe. It's particularly delicious when paired with my Chorizo Dirty Rice (page 200). The citrusy undertones of the chicken meet the piquant smokiness of the chipotles, and the gentle heat of the chiles balances the hearty flavor of the chicken livers in the rice.

1 chicken (4–4 ½ pounds)
4 tablespoons unsalted butter, at room temperature
2 tablespoons minced chipotle chiles in adobo (use less if less heat is desired)
1 teaspoon adobo
1 tablespoon grated lime zest
1 teaspoon salt
½ teaspoon freshly ground black pepper
1 whole lime, pricked with a fork several times

Preheat the oven to 400°F. Pat the chicken dry with paper towels. In a small bowl, combine the butter, chipotle, adobo, lime zest, salt, and pepper; blend until you have a smooth paste. Slide your fingers underneath the skin of the chicken (being careful not to tear it) to loosen it. Using a small spoon, slide the flavored butter under the skin, and use your hands to distribute it evenly. Place the lime inside the cavity of the chicken. Using kitchen twine, tie the legs of the chicken together and place the chicken, breast side up, on a roasting pan. Sprinkle the chicken with salt and pepper.

Roast the chicken for 1 hour and 45 minutes, or until an instant-read thermometer inserted into the thigh of the chicken registers between 180°F and 185°F (or the juices run clear when the chicken is pierced with a fork). Remove the chicken from the oven; tent loosely with aluminum foil and let it rest for 15 minutes before carving. To serve, remove the lime from the cavity and cut the chicken into the desired number of pieces. *Serves 4-6*

new southern-latino turkey with bourbon gravy

This festive bird is tender and juicy, full of bold flavor imparted by a combination of gutsy spices and a touch of the tropics. Wine lends a fruity taste and serves as a basting liquid. The turkey is "steam-roasted"—a favorite Central American cooking technique—and stays moist throughout the cooking process, yielding some of the most succulent flesh you'll ever taste. Turkeys were first domesticated in Central America, and by the time European *conquistadores* arrived in the New World, wild turkeys had themselves conquered a vast territory—no small feat for such awkward birds! Turkeys grace holiday tables throughout the Latin American continent, especially at Christmastime. The rich, succulent gravy features the ultimate blend of Latin spices and Creole flavors. It makes use not only of the fat drippings and giblet broth featured in most traditional gravies but also of the vegetable base that's cooked with the turkey. Inspired by the cuisine of Louisiana, parts of which were governed by Spain in the eighteenth century, this gravy begins with a dark, nutty roux. The result is a piquant sauce, sweetened with wine and aromatized with bourbon. The Creole culinary history of Latin and Southern cultures melts together once more and results in gravy with complex flavors that explode across the palate. I recommend that you serve this with my Green Bean Casserole (page 180) and New Southern-Latino Cornbread Dressing (page 186).

FOR THE TURKEY
- 1 turkey (12–14 pounds)
- 2 large celery ribs (with leaves)
- 2½ cups roughly chopped red onion, divided
- 1 bay leaf
- ½ cup (1 stick) unsalted butter, softened
- ½ cup Creole mustard
- 2 teaspoons salt
- 1½ teaspoons dried sage
- 1 teaspoon dried thyme
- 1 teaspoon freshly ground black pepper
- ½ teaspoon ground cumin
- ½ teaspoon dried oregano
- ½ teaspoon garlic powder
- ½ teaspoon smoked Spanish paprika

3 cups roughly chopped plum
   tomatoes
1 cup roughly chopped green
   bell pepper
2 large garlic cloves, thinly sliced
3 cups white wine (such as
   Chardonnay or Sauvignon Blanc)
3½–4 cups chicken stock
1 cup guava jelly

FOR THE GIBLET BROTH
Neck and giblets from the turkey
   (discard the liver)
1 bay leaf
3 cups chicken broth
2 cups white wine (such as
   Chardonnay or Sauvignon Blanc)
½ cup roughly chopped yellow onion
1 celery rib, roughly chopped

Preheat the oven to 350°F. Remove the giblets and neck from the cavity of the turkey; set aside. Pat the turkey dry with paper towels and set in a roasting pan; place the celery, ½ cup of the onions, and the bay leaf in the cavity. In a small bowl, make a paste with the butter, mustard, salt, sage, thyme, pepper, cumin, oregano, garlic powder, and paprika; rub the paste thickly all over the turkey and inside the cavity. Surround the bird with the tomatoes, the remaining red onions, the bell pepper, and garlic; pour the wine and stock over the vegetables. Cover the turkey loosely with aluminum foil and roast for 3–3½ hours (or until a thermometer inserted in the thickest part of the thigh registers 170°F), basting with the juices every 30 minutes.

Make the giblet broth while the turkey roasts. Place the neck and giblets in a medium saucepan; add the bay leaf, broth, wine, onions, and celery. Bring the liquid to a boil over medium-high heat; cover, reduce the heat, and simmer for 1½ hours. Remove from heat; cool slightly. Remove the giblets; pull as much neck meat as you can and chop finely. Chop the rest of the giblets finely; set aside. Strain the giblet broth—you should have about 3 cups—and reserve 1 cup (discard the remaining broth or freeze it to make soup later).

Remove the turkey from the oven. In a small saucepan, heat the guava jelly until it liquefies. Remove the foil from the turkey and brush the top with jelly; bake, uncovered, for 30 more minutes, stopping to brush with more of the jelly every 10 minutes. The turkey is completely done when the temperature measured at the thickest part of the thigh reaches 185°F and the skin is golden and shiny. Transfer the bird to a platter. Save the drippings and solids to make the gravy. Let the turkey rest for 20 minutes before carving.

FOR THE GRAVY

½ cup (1 stick) unsalted butter

½ cup all-purpose flour

Drippings and solids (vegetable base) left from roasting turkey

⅓ cup bourbon

Salt and freshly ground black pepper, to taste

Make the gravy: In a large, heavy-bottomed saucepan, melt the butter over medium-high heat; when it foams, reduce the heat to low. Whisk in the flour and cook, stirring, for 20–25 minutes, or until the mixture turns the color of peanut butter; remove from heat and set aside (this step may be done up to 4 hours ahead). Keep in mind that the darker the roux is, the less it will thicken sauces.

Set a strainer over a large bowl and strain the vegetable solids from the turkey drippings; reserve the vegetable solids. Use a degreaser to remove the fat from the drippings; place the fat in a jar, seal, and discard. Pour enough of the reserved giblet broth into the degreased drippings to make 3 cups of liquid; set aside.

Transfer the reserved vegetable solids into a blender and puree until smooth. Stir 2 cups of the blended vegetable solids into the roux in the pan (discard the rest or freeze and use as a soup base); whisk in the 3 cups of the reserved liquid. Bring the gravy to a boil over medium heat, stirring as it thickens (about 5 minutes). Stir in the bourbon and simmer for 3 minutes. Stir in the chopped giblets and neck meat and season with salt and pepper. Keep warm until ready to serve over sliced roast turkey.

Serves 6–8

pecan milanesas with corn and blueberry salsa

The crunchy crust on this chicken gives way to tender flesh, delicately dressed with a refreshingly sweet salsa embellished with hints of mint and honey. Milanesas, or breaded cutlets, are to Latin Americans what fried chicken is to Southerners. They became ever-present in Latin cuisine after Italian immigrants introduced them to South America in the nineteenth century. German immigrants brought their version, Wiener schnitzel, to the communities that welcomed them in large numbers, but it was the Italian term that has been absorbed into Latin American culinary lingo. They're usually topped with lime juice and often served stuffed into sandwiches. In my version, pecans, which are native to the South, add a satisfying crunch and a touch of sweetness to the crust. Corn and blueberries work together in a colorful salsa that pops with sweet and tart flavors.

FOR THE MILANESAS

6 boneless, skinless chicken breasts
½ cup all-purpose flour
½ teaspoon salt
½ teaspoon paprika
⅛ teaspoon freshly ground
   black pepper
1½ cups pecans, toasted and ground
   (see note)
½ cup dried bread crumbs
2 eggs, lightly beaten
½ cup vegetable oil

FOR THE SALSA

1½ cups corn kernels (fresh or
   frozen and thawed)
1 cup blueberries
¼ cup minced Vidalia onion
   (or other sweet onion)
1 minced serrano chile (seeded and
   deveined if less heat is desired)
2 tablespoons finely chopped cilantro
   (leaves and tender stems)
1 tablespoon finely chopped mint
1 tablespoon lime juice
2 teaspoons honey
   Salt and freshly ground black
   pepper, to taste

Preheat the oven to 350°F. Fit a baking sheet with a metal cooling rack; set aside. Pound the chicken breasts with a meat mallet to ¼-inch thickness; set aside. On a plate, combine the flour, salt, paprika, and pepper. On another plate, combine the pecans and bread crumbs. In a medium bowl, whisk together the eggs and 2 tablespoons water. Dredge each cutlet in the flour mixture, shaking off the excess, and dip both sides of the cutlet into the eggs. Dip both sides of the cutlet into the pecans, pressing gently so they adhere well. In a large skillet, heat ¼ cup of the oil over medium-high heat. Working in batches, fry the cutlets for 2–3 minutes per side, or until golden brown (add more oil as needed; reduce the heat if they brown too quickly). Transfer the cutlets to the prepared baking sheet and bake for 10–12 minutes, or until cooked through (no longer pink).

In a medium bowl, combine the corn, blueberries, onions, serrano, cilantro, mint, lime juice, and honey and stir until well incorporated; season with salt and pepper. Serve the chicken topped with salsa. *Serves 6*

NOTE: Toast pecans on a baking sheet in a 350°F oven for 5–8 minutes, or until fragrant. Transfer them to a plate to cool completely. Once toasted, pecans can be frozen in an air-tight container for up to 4 months. To grind pecans, place them in the bowl of a food processor fitted with a metal blade and pulse on and off until some pieces are ground to a meal and others remain a bit larger (about ten 1-second pulses); don't overgrind, or you'll end up with an oily meal. Alternatively, chop them very finely with a sharp knife.

pork tenderloin with cocoa, chile, and bourbon mole

This moist and perfectly tender pork is enveloped in a dark, sweet sauce that melds classic flavors of the Deep South with exotic tastes of the ancient Aztec civilization. Mole means "sauce" in Nahuatl. The most well-known mole, mole poblano, is unique in that it's the only Mexican mole that contains chocolate. Making moles is a many-step process requiring a long list of ingredients, including spices, seeds, chiles, and vegetables. Here, however, I simplify the matter by reducing the necessary steps. The result is a richly flavored sauce, luxurious enough to serve in your fine china. Be sure to use dark cocoa powder (or a blend of dark and Dutch) for depth of flavor. The chiles add a delicious complexity and sweetness to this mole without imparting too much heat. Serve this dish with steamed rice, creamy grits, or Collard Green Tamales (page 203).

FOR THE PORK

2 pork tenderloins (about 2 pounds total)

4 large garlic cloves, slivered (they should look like slivered almonds)

2½ tablespoons olive oil, divided

2 tablespoons dark cocoa powder

2 teaspoons salt

1 teaspoon freshly ground black pepper

2 teaspoons finely chopped fresh sage (or 1 teaspoon dried)

½ teaspoon Mexican cinnamon (canela) (see note)

Preheat the oven to 400°F. With a sharp knife, trim the fat and remove the silverskin from the tenderloins. With the tip of a very sharp knife, make several deep incisions in the tenderloins; insert one garlic sliver into each incision. Brush the pork with 1 tablespoon of the oil. In a small bowl, combine the cocoa, salt, pepper, sage, and cinnamon and rub the mixture all over pork.

In a large skillet, heat the remaining oil over medium-high heat; brown the pork, on all sides, about 4 minutes total. Transfer the pork to an oven-safe baking dish. Roast for 20–25 minutes, or until an instant-read thermometer inserted into the center of the tenderloin registers at least 140°F (for medium). Remove the roast from the oven, tent loosely with aluminum foil, and let rest for 10 minutes.

FOR THE MOLE

- 3 tablespoons unsalted butter
- 2 cups sliced Vidalia onion
- 3 large garlic cloves, minced
- 2 ancho chiles, seeded, deveined, and toasted (see sidebar, page 116)
- 1 guajillo chile, seeded, deveined, and toasted (see sidebar, page 116)
- 1 teaspoon minced chipotle chiles in adobo
- 1 teaspoon adobo
- 2 tablespoons raw, unsalted pepitas
- 1½ cups chicken broth
- ¼ cup bourbon
- ¼ cup molasses
- Salt and freshly ground black pepper, to taste

To make the mole: In a medium saucepan, melt the butter over medium-high heat; add the onions and sauté for 15 minutes, or until caramelized. Add the garlic and cook for 30 seconds; remove from heat. Transfer the onion mixture to a blender. Add the chiles, adobo, pepitas, and chicken broth; blend until smooth. Return the sauce to the pan; cover and simmer for 20 minutes over medium-low heat. Add the bourbon and molasses; simmer for 10 minutes. Season with salt and pepper.

Slice the tenderloins thinly on the bias; divide onto serving plates and drape with the mole sauce. *Serves 8*

NOTE: Since Mexican cinnamon is sold only in stick form, you'll need to grind it yourself. Break the stick into pieces and grind in a spice or coffee grinder or a mortar and pestle until smooth.

rib eyes with pimiento cheese butter and chimichurri

Few things are more delicious to me than juicy, tender steak laced with spices. Here, it's topped with pimiento cheese and an herb sauce called chimichurri. In the South, barbecue involves a whole pig; in Latin America, however, barbacoa is all about beef. Cattle were brought to the New World by conquistadores and quickly multiplied, making beef central to Latin cuisine. Today, Argentine beef is renowned worldwide, and Brazilians are famous for churrasco, beef cooked over coals on giant spits. Venezuelan guasacaca (avocado paste), Central American chirmol (charred tomato salsa), and Chilean pebre (spicy tomato sauce) are common accoutrements. Few barbecue sauces are more familiar than South American chimichurri. Made with parsley, vinegar, and spices, this sauce adds luscious pungency to the steak. The marriage of Southern and Argentinean flavors create a light sauce that dresses every bite.

4 rib-eye steaks (8–10 ounces each)
2 teaspoons vegetable oil
2 teaspoons grated lemon zest
½ teaspoon ground cumin
½ teaspoon ground coriander
½ teaspoon garlic powder
½ teaspoon dried thyme
½ teaspoon salt (I prefer sea salt)
¼ teaspoon freshly ground
    black pepper
Pimiento Cheese Butter (page 28)
Classic Argentinean Chimichurri
    (page 26)

Rub the steaks with oil on all sides. In a small bowl, combine the lemon zest, cumin, coriander, garlic powder, thyme, salt, and pepper and rub the mixture on all sides of the steaks; set aside for 20 minutes at room temperature (or chill for up to 12 hours; bring to room temperature before grilling). Heat an outdoor grill (or indoor grill pan) until hot. For medium-rare, grill the steaks for 4–6 minutes on each side, or until a thermometer inserted into the thickest part of a steak registers 145°F. Top each steak with a generous slice of Pimiento Cheese Butter and a few spoonfuls of the Chimichurri. *Serves 4*

shrimp 'n' grits

Caribbean flavors marry Low Country tradition in this succulent stew, featuring plump, briny shrimp swimming in a light sauce, boldly infused with the color of golden achiote. When I first arrived in the Carolinas, I was fresh out of college and a newlywed, eager to cook for my husband. He absolutely loved grits. I, on the other hand, had never heard of grits. It didn't take long for me to learn how to make them and to fall in love with this hearty meal. There are many ways to prepare this popular dish, and my twist on this Southern specialty builds upon classic ingredients with new elements. Here, Creole trinity (the mixture of onions, green bell peppers, and celery at the foundation of Creole cuisine) meets sofrito and produces a scrumptious base reminiscent of bacalao a la vizcaína (a traditional Basque dish of dried cod stewed in tomatoes, enjoyed throughout Latin America during Lent). Bacon, which is traditional to this dish, adds smokiness. I suggest you make the grits first and keep them warm while you cook the shrimp.

Basic Grits (page 16)

4 thick-cut slices of bacon

3 tablespoons achiote oil, divided
  (page 14)

1 cup finely chopped Vidalia onion

1 cup finely chopped celery

1 cup finely chopped green
  bell pepper

4 large garlic cloves, minced

1-1½ teaspoons ground chiles de árbol
  or red pepper flakes, or to taste
  (see note)

1 pound large (16–20 count) shrimp,
  peeled and deveined

½ cup white wine (such as Chardonnay)

1 cup pimiento-stuffed olives

1 tablespoon capers, drained and rinsed
  under cold water

1 cup grape tomatoes

¼ teaspoon salt

Freshly ground black pepper,
  to taste

Place the bacon slices in a large, dry skillet with high sides. Cook the bacon over medium-high heat until all the fat is rendered and the bacon is crispy (about 1½ minutes on each side). Remove the bacon and set it on paper towels to drain; when cool enough to handle, chop coarsely and set aside.

Remove all but one teaspoon of the bacon fat from the skillet and add 2 tablespoons of the achiote oil. Add the onion, celery, and bell pepper; sauté for 4 minutes, stirring often and scraping the bottom of the pan to remove the brown bits, until the vegetables are soft. Add the garlic and chiles de árbol and cook for 30 seconds, or until fragrant. Add the shrimp and cook, stirring, for 3–4 minutes, or until they begin to turn pink. Add the wine, olives, capers, and tomatoes and cook for another 2 minutes. Stir in the bacon and salt; season with pepper. Serve immediately over the grits. *Serves 4–6*

NOTE: This dish is spicy! You can reduce the heat by cutting down on the chiles de árbol. Remember that it's impossible to remove heat from a dish; so start with a small amount and add more in small increments until you've reached the desired heat.

spice-crusted tuna with peach salsa and yuca fries

Fresh fish meets colorful salsa speckled with bright herbs and citrus in this light and invigorating dish that provides sensory contrast: sweet, savory, sour, and spicy. Here, an adobo, a spice mixture reminiscent of the cooking traditions brought by Africans to

Brazil in the seventeenth century, brings a combination of sweet and pungent flavors. The golden fries are made of yuca (also known as cassava) instead of potatoes. This starchy tuber is abundant in Latin America and cooks the same way that potatoes do. Yuca, however, yields a heartier, denser fry with sweeter flavor and a meaty texture that stands up to all of the other ingredients. The honey flavor of the peaches foil the heat imparted by chile powder. The trick here is not to overcook the tuna. It should be seared quickly so it stays pink and cool in the middle.

2-inch piece Mexican cinnamon
   stick (canela)
1 teaspoon toasted cumin seeds
1 teaspoon toasted sesame seeds
1 teaspoon toasted coriander seeds
½ teaspoon pasilla chile powder
   (or ancho chile powder)
½ teaspoon salt
2 teaspoons olive oil
4 (6-8 ounce) sashimi-grade tuna fillets
   Peach salsa (page 33)

FOR THE YUCA FRIES
3 garlic cloves, peeled and left whole
1 bay leaf
1 tablespoon salt
   Vegetable oil for frying
2 pounds fresh yuca, washed, peeled, and sliced into fries (about ⅓ inch thick) (see note)

NOTE: Use fresh or frozen yuca (if frozen, you'll have to boil it longer). Canned yuca will not work here as it's too mushy and will fall apart in the oil.

Preheat the oven to 250°F. Fit two baking sheets with metal cooling racks; set aside. In a coffee grinder (or a mortar and pestle), combine the cinnamon, cumin, sesame, and coriander; grind to a powder. Transfer the spices to a small bowl and stir in the chile powder and salt. Rub both sides of the tuna with the olive oil and then rub both sides with the spice mixture and set on a plate; cover and chill for 30-40 minutes.

In the meantime, make the fries. Fill a large pan with water (about 3 quarts) and set it over high heat. When the water comes to a boil, add the garlic, bay leaf, and salt; bring the water back to a boil. Add the yuca and cook until tender and easily pierced with a knife, but not mushy (10-12 minutes); remove with a slotted spoon and lay on clean kitchen towels. When cool to the touch, pat the yuca dry and transfer to cooling racks. Let stand for 10 minutes (up to 30 minutes).

In a heavy-bottomed Dutch oven or large skillet with high sides, heat 2-3 inches of oil to 360°F. Working in batches, fry the yuca until golden (about 5-6 minutes). Using a slotted spoon, transfer the fries to the prepared racks. Sprinkle with salt while hot. Place the fries in the warm oven (for up to 1 hour) and grill the fish.

Heat an outdoor grill (or indoor grill pan) until very hot; for medium-rare, grill the tuna for 3 minutes on each side; for medium, 5 minutes per side.

Top the tuna fillets with a generous amount of peach salsa. Serve with the yuca fries on the side. *Serves 4*

whiskey and tamarind–glazed baby back ribs

These fall-off-the-bone pork ribs are sweet, sticky, and moist, with just a hint of heat. To speed up the cooking process and to imbue them with flavor, they're first steamed and infused with a Cuban marinade called *mojo*, featuring citrus juice and garlic. On the grill, they're brushed with a sweet-and-sour glaze made with traditional Southern ingredients and with some of Latin American cuisine's gutsier flavors. Tamarind is a tangy, reddish-brown fruit that grows in pods. Because of its large seeds, and for easier consumption, its pulp is often transformed into extracts and pastes. Native to Africa, it was introduced to South America by the European conquerors. Tamarind is a very popular flavoring in Latin America, where it's used in popsicles, juices, candies, and sauces. Find tamarind extract in Latin tiendas or in stores that specialize in Indian cuisine.

2 racks of baby back ribs
   (3–3½ pounds each)
¾ cup orange juice
¼ cup lemon juice
3 garlic cloves, thinly sliced
½ cup unsulfured molasses
¼ cup whiskey (or bourbon)
¼ cup tamarind extract (or concentrate)
¼ cup tomato ketchup
1 tablespoon Dijon mustard
2 teaspoons minced ají amarillo or
   chipotle chiles in adobo
1½ teaspoons Worcestershire sauce
½ teaspoon salt
¼ teaspoon freshly ground black pepper

NOTE: You may also broil the steamed ribs, glazing them on each side for 4–5 minutes, or until the glaze has caramelized.

Preheat the oven to 375°F. In a small bowl, combine the orange juice, lemon juice, and garlic; set aside. Place each rack of ribs on a large sheet of aluminum foil (large enough to form a package around the ribs). Pour half of the marinade on each rack and enclose the foil around them, forming two large packages. Place the foil packages on a large, rimmed baking sheet and bake for 45 minutes, or until the ribs are soft and tender. Carefully remove the ribs from the foil packages; reserve ¼ cup of the cooked juices from the ribs and discard the rest.

Preheat an outdoor grill to high heat (see note). In a medium, nonreactive bowl, whisk together the molasses, whiskey, tamarind, ketchup, Dijon mustard, ají amarillo, Worcestershire sauce, salt, pepper, and reserved juices from the steamed ribs. Place the ribs, meat side down, on the grill and brush the glaze over them. Grill for 5–6 minutes, adding more glaze every minute or so (be generous; it will thicken as it heats). Turn the ribs over and continue brushing with the glaze generously every minute; cook for 5–6 minutes, or until the glaze is thick and sticky. Remove the ribs from the grill and let them sit for 5 minutes. Divide them into individual portions and serve. *Serves 8*

yucatán fish cartuchos with maque choux

Here, fish is marinated in citrus and achiote, sits on a bed of colorful vegetables, and is elegantly presented in individual packages (cartuchos) for each guest to unwrap at the table. When the packages are unwrapped, the sweet, sour, and smoky aromas—a mixture of oranges, bacon, and corn—escape, permeating the air and enticing the palate to savor. This method of marinating fish is typical of the Yucatán Peninsula, where it's customary to wrap foods in banana leaves before setting them on the grill. Here, a Louisiana Cajun corn stew flavored with bacon bits and chiles (maque choux) serves as the bed for the delicate fish. The fish is steamed in its own juices while the colorful marinade infuses it with flavor and paints it a deep red hue. This dish is as much of a feast for the eye as it is for the appetite.

4	tilapia fillets (6–8 ounces each)
⅓	cup orange juice
¼	cup white vinegar
1	ounce achiote paste
3	garlic cloves, finely chopped
1	teaspoon salt
⅛	teaspoon freshly ground black pepper
4	slices of bacon
2	cups corn kernels (fresh or frozen and thawed)
¾	cup finely chopped shallots
¾	cup finely chopped red bell peppers
2	tablespoons finely chopped jalapeños (seeded and deveined if less heat is desired)
	Salt and freshly ground black pepper, to taste
4	(14 × 16-inch) sheets of parchment paper
2	egg whites, lightly beaten

Place the fish fillets in a nonreactive baking dish. In a medium bowl, combine the orange juice, vinegar, achiote paste, garlic, salt, and pepper; stir until the achiote paste dissolves. Pour the marinade over the fish, ensuring that both sides are coated; cover and chill for 20 minutes.

Preheat the oven to 425°F. Place the bacon slices in a large, dry skillet with high sides. Cook the bacon over medium-high heat until all the fat is rendered and the bacon is crispy (about 1½ minutes on each side). Remove the bacon and set it on paper towels to drain; when cool enough to handle, chop coarsely and set aside. Remove all but 2 teaspoons of the bacon fat from the skillet and add the corn, shallots, bell peppers, and jalapeños; sauté for 3–4 minutes, or until the vegetables are tender, and season with salt and pepper. Toss the bacon with the vegetables; set aside.

Fold each piece of parchment paper in half crosswise; starting from the folded edge, cut the largest half-heart shape you can from each piece (when open, the parchment will be heart shaped). Working with one heart at a time, place $\frac{1}{4}$ of the corn mixture on one half of the heart. Top with a fillet and drizzle with 1 tablespoon of the marinade. Fold the other half of the parchment paper over the ingredients. Starting at the top of the heart, make small, overlapping folds along the edges to seal the package; when you get near the pointed end of the heart, fold the parchment underneath. Place the packages on two baking sheets; brush the tops with egg whites. Bake for 25 minutes. Transfer the packages to individual plates; to open, cut an X in the top of each with a pair of scissors (being careful not to burn yourself with the steam). Serve with white rice on the side, if desired. *Serves 4*

soups, stews, & braises

One of the common misconceptions about people who live
in tropical climates is that they must not eat hot foods. Of
course, not every Latin American country enjoys year-long
warm weather—the snow-dusted tips of volcanoes throughout the
landscape attest to this. But even people who live in the hottest climates
without air conditioning enjoy hot food. When you eat a warm dish, your
body temperature goes up, so the weather suddenly seems cooler.

If you ask me, few places get warmer than the South on a hot, muggy,
summer's day, and yet who in this area has not experienced the joyfully
cooling effect that a summer rainstorm can bring? This is the chapter to
turn to when you long for warm and comforting dishes that are perfectly
suited for year-round enjoyment. Whether you find yourself huddled
under a blanket in the middle of a winter storm or sitting in a tropical
paradise after a cooling rain, these recipes will bring you comfort.

The South is home to exquisite soups: the gumbos of Louisiana, the
chowders of Hatteras Island, and the muddles of North Carolina's Outer
Banks first come to mind. Likewise, Latinos enjoy tapados in Honduras, menestras in Argentina, and ch'airos in Bolivia. When I set out to
create the recipes for this chapter, I went back to childhood memories
of lunches at my grandmother's house. Every meal began with a soup.
The beauty of soup is that no matter how simple it is, it always sets an
elegant tone to a meal. Soups served as a first course calm the appetite to make way for the rest of the meal. But many are served as a main
course; they contain meats, vegetables, and starches all in the same
pot. The locros of Paraguay and Bolivia, the sancochos of Panama and

Ecuador, and the asopaos of Cuba, Puerto Rico, and Central America are analogous to the burgoos made in Kentucky and the gumbos of Louisiana. My Shrimp and Okra Asopao reflects this shared cuisine. In addition, Southerners and Latin Americans share a love of seafood chowder. My Crab Soup with Artichoke Fritters celebrates this commonality.

I like to dress soups with garnishes that add contrasting textures and colorful accents. A good example is my Creamy Potato-Leek Soup with Chimichurri and Country Ham. Garnishes can be very simple: a few floating croutons, some chopped herbs, or even a dollop of cream. The addition of garnishes, as well as the use of aromatic bases and flour thickeners in soups, reflect the European influence in the modern-day cuisines of Latin America and of the South.

The same can be said of the many stews that grace the tables of the peoples of the Americas. Fricassees abound in both culinary cultures— a clear reflection of European influence over our cuisines—as do hearty pots of stewed seafood, meats, and vegetables. In Louisiana you can feast on crawfish or shrimp boils with corn, potatoes, and andouille sausage. The pucheros and cocidos prepared throughout Latin America beg comparison. Although their interpretations vary, rich meat stews featuring dumplings are another common dish to both cultures. For example, flour dumplings often fortify the chicken stews eaten in the South, whereas corn dumplings add depth to the Paraguayan bori-bori soup.

Bean dishes are a prominent part of both the Southern and Latin culinary landscapes. While they often appear deliciously prepared in combination with pork and rice (as they are in my Nuevo Red Beans and

Rice with Chiltepín Gremolata in this chapter), certain types of beans
are commonly associated with certain regions. For example, pinto beans
are mostly associated with Mexico, but they're actually eaten throughout Mesoamerica; and while black beans are most commonly connected
to the cuisines of Cuba and Brazil, they're just as popular in Florida
and Guatemala. Likewise, black-eyed peas are a staple in the South,
but they're also used copiously in the Latin countries of the Caribbean
and in Brazil (a clear reflection of the influence Africans had on these
cuisines).

Braising is perhaps my most favorite cooking technique because
it frees me to do other things while my meal cooks and fills my home
with the most wonderful aromas. This method is ideal for preparing the
least expensive cuts of meats—those that are too tough to be grilled or
roasted. When you braise meats, you brown them in a little bit of fat,
and then cook them in a small amount of liquid slowly, over low heat.
This slow and low cooking method breaks down the tougher cuts of
meat until they become tender and fall off the bone. The Beef Short Ribs
with Roasted Tomato and Molasses Gravy and the Cola Brisket with
Dried-Chile Gravy found in this chapter are my interpretations of this
classic cooking method.

beef short ribs with roasted tomato and molasses gravy

A sweet, robust, richly seasoned gravy dresses these tender, fall-off-the-bone short ribs. This is one of the easiest braised dishes you'll ever make. The idea is to let your stove do the work. Many Mayan and Aztec recipes feature the technique of charring vegetables for sauces. Here, fire-roasted tomatoes are used for their smoky flavor and sweet succulence, which are further enhanced with molasses. Canned fire-roasted tomatoes can be found in most grocery stores. The combination of sweet spices and tomatoes is still prevalent in Central American cuisine and is a clear reflection of the Arab influence over the region's gastronomy. Be sure to dry the meat well by blotting with paper towels; if you skip this step the meat will steam rather than caramelize, and the final dish will lack depth of flavor.

3½ pounds (8 large) beef short ribs

1 teaspoon salt

¼ teaspoon freshly ground
   black pepper

2 tablespoons vegetable oil

1 (28-ounce) can crushed
   fire-roasted tomatoes

2 cups chopped white or yellow onion

2 cups cilantro (leaves and tender
   stems), packed

4 large garlic cloves, peeled and
   left whole

½ cup unsulfured molasses

1 large or 2 medium jalapeños,
   chopped (seeded and deveined
   if less heat is desired)

1 tablespoon ancho chile powder

2 teaspoons ground cumin

1 teaspoon ground coriander

½ teaspoon ground cloves

Pat the ribs dry with paper towels and season on all sides with salt and pepper. In a large Dutch oven, heat the oil over medium-high heat. Working in batches, being careful not to crowd the ribs in the pan, brown the ribs on all sides (about 10 minutes total for each batch—they should be a deep golden color on all sides). Turn off the heat and transfer the browned ribs to a plate and remove all but 2 teaspoons of the fat from the pan.

In a blender, combine the tomatoes, onions, cilantro, garlic, molasses, jalapeños, chile powder, cumin, coriander, and cloves; blend until smooth. Heat the fat in the Dutch oven over medium-high heat; when it's hot, add the blended sauce and stir well (be careful; the sauce will splatter briefly). Return the ribs to the pan (and any juices that accumulated in the bottom of the plate); stir to combine. Bring the liquid to a boil and cover; reduce the heat to low and simmer gently for 1½ hours. Taste and adjust the salt and pepper to your liking; cover and simmer for an additional 30 minutes. Serve hot. *Serves 4*

braised lentils

The Creole trinity (onion, bell pepper, and celery), chiles, and red wine provide the flavor highlights in this easy-to-make, tasty stew. Cayenne pepper adds a hint of heat that does not overpower. European conquerors brought lentils into the New World. Today, they're very common in the South American diet and are often used in braises and soups called *menestras*. Lentil dishes can be put together quickly because they don't require any soaking before cooking (as is the case with many legumes). You can use any kind of lentil in this dish, but I prefer the French green variety because they hold their shape better (even when overcooked) and are easy to reheat. They also have a distinctively nutty taste. Serve the lentils over a scoop of cooked rice or as a bed for Whiskey and Tamarind-Glazed Baby Back Ribs (page 138).

2	tablespoons extra-virgin olive oil
½	cup finely chopped yellow onion
½	cup finely chopped celery
½	cup finely chopped green bell pepper
½	cup peeled and finely chopped carrots
2	tablespoons minced garlic
2	tablespoons seeded, deveined, and minced jalapeños
½	cup seeded and finely chopped tomatoes
1	cup red wine
2	cups dried French green lentils
5	cups chicken broth or water
¼	teaspoon cayenne pepper
½	teaspoon dried thyme
1	bay leaf
2	teaspoons salt
¼	teaspoon freshly ground black pepper

In a large Dutch oven, heat the oil over medium-high heat; add the onion, celery, bell pepper, and carrots; cook, stirring often, for 3–4 minutes, or until the vegetables are soft. Add the garlic and jalapeño; cook for 30 seconds. Add the tomatoes and cook for 30 seconds. Add the wine and cook, stirring, for 2 minutes. Add the lentils, broth, cayenne, thyme, bay leaf, salt, and pepper; stir well. Bring to a boil; cover, reduce the heat to low, and simmer gently for 30–35 minutes, or until the lentils are tender. Discard the bay leaf, adjust the salt and pepper, and serve. (These taste even better a day after you've made them; reheat over medium-low heat until bubbly.)

Serves 6

butternut squash soup with chipotle and bacon

This warm, creamy, spicy soup gets a smoky kick from the crispy bacon used to garnish it. Latin Americans have a saying that translates roughly into this: "When impromptu guests arrive, just add more water to the soup"; in other words, there is always room for another person at the table. Anyone who has ever been lucky to live south of the Mason-Dixon line knows about Southern hospitality. The spirit of generosity at the cornerstone of both Southern and Latino cultures originates from a history of communal strife in which neighbors cared for one another. No matter the country, when people open up their home and feed you, they're offering you more than a warm meal. This soup, paired with my fluffy Buttermilk and Pork Rind Biscuits (page 18) and the Collard Greens, Oranges, and Pepita Salad with Buttermilk Dressing (page 87), makes a comforting meal.

4 slices of bacon
2 (2-pound) butternut squash
1¼ teaspoon salt
½ teaspoon freshly ground black pepper, or to taste
1 cup roughly chopped onion
2 teaspoons minced garlic
¾ teaspoon dried sage
1 chipotle chile in adobo, minced into a paste
1 teaspoon adobo
4½ cups chicken broth
½ cup heavy whipping cream

Preheat the oven to 400°F. Line two baking sheets with parchment paper; set aside. Place the bacon slices in a large, dry skillet with high sides. Cook the bacon over medium-high heat until all the fat is rendered and the bacon is crispy (about 1½ minutes on each side). Remove the bacon and set it on paper towels to drain; reserve 1 tablespoon of rendered fat. When the bacon is cool enough to handle, chop it finely; set aside. Trim both ends of the squash, halve them lengthwise, and discard the seeds. Lay the squash halves, cut side up, on the prepared baking sheets; season with the salt and pepper and roast for 45–60 minutes, or until soft and easily pierced with a fork. Scoop out the flesh and mash until smooth with a potato masher (or process in a food processor); set aside.

In a Dutch oven, heat the rendered fat over medium-high heat; add the onions and sauté, stirring often, for 3–4 minutes, or until soft. Add the garlic, sage, chipotle, and adobo and cook, stirring, for 30 seconds. Add the squash and broth and bring to a boil; cover, reduce the heat, and simmer gently for 20 minutes. When ready to serve, stir in the cream and heat through (being careful not to let the soup boil or the cream will curdle). Adjust the salt and pepper. Ladle into bowls and garnish with the crumbled bacon.

Serves 4-6

chicken and dumplings

Hearty and fragrant, this thick stew with vegetables is very satisfying. Best of all, it's a one-pot meal. Dumplings, common in both Latino and Southern cuisines, are featured as soup garnishes or are stuffed with fruit, wrapped in banana leaves (tamales), and fried. But pairing them with chicken is classic. Here, they're made with yuca (cassava) and instead of being rolled thinly and cut into strips, as is customary in the South, these are cut into small pieces. A food processor cuts the preparation time in half, but they're also easy to make by hand. If you're short on time, use rotisserie chicken and prepared broth. Dumplings can be made ahead and frozen; if they're frozen, you'll have to cook them a little longer.

FOR THE DUMPLINGS

- 2 pounds cooked yuca, peeled, halved, and tough inner vein removed (see note)
- 2 eggs
- ½ teaspoon salt
- 1½ cups all-purpose flour

FOR THE STEW

- 5 tablespoons unsalted butter
- 1 cup finely chopped onion
- 1 cup cooked carrots, diced
- 1 (4-ounce) jar diced pimientos, drained
- ¼ cup all-purpose flour
- 4½–5 cups warm chicken broth
- 1½ teaspoons salt, or to taste
- ½ teaspoon freshly ground black pepper
- ¼ teaspoon freshly grated nutmeg
- 6 cups cooked chicken, diced into 1-inch cubes
- ¾ cup milk
- ¼ cup finely chopped parsley, for garnish

Line 2 baking sheets with parchment paper. Place the yuca in the bowl of a food processor fitted with a metal blade. Pulse for 30–45 seconds, or until yuca is pureed (if it's dry, it will turn into a meal, which is okay). Add the eggs and salt and pulse for 30 seconds. On a clean surface, dump the flour; make a well in the middle. Dump the yuca mixture into the center of the well; with your hands, gently incorporate the flour into the yuca mixture until a soft dough is formed. Knead the dough for 6–8 minutes, dusting with a bit more flour to prevent the dough from sticking to the work surface. The dough is ready if it springs back when pressed down lightly. Form the dough into a ball, cover with a damp towel, and let rest for 20 minutes.

Divide the dough into 6 equal pieces. Working with one piece at a time (and keeping the others covered with the towel), roll the dough into 1-inch-thick ropes. Cut the ropes into ½-inch pieces and place them on the prepared sheets; cover with the damp towel and set aside.

In a large Dutch oven, melt the butter over medium-high heat. Add the onions, carrots, and pimientos; cook for 4–5 minutes, or until the carrots are tender. Add the flour and cook, stirring, for 1–2 minutes (be careful not to let it brown). Add 4½ cups of the chicken broth,

NOTE: You can use canned yuca for the dumplings; drain and pat it dry before using. You'll need 2 (15-ounce) cans.

the salt, pepper, and nutmeg; stir well. Bring to a boil. Reduce the heat and add the chicken and dumplings; simmer, partially covered, for 12–15 minutes, or until the dumplings are cooked through (and the sauce has thickened to the consistency of gravy). Add the milk and simmer for an additional 5 minutes (if the sauce thickens too much, add the rest of the broth). Ladle into bowls and sprinkle with parsley. *Serves 6-8*

chicken and mango braise

Tropical sweetness and homey goodness envelop tender chicken in this bubbly and comforting one-pot dish. This is my idea of dinner on the lazy fall evenings in the South when cooler temperatures announce the arrival of the winter months. The lovely orange tint of the sauce matches the beautiful colors of autumnal leaves, and the sultry and mildly sweet flavors of mangoes bring to mind the palm trees of the Latin coastline. This tastes as if it took a long time to cook, but it only takes a few minutes to prepare, which makes it one of my favorite dishes to make on busy days. Braises usually require lengthy cooking periods, but since chicken cooks so quickly, this one can be ready in just a short time. The sauce, though complex in flavor, is actually a cinch to make and can be prepared in minutes—simply blend and cook.

1 large mango, peeled, seeded, and roughly chopped
1 cup roughly chopped Vidalia onion
1 (14.5-ounce) can diced tomatoes, with juices
1 teaspoon achiote (annatto) powder
1 chipotle chile in adobo
1 teaspoon adobo

1 large garlic clove, quartered
2 teaspoons Worcestershire sauce
2 teaspoons olive oil
1 chicken (4–4½ pounds), cut into 8 portions and patted dry
1½ teaspoons salt
½ teaspoon freshly ground black pepper
½ teaspoon dried Mexican oregano

149

In a blender, combine the mango, onions, tomatoes, achiote powder, chipotle, adobo, garlic, and Worcestershire sauce; blend until smooth and set aside. In a large Dutch oven, heat the oil over medium-high heat. Working in batches, and being careful not to crowd the pieces in the pan, brown the chicken well on all sides; they should be a deep golden color. Turn off the heat and transfer the chicken to a platter; set aside.

Remove all but 2 teaspoons of the rendered fat from the pan. Heat the fat in the pan over medium-high heat, add the sauce (be careful; the sauce will splatter briefly), and stir well, making sure to scrape all the brown bits from the bottom of the pan. Add the salt, pepper, and oregano; return the chicken pieces to the pan. Bring the liquid to a boil; cover, reduce the heat to low, and simmer for 30 minutes, or until the chicken is cooked through (the juices will run clear when the chicken is pierced with a fork). Serve over white rice. *Serves 4-6*

chilled avocado-buttermilk soup with crab salad nacho

This is a classic soup with a twist: refreshing, smooth, and sinfully delicious. Every spoonful is like a collision of textures in which buttery liquid meets crunchy chips and tender seafood. Sherry imparts depth of flavor; cayenne lends subtle spiciness that lingers on the tongue. The lime juice seasons this soup lightly without overpowering the flavor of the avocados. Chileans serve palta *reina*, an avocado filled with creamy salad (most often chicken or seafood), as a first course, and I couldn't resist transforming this combination of ingredients into an enticing soup that is as easy to make as it is impressive to serve. For a stunning presentation, serve this soup well chilled in glasses.

FOR THE SOUP

2 Hass avocados
2 cups chicken broth
1 cup buttermilk
¼ cup dry sherry
¼ cup minced onion
1 garlic clove, minced
Salt and freshly ground black
pepper, to taste
1½ tablespoons lime juice, or to taste

FOR THE CRAB SALAD

1 cup crabmeat (claw meat only),
picked for shell fragments
¼ cup mayonnaise
1 teaspoon lime juice
1 tablespoon minced white onion
2 tablespoons flat-leaf parsley
(leaves and tender stems)
Pinch cayenne pepper
Salt and freshly ground black
pepper, to taste

FOR THE NACHOS

8 corn tortillas, quartered
½ cup vegetable oil

Halve and pit the avocados; scoop out the flesh with a spoon into a blender. Add the chicken broth, buttermilk, sherry, onions, and garlic; blend until smooth. Transfer the avocado soup to a nonreactive bowl. Season with salt, pepper, and lime juice; cover well with plastic wrap. Chill for at least 1 hour (or up to 6 hours).

Make the crab salad: In a medium bowl, combine the crabmeat, mayonnaise, lime juice, onions, and parsley, being careful not to break up the crabmeat; add the cayenne and season with salt and pepper. Chill the salad until ready to serve.

Fry the tortilla chips: Fit a baking sheet with a metal cooling rack. In a medium skillet, heat the oil over medium-high heat to 360°F. Working in batches, carefully add the tortilla pieces to the oil. Fry them, turning halfway through, until golden and crispy on both sides (2–3 minutes). Using a slotted spoon, transfer the fried chips to the prepared cooling rack; sprinkle with salt.

To plate: ladle the soup into chilled bowls. Top each tortilla chip with crab salad and float one in every soup bowl; serve the rest on a platter. Serve immediately.
Serves 4–6

cola brisket with dried-chile gravy

In this delicious dish, sweet and smoky beef brisket is cooked until tender enough to pull apart with a fork. The braised beef, embellished with thick gravy, features the deep, hearty flavor of dried chiles. Since the chiles are seeded, this dish is not overly spicy; the natural pectin in chiles helps to thicken the sauce. Although brisket is one of the most underused cuts of meat, maligned for its fibrous texture and a reputation for being tough, it yields some of the most succulent meat when it's cooked slowly in simmering liquid. Brisket is featured widely in Latin cuisine. Here, I juxtapose the flavors of the South's native colas (Pepsi Cola was invented in North Carolina and Coca-Cola in Georgia) with Latin spices. Serve it with steamed rice or over grits. Leftovers are great shredded and stuffed into sandwiches and quesadillas.

1 beef brisket (4–5 pounds)
1 tablespoon vegetable oil
3 dried ancho chiles, stem removed, seeded, and sliced in half
1 dried mulato chile, stem removed, seeded, and sliced in half
3 cups thinly sliced white onion
2 garlic cloves, peeled and left whole
3 plum tomatoes, quartered
4 medium tomatillos, halved
2 cups cola-flavored soft drink
1 teaspoon achiote (annatto) powder
¼ teaspoon ground cloves
1 bay leaf
1 stick Mexican cinnamon (canela)
1½ teaspoons salt
½ teaspoon freshly ground black pepper

Pat the brisket dry with paper towels. In a large Dutch oven, heat the oil over medium-high heat; brown the brisket well on both sides (3–4 minutes per side). Transfer the brisket to a platter. Add the chiles, onion, garlic, tomatoes, and tomatillos to the pan and sauté for 3–4 minutes, or until soft. Return the brisket to the pan (along with any juices that collected in the platter). In a large bowl, combine the cola, achiote powder, and cloves and pour over the brisket. Add the bay leaf, cinnamon, salt, and pepper; stir well. Bring the liquid to a boil. Reduce the heat to low, cover tightly, and simmer for 2½ hours, or until the meat is very tender and soft. Turn off the heat, uncover the pan, and let the brisket cool in the sauce for 10 minutes. Carefully transfer the brisket to a large platter; tent with aluminum foil and set aside while you finish the sauce.

Using a slotted spoon (or a degreaser cup), remove the top layer of fat from the sauce; discard. Working in batches, transfer the sauce and solids (including the bay leaf and cinnamon stick) to a blender; blend until smooth. Return the sauce to the Dutch oven and bring it to a boil over medium-high heat; boil the sauce for 20–25 minutes, or until thickened to your taste; season with salt and pepper, to taste. Return the brisket to the sauce, reduce the heat, and simmer for 15 minutes, or until the brisket is warmed through. Remove the brisket from the sauce and slice thinly against the grain. Serve topped with a generous amount of sauce. Serve extra sauce on the side.

Serves 12

crab soup with artichoke fritters

Velvety and silken seafood chowders such as this one, reminiscent of those I've encountered in my travels to the coastal towns in the South, are also commonly prepared
in South America. This one has a delicate, luxurious flavor and is easy to make. Coconut
milk, often featured in Brazilian cuisine, is used here to provide thickness and a hint of
sweetness. Garnishes, which are frequently featured in Latin soups, add visual interest and textural diversity. They're usually unassuming—a few slices of avocado, some
fried tortilla strips, a sprinkling of chopped herbs, or finely chopped vegetables—and I
always add them to mine. Here, fritters offer crispiness and a welcomed contrast. Make
this soup just before you plan to serve it and simmer it ever so gently so as not to curdle the cream. You'll have to make your own fish or shrimp stock. My recipe for Pickled
Shrimp (page 68) has easy instructions for making shrimp stock.

FOR THE FRITTERS
½ cup self-rising flour
   Pinch cayenne pepper
¼ cup plus 2 tablespoons water
 1 tablespoon vegetable oil
 1 (15-ounce) can artichoke hearts,
      drained and finely chopped
   Vegetable oil for frying

FOR THE SOUP
 4 tablespoons (½ stick) unsalted butter
 1 cup minced leeks (white and light
      green parts only), rinsed well
      (see cook's tip, page 65)
½ cup peeled, seeded, and minced
      tomatoes
½ cup dry sherry
 2 cups fish or shrimp stock
 1 cup heavy whipping cream
 1 cup coconut milk

Preheat the oven to 250°F. Line a baking sheet with a
metal cooling rack. In a medium bowl, combine the flour
and cayenne. In a small cup, combine the water and oil
and gradually add the mixture to the dry ingredients; stir
until smooth. Stir in the artichokes; allow the batter to
rest for 10 minutes.

In a medium saucepan, heat 3 inches of oil to 360°F
(or use a deep fryer according to the manufacturer's
instructions). Carefully drop the artichoke batter by tablespoon into the oil and fry for 2–3 minutes, or until golden.
Remove the fritters with a slotted spoon and place them
on the prepared racks. Keep them warm in the oven (for
up to 1 hour) while you prepare the soup.

In a medium Dutch oven, melt the butter over medium-
high heat; add the leeks and cook for 3–4 minutes, or until
soft (but don't let them brown—reduce the heat if they're
cooking too quickly). Stir in the tomatoes and cook for
2 minutes; add the sherry and cook for 2 minutes, or until
the liquid is slightly reduced. Add the stock and bring to a
simmer; cook for 5 minutes. Add the cream, coconut milk,
crabmeat, Worcestershire sauce, and hot sauce; season

2 cups lump crabmeat, picked for
    shell fragments (I prefer claw meat)
2 teaspoons Worcestershire sauce
1 teaspoon hot sauce (such as
    Tabasco), or to taste
  Salt and freshly ground black
    pepper, to taste
2 cups Yukon Gold potatoes, peeled
    and chopped into ½-inch dice
  Vegetable oil for frying

with salt and pepper; reduce the heat and simmer gently for 5 minutes. Stir in the potatoes and continue simmering gently for 10–15 minutes, or until the potatoes are fork-tender.

Ladle the soup into bowls; top each with a fritter and offer the rest on the side. *Serves 6*

creamy potato-leek soup with chimichurri and country ham

This scrumptious soup is pureed until silky and dressed with vibrant garnishes that awaken the palate one delectable spoonful at a time. Featuring the classic combination of aromatic leeks and creamy potatoes that has been adopted by many world cuisines, it can be served easily as a main dish. Soups like this one are common fare in South American countries, where the chill of winter beckons a need for heartier flavors to warm the body and comfort the soul. Mashed spuds are very popular in the South, often served as a side dish to baked ham. Here, I reverse their roles and use the country ham to garnish the potatoes instead. I always tell my cooking students that the easiest way to add a touch of elegance to soups is to add contrasting elements of texture and color with the help of garnishes, and this recipe proves my point.

3 tablespoons unsalted butter
5 garlic cloves, peeled and left whole
4 cups sliced leeks (white and light
    green parts only), rinsed well
    (see cook's tip, page 65)
2 pounds Yukon Gold potatoes,
    peeled and cut into 1-inch cubes
5 cups chicken broth

In a large Dutch oven, melt the butter over medium-high heat; add the garlic and leeks and cook for about 5 minutes, or until very fragrant and the garlic begins to turn a golden color (don't let them get brown or they'll turn bitter). Add the potatoes, broth, salt, and pepper; bring to a boil. Reduce the heat, cover, and simmer gently for 30 minutes or until the potatoes are very tender.

1 teaspoon salt, or to taste
½ teaspoon freshly ground black
    pepper, or to taste
2 teaspoons olive oil
6 ounces country ham, cut into
    ¼-inch cubes
½ cup heavy whipping cream
    Chimichurri (page 26)

In the meantime, in a small skillet, heat the oil over medium-high heat. Add the ham and fry until the cubes have rendered their fat and are starting to crisp; remove with a slotted spoon and place on paper towels to drain.

Puree the soup using an immersion food blender (or cool slightly and transfer in batches to a food processor or blender). Return the soup to the heat and add the cream; adjust the salt and pepper and heat through.

Ladle the soup into serving bowls, swirl a spoonful of chimichurri in the surface of the soup, and sprinkle with some of the country ham bits. Serve immediately. *Serves 6*

creole black bean soup with rum

Pork and beans are a classic combination. This hearty, stick-to-your-ribs black bean soup combines the deep, earthy flavors of three very different places: Cuba, Guatemala, and Louisiana. Dried beans are a staple of Latin American cuisine. They need to be soaked overnight to soften their skins and reduce the cooking time; this also removes the enzymes that cause that uncomfortable reaction that beans are maligned for! You can make a quicker version of this soup by using canned beans instead. Andouille sausage takes the place of the chorizos and pork ribs normally found in Guatemalan bean stews; it lends luscious spice and garlicky undertones. I like to serve this soup year-round with a basket of Chicharrón Biscuits (page 18).

1 pound black beans (turtle beans),
    picked over and rinsed
1 (6-ounce) piece of salt pork
1 bay leaf
½ white onion, plus ½ cup finely
    chopped white onion
2 tablespoons vegetable oil
1 garlic clove, minced
½ cup finely chopped celery
½ cup finely chopped green bell pepper
1 tablespoon finely chopped jalapeño
1 cup finely chopped andouille sausage
1 teaspoon salt
¼ teaspoon freshly ground black pepper
2 tablespoons dark rum
3 cups cooked white rice

COOK'S TIP: To quick-soak beans, place the beans in a large pan and cover with 2 inches of water; bring the water to a boil and cook the beans at a rolling boil for 2 minutes. Turn off the heat, cover the beans, and let them soak for 1 hour; drain and discard the liquid and continue with the recipe.

Place the beans in a glass bowl and cover with water; soak overnight (or use the quick-soaking method described in the cook's tip at left). Drain and rinse the beans and place them in a Dutch oven; cover with 6 cups of water. Stir in the salt pork, bay leaf, and ½ onion. Bring the beans to a boil over high heat; cover, reduce the heat, and simmer for 1–1½ hours, or until soft. Remove the pork, bay leaf, and onion; discard.

In a medium skillet, heat the oil over medium-high heat; add the chopped onion, garlic, celery, bell pepper, and jalapeño; sauté for 5 minutes, or until the vegetables are tender. Add the chopped sausage and sauté until heated through, about 3–4 minutes; set aside.

Transfer 2 cups of the beans and 1 cup of the bean liquid to a food processor; pulse until the beans are smooth. Return the pureed bean mixture into the pot with the rest of the soup; add the sausage mixture, salt, and pepper and stir well. Simmer the soup for 10 minutes. Add the rum and simmer for 5 minutes. Ladle the soup into bowls and top each with a scoop of rice. *Serves 6*

nuevo red beans and rice with chiltepín gremolata

Tender beans meet spicy sausage in this hearty stew with Cajun intonations. Served over fluffy white rice, it's finished with a fiery chile salsa. The combination of rice and beans is at the heart of the Latin American diet and is prepared in virtually every Latin country (from Mexico all the way to Brazil) and in many Southern states, a direct result of the multicultural background of both cuisines. Cuban *moros y cristianos*, Puerto Rican *arroz con gandúles*, and Nicaraguan gallo pinto are culinary cousins to Southern hoppin' John and red beans and rice. Soaking the beans helps them cook faster. Andouille sausage is the smoked, richly spiced pork sausage of Louisiana; if you cannot find it, select a similarly piquant sausage, such as Spanish chorizo. Serve this rich stew in deep bowls; offer plenty of corn tortillas.

1 pound dried red beans, soaked overnight (or use the quick-soaking method on page 156)

8 baby back ribs, divided into ribs (about 3½ pounds)

2½ teaspoons salt

2 bay leaves

1 (14.5-ounce) can diced tomatoes

1 cup chopped yellow onion

½ cup chopped green bell pepper

4 garlic cloves, chopped

1 teaspoon cayenne pepper

1 teaspoon ground cumin

½ teaspoon dried oregano

½ teaspoon dried thyme

2 teaspoons achiote oil (page 14)

2 andouille sausages (about 1 pound), sliced into 1-inch-thick rounds

8 cups cooked white rice

Chiltepín Gremolata (page 24)

Place the beans and 4 cups of water in a large Dutch oven. Bring to a rolling boil over high heat; cover, reduce the heat to low, and simmer for 30 minutes. Add the ribs, salt, and bay leaves; cover and simmer for 30 minutes.

In a food processor or blender, combine the tomatoes, onions, bell pepper, garlic, cayenne, cumin, oregano, and thyme. Pulse (or blend) until the mixture has a slightly chunky texture.

In a medium skillet, heat the achiote oil over medium-high heat and add the sausage; cook for 4 minutes, or until the sausage begins to brown. Remove all but 1 tablespoon of the oil left in the skillet; add the processed vegetables and cook for 3 minutes, stirring often. Add the sausage mixture to the beans and stir well. Simmer the beans, uncovered, for 30 minutes. Adjust the salt to taste. Serve over white rice and garnish with the gremolata.

Serves 8

shrimp and okra asopao

Asopao, redolent of spices and sofrito—a base of seasoned tomatoes, onions, and peppers, used in Latin cuisine—is a close cousin to Spanish paella. In my version, cloves, allspice, and paprika aromatize the broth with sweet and spicy undertones; okra thickens it. Too thick to be a soup, yet too soupy to be a stew, asopao is prepared with many variations throughout Latin America. African slaves introduced okra, a key component of Southern cuisine, into Latin American countries, including Brazil, Venezuela, and Cuba (where it's known as *quimbombó*). This dish is the marriage of two classics: gumbo and asopao. In Cajun cooking, roux is traditionally used as a thickener, but here the starch in the rice and the okra thicken this stew. Annatto seeds enhance the broth with a bright, golden color reminiscent of a sunset. When you need a cup of comfort, make a batch of this steamy soup. It will feed your soul and warm your body.

12 cups chicken broth
2 cups cooked and cubed chicken
2 cups finely chopped carrots
1½ cups finely sliced green beans
1 cup Valencia rice (or short-grain rice such as Arborio)
1 cup chopped, cooked chicken giblets (hearts, gizzards, and liver) (see note)
1 (4-ounce) jar diced pimientos, drained
¼ cup olive oil
2½ cups minced plum tomatoes
1 cup minced yellow onion
1 cup minced green bell pepper
1 garlic clove, minced
1½ teaspoons achiote (annatto) powder
1 teaspoon paprika
½ teaspoon cayenne pepper

In a large soup pot, heat the chicken broth over medium-high heat; add the cooked chicken, carrots, green beans, rice, giblets, and pimientos. When the liquid comes to a boil, cover, reduce the heat, and simmer for 20 minutes, or until the rice is tender.

In the meantime, in a small skillet, heat the oil over medium-high heat; add the tomatoes, onions, bell pepper, garlic, achiote powder, paprika, cayenne, allspice, and cloves. Cook, stirring, for 10 minutes; transfer the mixture to a blender and blend until smooth (it will be a bright orange color). Add it to the simmering soup; stir in the shrimp and okra and simmer for 10 more minutes, or until the shrimp turns pink and the okra has begun to soften. Serve hot. *Serves 8*

¼ teaspoon allspice
  Pinch of ground cloves
1 pound large (16–20 count) shrimp,
  peeled and deveined (leave tails on)
2 cups very thinly sliced okra (about
  22 pieces)

NOTE: To cook the giblets, place in a pan, cover with water, and simmer for 1 hour; cool and chop. As is often the case with soups and stews, this dish tastes even better the next day. You'll have to add more broth to thin it out since the rice will absorb all the liquid as it chills.

sweet corn soup with cinnamon hushpuppies

This dessert soup is smooth and custardy. Crispy and sugary hushpuppies provide delicious contrast—a delightful shock to the palate that defies stereotypical ideas of what a soup must be. This one is sweet and is based on the ancient Mayan drink called atole. The cooking process required to make this traditional drink is laborious and calls for a long period of simmering at a low temperature. Here, I remove all difficulty from the equation. Hushpuppies, or what I consider rustic corn fritters, are beloved in the South. Although typically laced with onion and served alongside Southern barbecue, these are more like doughnuts and are reserved for the end of the meal. Serve this luxurious and comforting soup piping hot.

FOR THE SOUP
2 (14.75-ounce) cans creamed corn
2 cups milk
½ cup sugar
¼ cup cornstarch
⅛ teaspoon salt
1 stick Mexican cinnamon (canela)

Line a baking sheet with a metal cooling rack; set aside. In a blender, combine the corn, milk, ½ cup sugar, cornstarch, and salt; blend until smooth; strain the mixture through a fine sieve; discard the solids. In a medium saucepan, heat the corn mixture over medium heat. Add the cinnamon stick and simmer slowly, stirring constantly, for 10–12 minutes, or until thickened (be careful not to let it come to a boil). Remove the cinnamon stick and discard; cover the soup and keep it warm.

FOR THE HUSHPUPPIES

2 cups plus 2 tablespoons stone-
ground yellow cornmeal

¼ cup plus 2 tablespoons sugar,
divided

½ teaspoon salt

1 teaspoon baking soda

½ teaspoon baking powder

1¼ cups buttermilk

1 egg

1 teaspoon ground cinnamon
Vegetable oil for frying

In a large bowl, combine the cornmeal, 2 tablespoons sugar, the salt, baking soda, and baking powder. In a small bowl, whisk together the buttermilk and egg; add to the dry ingredients and stir just until combined. Set aside for 5 minutes. In a medium, heavy-bottomed skillet, heat 2–3 inches of oil to 360°F (or use a deep fryer according to the manufacturer's directions). Using a 2-inch ice cream scoop, carefully drop the batter into the oil. Fry the hushpuppies for 2–3 minutes, or until golden, turning them over halfway through. Using a slotted spoon, transfer them to the prepared cooling rack to drain. On a plate, combine the remaining sugar and the cinnamon; roll the warm hushpuppies in this mixture; return to the cooling rack.

Serve the soup in bowls or mugs with a basket of hushpuppies on the side. *Serves 4*

sweet potato posole

This one-pot meal is spicy, steamy, and totally satisfying. Like chili, posole is a chunky, hearty, and filling stew. Here, tender chunks of plump pork swim in broth that has been aromatized with a mixture of smoky, dried chiles, sweet spices, and gutsy oregano. Hominy is at the heart of this traditional Mexican soup, which is given a Southern twist with the addition of sweet potatoes. Tomatoes and tomatillos lend a slight hint of acidity that creates a delicate balance of flavors, and the chiles provide the sweet and earthy undertones that give this recipe its distinguishing taste. Vibrant and refreshing raw toppings temper the richness of the stew. This is a great party dish for any crowd. It tastes even better a day after it's made.

1	pork butt/shoulder with bone
	(3 ½ pounds)
6	garlic cloves, peeled and
	left whole
1	small, unpeeled yellow onion,
	halved
1	bay leaf
5	dried guajillo chiles
2	dried ancho chiles
4–6	dried chiles de árbol, or to taste
3	large Roma or plum tomatoes,
	quartered
4	medium tomatillos (or 1 green
	tomato), husks removed,
	washed and quartered
	2-inch piece Mexican cinnamon
	stick (canela)
2	allspice berries
2	whole peppercorns
2	teaspoons salt
1	teaspoon ground cumin
½	teaspoon dried oregano
	(preferably Mexican)
¼	teaspoon ground cloves
2	sweet potatoes, peeled and
	cut into ½-inch cubes
2	(29-ounce) cans hominy,
	drained and rinsed
2	cups thinly sliced radishes
1 ½	cups sour cream
1	cup finely chopped cilantro
	Lime wedges
20	corn tortillas, warm

In a large Dutch oven, cover the pork with 7 cups of cold water. Add the garlic, onion, and bay leaf. Set the pan over medium-high heat and bring the liquid to a boil. Cover, reduce the heat, and simmer for 10 minutes. Remove the cover and skim off any foam that has floated to the top. Cover and simmer for 1 ½ hours.

In the meantime, place the chiles in a medium bowl; cover them with 4 cups of boiling water and weigh them down with a plate to keep them submerged. Soak the chiles for 15 minutes, or until soft. Drain the chiles, reserving ¼ cup of the soaking liquid. Remove the stems, seeds, and veins; set aside.

In a blender, combine the chiles, reserved soaking liquid, tomatoes, tomatillos, cinnamon, allspice, peppercorns, salt, cumin, oregano, and cloves; blend until smooth and set aside until the pork is cooked.

Transfer the pork to a platter, reserving the cooking liquid in the pan. Discard the garlic, onion, and bay leaf. When the pork is cool enough to handle, cut it into 1-inch cubes, discard the bone, and return the pork to the pan. Stir in the sweet potatoes, hominy, and blended sauce. Bring the liquid back to a simmer and cook, uncovered, for 30 minutes, or until the sweet potatoes are easily pierced with a fork. Season with more salt and pepper, if needed.

Ladle the posole into bowls. Serve with the radishes, sour cream, cilantro, lime wedges, and warm tortillas on the side. *Serves 10*

three vegetables, two cultures

There are three important vegetables favored in the cuisines of both Latin America and the American South. They're sometimes used in identical fashion and other times with differing interpretations, but their similarities are stronger than initially meets the eye.

Okra: Originating in Africa, okra (or *quimbombó* in Spanish) is an important food in the cuisines of both the Deep South and countries such as Brazil, Venezuela, Cuba, Puerto Rico, and the Dominican Republic. In the South, okra is often breaded and fried. In Latin America, it's commonly featured in rice dishes. In both places, stewed okra and tomatoes is a popular dish. Fragrant Brazilian *carurú* stew, made with okra, onion, shrimp, and toasted nuts, is very similar to the vibrantly flavored shrimp and okra stews of Louisiana.

Greens: Native to the Mediterranean, these members of the kale family, sometimes called Old World cabbages, include chard, collards, and kale. In the South, greens are often boiled with a piece of irresistible smoked pork until they're very soft. In contrast, Latin Americans often briefly sauté them with garlic in oil and serve them still crispy. They're also used to flavor stews, such as Brazilian *caldo verde*, chopped into batter for buñuelos, and cooked in cream. In Argentina, creamed greens are stuffed into hollowed-out onions and baked.

Sweet potatoes: Native to Central and South America, these tubers get a sweet treatment in both cultures. They're candied, baked into pies (or empanadas), and featured in casseroles. Southern sweet potato salads dressed with mayonnaise remind me of Peruvian causas (layered potato salads) flavored with spicy chiles and lime.

sweet potato soup

This subtly scented soup with hints of cinnamon and Latin spices yields a creamy and smooth texture that warms the body and teases the palate. It's not a dessert soup, but the carefully balanced combination of ingredients is mildly sweet. Known as *camote* or *batata*, the sweet potato is as widely used in Latin kitchens as it is in the South. Sunday lunches at my grandmother's home always started with a tasty soup. During the autumnal months in North Carolina, I continue the tradition by serving this version, which takes on a magical, orange tone from the combination of sweet potatoes and sultry achiote oil, at my special family gatherings, often accompanied by a basket of freshly baked Chile-Cheese Biscuits with Avocado Butter (page 21). For a vegetarian version, simply substitute low-sodium vegetable broth for the chicken broth.

3 tablespoons achiote oil (page 14)
6 cups peeled and chopped sweet potatoes
1½ cups chopped celery
1½ cups chopped carrots
1 cup chopped yellow onion
1 tablespoon minced garlic
4 cups chicken broth
3-inch piece Mexican cinnamon stick (canela)
2 tablespoons unsulfured molasses
1 teaspoon salt
½ teaspoon ground cumin
¼ teaspoon freshly ground black pepper
¾ cup buttermilk (plus more for garnish)

In a large Dutch oven, heat the oil over medium-high heat; add the sweet potatoes, celery, carrots, and onions and cook for 5–6 minutes, or until the vegetables begin to soften. Add the garlic and cook for 1 minute; add the broth, cinnamon, molasses, salt, cumin, and pepper. Bring the liquid to a boil; cover, reduce the heat to low, and simmer gently for 15–20 minutes, or until all the vegetables are fork tender. Remove the cinnamon stick and discard. Cool the soup slightly and, working in batches, transfer it to a blender (or food processor) and blend until smooth. Return the soup to the pan and bring to a simmer; add the buttermilk and heat through, about 2–3 minutes (be careful not to let it come to a boil).

Ladle the soup into bowls; add a few drops of buttermilk into each bowl and swirl with a wooden skewer. Serve immediately. *Serves 6-8*

vidalia, poblano, and asparagus soup

Velvety, creamy broth serves as a flavorful backdrop to tender asparagus tips in this elegant first course perfect for entertaining. Asparagus, known colloquially during colonial times by its old English name of sparrow grass, has been a Southern staple since the 1700s, particularly in Virginia and in the Carolinas. Although it's not a traditional ingredient in Latin America, it's commonly used in modern Latin American cuisine. I'm partial to pairing asparagus with another one of the South's springtime delicacies, the subtly sweet Vidalia onion. Grown in Georgia, these members of the allium family grow in sandy, low-sulfur soil that yields sweet-fleshed bulbs that lack the pungent bite of other onions. Roasting poblanos, which are typically mild (although some occasionally and unpredictably carry heat), elevates their sweetness. A touch of cream adds rich, luxurious flavor and simple elegance to this irresistible soup.

4 tablespoons unsalted butter

3 cups chopped Vidalia onion

1½ cups finely sliced leeks (white and light green parts only), rinsed well (see cook's tip, page 65)

1 pound asparagus, chopped into 1-inch pieces, about 3 cups (tough ends discarded and tips reserved)

2 poblano chiles, roasted, peeled, seeded, deveined, and chopped (see sidebar, page 116)

3 cups chicken broth or vegetable stock

¾ teaspoon salt, or to taste

¼ teaspoon freshly ground black pepper, or to taste

¼ cup heavy whipping cream

¼ cup finely chopped chives

In a large Dutch oven, melt the butter over medium-high heat. Add the onions and leeks and cook for 4 minutes, or until soft. Add the asparagus stalks and cook for 4–5 minutes, or until bright green. Stir in the chiles, broth, salt, and pepper. Bring the mixture to a boil; cover, reduce the heat, and simmer gently for 15–20 minutes, or until the asparagus is tender. Cool slightly. Working in batches, transfer the soup to a blender (or food processor) and blend until smooth; return the soup to the pan and bring it to a simmer over medium heat. Add the asparagus tips. Reduce the heat, cover, and simmer the soup for 4–5 minutes, or until the tips are tender. Stir in the cream, garnish with chives, and serve immediately. *Serves 6*

Sweet Corn Soup with Cinnamon Hushpuppies (page 159)

Jalapeño Deviled Eggs (page 59)

Peach Salsa
(page 33)

Drunken Chicken with Muscadine Grapes and White Wine (page 122)

Grits and Pino Casserole (page 182)

Rolled Ham Salad
Cake (Pionono)
(page 69)

Crab Soup with Artichoke Fritters (page 153)

Latin Fried Chicken
with Smoky Ketchup
(page 125)

covered dishes & casseroles

The first British settlers brought casseroles into the South. These consisted of molded rice paste stuffed with minced meats or vegetables that were slowly steamed. Casseroles, as we define them today, are mixtures of ingredients placed in a glass ceramic dish and cooked slowly in the oven. Foods are prepared this way in many cultures; the Moroccan tagines and the French cassoulets are two great examples.

Casseroles or covered dishes, as they're sometimes called, became popular in the South during the early twentieth century. When rationing occurred after World War I, casseroles proved to be a convenient and economical way to use leftovers. When the Campbell's Soup Company introduced creamy soups in the 1930s with instructions on how to convert them into sauces, casserole recipes multiplied. Although my recipe for Green Bean Casserole doesn't call for canned soup, as the traditional recipe does, and is seasoned with Latin spices, it was inspired by the classic.

Potluck suppers are an American tradition, and casseroles play a huge role in them. The term "potluck," coined in sixteenth-century England, indicated to impromptu guests that they had to eat whatever the family's dinner pot held that day. Some days, dinner could be hearty and delicious, but on other days the pot could hold a meager and tasteless fare. Unannounced guests had to be content with whatever they were served, depending on their luck. Today, however, potluck means something altogether different: a communal meal in which participants bring their own specialty dishes to share.

Latin Americans had no such concept until very recently. In fact, until the late twentieth century, it was seen as uncouth to ask guests to bring part of the meal with them. It simply was not done because old Latin American traditions dictated that guests had to be catered to in every way, even if this meant serving them a very humble repast (which goes back to the original meaning of the term "potluck"). Back then, if guests brought with them a prepared dish that was meant to be included during the main meal, it was considered an insult because the gesture implied that the host was incapable of offering the proper hospitality.

Centuries of culinary history in Latin America, however, paint a picture in which guests would bring small edible gifts, meant to be enjoyed at a later time and always given as a sign of appreciation for troubles caused. This tradition continues today, particularly when guests are dropping by unexpectedly. Homemade cakes, seasonal fruits, jars of preserves, or boxes of assorted sweets are typical gifts. These ensure that the host has something to offer in case there is nothing else suitable for entertaining in the house. However, it's still not customary to bring casseroles or main dishes to a dinner party. The host is expected to cater to the guest and not the other way around.

The concept of the potluck dinner, as it's defined here in the United States, however, is beginning to grow in popularity among younger generations of Latin Americans, as are many North American traditions—such as celebrating Halloween—that are making their way into Latin culture through the media. In my opinion, the potluck dinner is an ideal solution for young Latinos, who, like their North American counterparts, are busier than ever, as it offers an opportunity to organize impromptu get-togethers, without putting a dent in their schedules (and in the case of many, their pocketbooks). Nevertheless, the potluck dinner still has a way to go before it gains full acceptance among Latin American society as a whole, particularly among the older generations.

In Latin America, casseroles, such as the Pimiento and Cheese Chilaquiles I feature here, are generally served to family or as an elegant offering to visitors, whereas in the South they play a much larger role. In the South, they're toted along to church suppers, brought to homes when there has been a death in the family, carried to picnics, offered as a comfort to ailing friends, or presented to new neighbors as a welcome gift. Casseroles denote comfort, friendship, and hospitality.

When I moved back to this country, it didn't take me long to become enamored of potluck dinners. They're an easy way to entertain at the spur of the moment. They also represent to me the quintessence of America's melting pot because ethnicities come together and flavors mingle without clashing.

When I'm invited to a potluck, I love to bring a casserole because they're easy to make, but even more so because I immediately feel welcomed along with everyone else. Sharing a meal around a communal table removes all pretense and formality and says "welcome."

My Green Rice and Corn Casserole and the Sweet Potato and Plantain Casserole feature familiar flavors. Tamale pies are common fare at Southern potlucks; for something different and truly comforting, try my version, Grits and Pino Casserole, which features Chilean flavors and a topping made out of grits.

Younger generations of Southerners have long been exposed to Latin flavors through the food they have enjoyed in school cafeterias, restaurants, and university eateries, albeit mostly Mexican dishes. I've created the recipes for traditional Chicken Enchiladas with Tomatillo Sauce and a contemporary version, Squash Casserole Enchiladas, featuring Southern and Latin flavors, with younger palates in mind so that your family can gather around the table and discover new flavors together.

Butternut Squash Canelones with Coconut Sauce and Praline Powder and my Kale Canelones with Country Ham and Mushrooms require a bit more effort but will impress, I assure you. These are two of my favorite covered dishes to bring to potluck dinners and are always received with great accolades.

Casseroles are synonymous with community. Make some of the recipes that follow for family and friends and help spread this important culinary tradition, so worth keeping.

bacon, vidalia, and chayote pie

The flaky crust in this pie is the perfect foil for the savory custard filling with smoky and spicy undertones. Tender vegetables and sweet aromatics complete this crowd-pleasing pie. This is equally sublime whether you serve it hot from the oven or at room temperature. The crust can be made well ahead of time. The custard is a simple mixture of eggs and sour cream dressed with savory flavors. The chayote, a pear-shaped member of the squash family, is widely used in Latin America and in the cuisine of New Orleans, where it's known as a mirliton.

FOR THE PASTRY

2 cups all-purpose flour
1 teaspoon salt
½ cup (1 stick) unsalted butter, cubed into ½-inch pieces and chilled
1 teaspoon white vinegar
4-6 tablespoons iced water

In the bowl of a food processor fitted with a metal blade, combine the flour and salt; pulse for 10 seconds. Add the butter; pulse for 30–40 seconds, or until the mixture resembles coarse sand. Add the vinegar; pulse for 10 seconds. Gradually add 4 tablespoons of the iced water through the feed tube, pulsing briefly between additions, until the dough begins to hold together. Press some of the dough between your fingers; if it holds together, it's ready. If it doesn't, add a bit more water and pulse a few more seconds. Turn the dough out onto a clean surface and divide it in half. Press each half into a disk and wrap each tightly in plastic wrap; chill it for 30 minutes (up to 24 hours, or freeze for up to 2 months).

Preheat the oven to 425°F. Let the dough stand at room temperature for 10 minutes, or until soft enough to roll. On a lightly floured surface, roll out the dough into a circle 12 inches in diameter. Fit the dough into a 9-inch pie plate; trim the edges to leave a 1-inch overhang and crimp the overhang. Place a large piece of parchment paper over the dough (there should be a generous overhang to facilitate easy removal), press it into the shell, and weigh it down with pie weights (or use dried beans); bake for 25 minutes, or until the dough is slightly golden; lift out the parchment paper along with the pie weights.

FOR THE FILLING

1	tablespoon unsalted butter
6	slices thick-cut bacon (applewood- or hickory-smoked), chopped into ¼-inch cubes
3½	cups thinly sliced Vidalia onion (or other sweet onion)
2	chayotes, peeled, sliced, cored, and finely chopped
1½	tablespoons minced, rocotó peppers (or 2 tablespoons pimientos, plus 1 teaspoon hot sauce)
½	teaspoon salt
⅛	teaspoon pepper (freshly ground)
⅔	cup sour cream
2	tablespoons all-purpose flour
2	egg yolks

In a large saucepan, melt the butter over medium-high heat. Add the bacon and sauté until most of the fat is rendered and the bacon is golden (3–4 minutes). Remove all but 1 tablespoon of fat from the pan. Add the onions and chayote; sauté until soft (6–8 minutes). Add the rocotó peppers, salt, and pepper; cook for 1 minute. Set aside to cool. In a medium bowl, combine the sour cream, flour, and egg yolks; stir into the onion mixture. Pour the filling into the prepared crust and bake for 30–35 minutes, or until the filling is set in the middle and golden. *Serves 6*

COOK'S TIP: Freezing bacon for 15 minutes makes it easier to chop.

best potato casserole

Soft, comforting potatoes are given a tasty lift with a combination of cheese, herbs, and chiles in this extremely versatile casserole that can be doubled and tripled easily to feed a crowd. Whipped egg whites folded into the potato base gives it a light consistency. It's the ultimate side dish for any table. At breakfast, it pairs magnificently with ham and eggs, but it's also a delectable accompaniment to grilled meats or chicken dishes. Potatoes remain hot for a long time, so this is a great dish to tote along to church suppers and picnics. For elegant occasions, such as a bridal brunch, I often bake this casserole in individual-size ramekins.

2 ½ pounds Yukon Gold potatoes, cooked,
 peeled, and cut into 1-inch cubes

1 ¼ cups heavy whipping cream

1 cup sour cream

⅓ cup unsalted butter, melted

1 ½ cups grated Cotija cheese
 (or Parmesan cheese)

½ cup sliced green onions

½ cup finely chopped cilantro
 (leaves and tender stems)

½ cup finely chopped flat-leaf parsley
 (leaves and tender stems)

2 serrano chiles, finely chopped
 (seeded and deveined if less
 heat is desired)

1 teaspoon salt

¼ teaspoon freshly ground
 black pepper

4 eggs, at room temperature,
 separated

2 ¼ cups grated sharp cheddar cheese

Preheat the oven to 350°F. Butter a 9 × 13 × 2-inch casserole dish. In a large bowl, combine the potatoes, heavy whipping cream, sour cream, and butter. Using a potato masher (or large fork), mash the ingredients together until smooth. Add the Cotija cheese, green onions, cilantro, parsley, chiles, salt, and pepper, stirring to combine. In a small bowl, beat the egg yolks and then stir them into the potato mixture. In a separate bowl, using an electric mixer or a whisk, beat the egg whites until soft peaks form (about 2 minutes—see note). Fold the whites into the potato mixture just until combined. Spread the potato mixture evenly into the prepared pan; sprinkle with the cheddar cheese and bake for 40–45 minutes, or until the casserole is set in the middle and the cheese has begun to brown. Allow it to rest for 5 minutes and serve. *Serves 10*

NOTE: Beaten egg whites have reached the soft peak stage when the peaks droop slightly off the whisk (or beaters). They've reached the stiff peak stage when they're pointy and stand straight off the whisk.

COOK'S TIP: To bring cold eggs quickly to room temperature, place them in a bowl of hot (not boiling) water for 10 minutes.

making pastry by hand

Many recipes in this book, whether they're for empanadas, pies, or cobblers, involve making pastry dough. Pastry is made by combining flour, fat (lard, butter, or shortening), and liquid (cream, water, or milk). I use a food processor to make pastry simply because it makes my work easier. Also, I happen to have warm hands, and on hot, summer days, I can easily ruin the pastry. Pastry needs to remain very cold so that the tiny fat particles remain solid until baked. When cold pastry goes into a hot oven, these fat bits melt slowly and release steam, creating layers in the pastry. Of course, if you don't have a food processor, you can always make the pastry by hand. Here's how: Before you start, chill the fat, flour, and liquid needed for the recipe, as well as a large bowl. In the chilled bowl, combine the dry ingredients. Cut the fat into small pieces, and, using your fingers, two knives, or a pastry cutter, cut the fat into the flour until it reaches the consistency the recipe calls for (for example, until it resembles coarse sand). Stir in the liquid, a little bit at a time, just until the pastry begins to come together. Turn the pastry out onto a lightly floured surface and with the heel of your hand, knead it gently until it holds together. It's important not to overwork the pastry or it will get tough. You should still see tiny pieces of fat in the dough. Shape the pastry into a disk, wrap it tightly in plastic wrap, and chill it for at least 20 minutes (or freeze it for up to 2 months; thaw in refrigerator overnight). This allows the gluten (protein) in the flour to relax, making the pastry much easier to roll. Proceed with the recipe as directed.

butternut squash canelones with coconut sauce and praline powder

These tender crepes filled with smooth and creamy puree are slightly perfumed with herbs and then drenched in a bubbly, thick, and lavish tropical sauce. Sweet and savory flavors, as well as diverse culinary traditions, collide in this most elegant side dish. Squash, or zapallo, as it's known in some South American countries, is native to the Americas. The crepes commonly prepared in Latin cuisine have been influenced by the waves of German immigrants who settled in countries like Chile, Argentina, and Bolivia. The British colonists introduced molasses to the South, and it has remained a key element in Southern cooking. Here, I use it to infuse the filling with a touch of sweetness. Pralines, a favorite Southern confection made with sugar and pecans, are crushed into a powder and used as a last-minute topping that adds sweet crunch and an unexpected nutty flavor. Bake this in a large casserole dish or in individual gratin dishes.

1	butternut squash (about 1½ pounds)
1½	teaspoons salt
½	teaspoon freshly ground black pepper
½	cup sugar
½	cup chopped pecans
5	tablespoons unsalted butter
1	cup minced yellow onion
1	teaspoon dried thyme
⅓	cup molasses
	Basic Crêpes (page 15)
	Thin Béchamel Sauce (page 17)
1	(13.5-ounce) can coconut milk
½	cup shredded Parmesan cheese

Preheat the oven to 400°F. Line two baking sheets with parchment paper. Trim both ends of the squash and halve them lengthwise; discard the seeds. Lay the squash halves, cut side up, on one of the prepared sheets; season with salt and pepper and roast for 45–60 minutes, or until soft and easily pierced with a fork.

Make the praline powder: Butter a small baking sheet. In a small saucepan, melt the sugar over medium-low heat and cook, swirling occasionally, until it's a dark golden color (about 4 minutes). Remove from the heat, stir in the pecans, and spread on the second prepared baking sheet to about a ¼-inch thickness; let it harden at room temperature, about 45 minutes. Break it into pieces, transfer to a food processor, and pulse until it has become powder; set aside.

Cool the butternut squash slightly, scoop out the flesh into a medium bowl, and mash it with a potato masher until smooth (or process in a food processor); set aside. In a small skillet, melt the butter over medium-high heat; add the onions and cook, stirring often, for 3–4 minutes, or until soft; stir in the thyme and molasses. Combine this mixture with the butternut squash puree.

Spread ¼ cup of the filling on each crepe; roll up the crepes and place them seam side down in the prepared baking dish. Add the coconut milk to the béchamel sauce; pour the sauce over the crepes and bake for 40–45 minutes, or until the sauce is bubbly. Top with the cheese and praline powder and serve. *Serves 8*

chicken enchiladas with tomatillo sauce

The tender chicken in this casserole is wrapped in delicate corn tortillas and baked under a bubbly and vibrant sauce flavored with cilantro and chiles. Monterey Jack cheese blankets the enchiladas, adding a mellow counterpoint to the spicy chiles. A perfect main dish for a party, it's served with a variety of colorful, refreshing garnishes. The recipe is easy to multiply, freezes beautifully so you can prepare it ahead of time, and, once baked, keeps warm for a good while, making it an ideal addition to any buffet table. A favorite of children and adults alike, this is one of the most requested recipes by my cooking students.

20 tomatillos, husks removed

2 cups chopped white onion

2 large garlic cloves, peeled and left whole

1 cup water

4 serrano chiles, seeded and roughly chopped (leave seeds for more heat)

1 jalapeño, seeded and roughly chopped (leave seeds for more heat)

2 cups chopped cilantro (leaves and tender stems), packed
    Salt and freshly ground black pepper, to taste

12 warm corn tortillas (see note on page 115)

6 cups cooked and shredded chicken (dark and white meat)

2¼ cups shredded Monterey Jack cheese

Preheat the oven to 375°F. Butter a 13 × 9 × 2-inch baking dish (see note). In a large Dutch oven, combine the tomatillos, onion, garlic, water, chiles, and jalapeños; bring to a simmer and cook until the tomatillos have popped, about 15 minutes. Cool for 10 minutes. Working in batches, transfer the tomatillo mixture and cilantro to a blender (or food processor) and blend until smooth; season sauce with salt and pepper. Return the sauce to the pan and simmer, uncovered, until it has thickened, about 20 minutes.

Place ½ cup of the tomatillo sauce in the bottom of the baking dish. Working with 1 tortilla at a time, dip the tortillas into the warm sauce in the pan. Place ½ cup of the chicken on the tortillas, roll them up, and place them seam side down, snuggly together, in the baking dish. Cover with the remaining tomatillo sauce; sprinkle with the cheese. Bake for 30–35 minutes, or until the sauce is bubbly and the cheese has melted. Serve hot, with garnishes. *Serves 6*

GARNISHES (OPTIONAL)

2 cups shredded iceberg lettuce

1½ cups sour cream

1 cup seeded and finely chopped
plum tomatoes

¾ cup finely chopped cilantro
(leaves and tender stems)

¾ cup finely chopped red onion

¼ cup finely chopped serrano chiles
(with seeds)

NOTE: If you plan to freeze the casserole and serve it at a later time, line the casserole dish with heavy-duty aluminum foil and spray with cooking spray. Follow the recipe as directed and freeze the casserole until solid (about 2 hours). Carefully lift the enchiladas (foil and all) out of the dish and wrap them with plastic wrap; keep frozen for up to 2 months. To bake: Unwrap the enchiladas (removing the foil too), grease the casserole dish, and return the enchiladas to the dish. Bake for 60-65 minutes, or until the sauce is bubbly and the cheese has melted.

coconut, chayote, and corn bake

Moist and utterly mouthwatering, this comforting dish with subtle hints of cinnamon makes a good side dish or a dessert. The first thing you'll notice is its cakelike consistency, which reminds me of corn pudding. Chayotes, known in the South as mirlitons or vegetable pears, are native to Guatemala but widely used throughout Latin America and in the cuisine of Louisiana. In the Deep South, they're used in savory dishes—sometimes stuffed with seafood or chopped up in soups, but they're widely featured in Latin American desserts. Here, I shred them finely and use them in the same manner that bakers use zucchini: to provide moisture that gives breads a luxurious texture. The combination of cornmeal, fresh corn kernels, and cream-style corn makes this dish irresistible. You'll be hard-pressed not to eat the whole thing before you get to your party.

1 (14.75-ounce) can cream-style corn
1 small chayote, peeled, cored, quartered, and grated (about 1 cup)
1½ cups corn kernels (fresh or frozen and thawed)
1¼ cups coconut milk
1 cup sugar
3 eggs
1 teaspoon salt
1 teaspoon vanilla extract
½ teaspoon ground cinnamon
1½ cups stone-ground yellow cornmeal

Preheat the oven to 350°F. Butter a 9×13×2-inch baking pan. In a large bowl, combine the cream-style corn, chayote, and corn. In a blender, combine the coconut milk, sugar, eggs, salt, vanilla, and cinnamon; blend until the sugar is dissolved (about 1 minute). Pour the coconut milk mixture into the bowl with the other ingredients. Gradually add the cornmeal, stirring well after each addition, until well combined. Pour the batter into the prepared pan and bake for 55–60 minutes, or until the center is set and the top is golden brown. Let it cool for 15 minutes before slicing into squares. *Serves 12*

the southern-latino garden

A strong connection between the land and the table exists in both Southern and Latino cultures. The survival of most indigenous peoples of Latin America still depends upon their ability to grow their own food. Even those with the smallest piece of land are able to grow beans, chiles, potatoes, and corn. Yet modern suburban Latin American households rarely have their own edible gardens. In the South, however, gardens are a common sight, whether planted on acres in the countryside, in small plots in suburban back yards, or in pots on balconies in the city. For a change of pace in your garden, why not grow the kinds of herbs and vegetables that lend themselves to the Southern-Latino table?

For a salsa garden, choose a sunny section of your garden to plant a combination of tomatoes, cilantro, onions, garlic (or garlic chives), parsley, mint, green and red bell peppers, and a variety of chiles (including jalapeños, ají amarillo, chiltepines, and serranos).

For an herb garden, include herbs that would have been staples in colonial Southern gardens, such as rosemary, thyme, dill, chives, lavender, peppermint, chervil, fennel, sorrel, and sage. Include Latin favorites such as cilantro, spearmint, anise, chamomile, watercress, and oregano.

For a vegetable garden, plant vegetables beloved by Southerners such as asparagus, celery, cardoons, cauliflower, pumpkin, salsify, and carrots. Also plant Latin darlings such as tomatoes and chiles, leeks, fava beans, green beans, garlic, squash, and onions. Include mustard, collards, kale, lettuces, Swiss chard, or spinach.

green bean casserole

I love this casserole with tender vegetables in creamy sauce. In place of the classic fried onions, I prefer a crispy topping of bread crumbs, nutty cheese, and savory herbs and spices. Although the original casserole is not a Southern invention, I've encountered it innumerable times on the holiday tables of my Southern friends. My rendition leaves out the canned soup, replacing it instead with a slightly tangy sauce that thickens as the casserole bakes. This is a cinch to make, leaving you more time to concentrate on the Thanksgiving turkey or holiday ham. Citrus and garlic are commonly combined in Latin cuisine; here, they perfume the entire casserole, giving it a fresh taste that adds zing. Make the casserole ahead of time and reheat just before serving.

1½ pounds green beans
   (ends trimmed)
1 tablespoon vegetable oil
1 cup sliced shallots
2 large garlic cloves, chopped
½ teaspoon ancho chile powder
4 ounces cream cheese, softened
1½ cups sour cream
1 tablespoon Dijon mustard
1 teaspoon Worcestershire sauce
1 teaspoon salt
1 cup panko (Japanese-style)
   bread crumbs
⅓ cup finely chopped cilantro
   (leaves and tender stems)
½ teaspoon ground coriander
¼ teaspoon ground cumin
¼ teaspoon ancho chile powder
   Grated zest of 1 lemon
½ cup Cotija cheese
4 tablespoons unsalted
   butter, melted

Preheat the oven to 400°F. Butter an 8 × 8-inch baking dish. Fill a large bowl with iced water; set aside. Bring a large pan of water to a boil. Add the beans and cook for 3 minutes. Drain the beans and plunge them into the iced water; stir until chilled. Drain the beans and set aside.

In a large skillet with high sides, heat the oil over medium-high heat. Add the shallots and cook for 2–3 minutes, or until they start to caramelize. Add the garlic and chile powder and cook for 30 seconds, or until fragrant. Reduce the heat to medium-low and add the cream cheese, sour cream, mustard, Worcestershire sauce, and salt; stir until smooth. Stir in the green beans and transfer to the prepared baking dish. In a medium bowl, combine the bread crumbs, cilantro, coriander, cumin, chile powder, lemon zest, and cheese. Add the melted butter and stir to combine. Distribute evenly over the vegetables. Bake for 20–25 minutes, or until the topping is golden and the sauce is bubbly. *Serves 8*

green rice and corn casserole

This dish is a hidden treasure of deep shades of emerald green dotted with golden flecks. It sits under a heavy blanket of cheese, waiting to be uncovered. This creamy, sumptuous, and richly flavored vegetarian casserole has strong Mexican roots. Its green hue comes from a mélange of spinach and herbs that also lends luxurious mouth feel. Easy to make, this casserole can be prepared several days ahead of time and transports well. (But rice casseroles aren't suitable for freezing because they lose their texture.) I've found this to be a true crowd pleaser, enjoyed even by those who normally don't like greens. Long ago when my girls were small, I introduced them to spinach with this casserole, but if you're planning to serve it to kids you may want to make it without the chiles.

8 cups (8–9 ounces) fresh baby spinach

1 cup flat-leaf parsley (leaves and tender stems), packed

½ cup cilantro (leaves and tender stems), packed

⅓ cup finely chopped white onion

2 large garlic cloves, roughly chopped

¼ cup vegetable or corn oil

2 cups long-grain white rice

3½ cups chicken broth

1½ cups corn kernels (fresh or frozen and thawed)

½ teaspoon salt, or to taste

¼ teaspoon freshly ground pepper, or to taste

1½ cups sour cream

½ cup grated queso seco, Cotija, or Parmesan cheese

2 large (or 3 medium) poblano chiles, roasted, peeled, seeded, deveined, and chopped into ½-inch dice (see sidebar, page 116)

2 tablespoons unsalted butter

1½ cups shredded Monterey Jack cheese

Preheat the oven to 350°F. Butter a 9 × 13 × 2-inch casserole; set aside. Place the spinach and ¼ cup of water in a large skillet; cover and cook on low heat for 5–6 minutes, or until the spinach is wilted, stopping to stir once or twice. Transfer the spinach (and any remaining liquid) to a blender and add the parsley, cilantro, onion, and garlic; blend until smooth (if necessary to get the motor going, add a bit more water, a couple of tablespoons at a time); set aside.

In a medium skillet, heat the oil over medium heat; add the rice and sauté for 2–3 minutes, or until lightly golden. Add the spinach puree and cook for 1–2 minutes, or until it begins to thicken. Add the broth, corn, salt, and pepper, stirring well to combine. Bring the liquid to a boil; reduce the heat to medium-low, cover, and simmer for 20–25 minutes, or until the rice is tender and most of the liquid has been absorbed. Turn off the heat and keep the rice covered for 10 minutes (it will continue to absorb liquid). Add the sour cream, queso seco, and chiles and stir to combine.

Spread the rice mixture in the prepared casserole dish. Dot the top with butter. Cover the rice with foil and bake for 10 minutes. Remove from the oven and top with the shredded cheese and bake, uncovered, for 10–12 minutes, or until the cheese is melted and golden. *Serves 10*

NOTE: If you plan to chill this casserole before baking, don't add the shredded cheese until you're ready to bake. Bake the chilled casserole, covered, for 20–25 minutes, or until the rice is hot; add the cheese and continue baking, uncovered, for 10–12 minutes, or until the cheese is melted and golden.

COOK'S TIP: The best way to determine whether rice is seasoned properly is to taste the liquid it's cooking in. Since rice absorbs the flavored liquid as it cooks, be sure to adjust the seasonings both right after you add the liquid and before the rice is fully cooked.

grits and pino casserole

Cheesy, bubbly, creamy grits top spicy ground beef laced with sweet and salty undertones in this New Southern-Latino version of tamale pie. According to the Oxford Companion to American Food and Drink, tamale pies were invented and popularized in the early twentieth century in the Southwestern United States. However, I've encountered myriad interpretations in the South, with toppings ranging from pie crust to cornbread. The only Latin American dish that resembles the tamale pie is the Chilean pastel de choclo, which is made with a layer of pino (known as picadillo in some Latin American countries), a spicy beef concoction dotted with olives and raisins, and a layer of cooked chicken, topped with fresh, savory corn pudding. Here is my interpretation of this delicious concoction that combines the flavors of Chile with the beloved grits casserole of the South.

¼ cup extra-virgin olive oil

2 cups finely chopped yellow onion

4 garlic cloves, minced

2 pounds ground chuck (lean, if preferred)

2 teaspoons paprika

1½ teaspoons ground cumin

1 teaspoon dried oregano

½ teaspoon cayenne pepper

1½ teaspoons salt

½ teaspoon freshly ground black pepper

2 cups chopped pimiento-stuffed green olives

1¼ cups raisins

2 cups water

2 cups whole milk

1 cup stone-milled grits

2 cups shredded sharp cheddar cheese, divided

2 tablespoons unsalted butter

¾ teaspoon salt, or to taste

¼ teaspoon freshly ground pepper, or to taste

⅓ cup thinly sliced green onions (white and green parts)

In a large skillet, heat the oil over medium-high heat. Add the onions and cook for 4–5 minutes, or until soft. Add the garlic and cook for 1 minute. Add the chuck, paprika, cumin, oregano, cayenne, salt, and pepper; cook, stirring often and breaking up the beef with a wooden spoon, until the beef is browned. (If desired, drain the beef to remove excess fat and return it to the pan, but be aware that you may compromise flavor; the seasonings will be drained with the fat.) Stir in the olives and raisins. Reduce the heat to medium-low and cook for 5 minutes. Set aside to cool.

Preheat the oven to 375°F. In a large Dutch oven, bring the water and milk to a boil over medium-high heat (see cook's tip). Slowly add the grits to the boiling liquid in a thin stream while whisking vigorously; when the grits begin to thicken, reduce the heat to low and continue cooking, stirring often, for 20 minutes, or until the grits are soft and creamy. Remove from the heat; add the salt, pepper, 1 cup of the cheese, and the butter. Stir until the cheese is melted and the grits are smooth.

Place the meat mixture in the bottom of a 9×13×2-inch baking dish; spread the grits evenly over the meat mixture. Sprinkle with the remaining cheese and bake for 25–30 minutes, or until the cheese is melted and the casserole is bubbly. Cool for 10 minutes, top with green onions, and serve. *Serves 10-12*

COOK'S TIP: It's important to watch milk or cream as it boils. If it boils over, it can make a dangerous mess that can easily catch on fire. To prevent this, place a large ladle inside the pan; if the milk threatens to boil over, lift the ladle out of the pot and stir the milk.

hearts of palm and rice casserole

This casserole is the epitome of comfort: cheesy, creamy, and satisfyingly delicious. You'll love how straightforward this recipe is. It makes great use of leftover rice and you can prepare it with ingredients found in grocery stores. Hearts of palm, known in Spanish as palmitos, are harvested from the inner core of the cabbage palm, Florida's state tree. They taste a lot like artichoke hearts and are very popular in Latin America, but you can easily find them canned in U.S. grocery stores. They're traditionally used in salads, but, as you'll find out, they actually taste quite scrumptious when heated through. Mayonnaise is the ever-present ingredient in many Southern casseroles, and here it adds tanginess and moisture. Colorful and delightful, this casserole pairs beautifully with roasted meats.

6 cups cooked white rice

1¾ cups (about 8) hearts of palm, cut into ½-inch-thick slices

1½ cups sour cream

1 cup mayonnaise

1 cup grated Cotija cheese or queso seco (or Parmesan, in a pinch)

1 cup finely chopped parsley (leaves and tender stems)

½ cup finely chopped green onions

1 (4-ounce) jar diced pimientos, drained

1 teaspoon salt

¼ teaspoon freshly ground black pepper

1½ cups shredded queso fresco (or Monterey Jack)

Preheat the oven to 350°F. Butter a 9×13×2-inch baking dish. In a large bowl, combine the rice, hearts of palm, sour cream, mayonnaise, cheese, parsley, green onions, pimientos, salt, and pepper; mix well. Spread the rice mixture into the prepared baking dish; sprinkle with the queso fresco and bake for 30–35 minutes, or until the casserole is bubbly, the cheese has melted, and the top is golden. *Serves 10-12*

kale canelones with country ham and mushrooms

Kale and ham are a natural combination. In this elegant recipe, they come together in a flavorful and satisfying filling for delicate crepes. Garlic, nutmeg, and Parmesan infuse this dish with piquancy, while a luxurious béchamel sauce bathes the canelones as they bake. It's often said that Argentineans speak Spanish but eat in Italian. The sheer number of Italian immigrants that flocked into Argentina during the twentieth century changed its culinary landscape permanently. Beef and pasta go hand in hand in this South American country. Menus regularly feature pasta dishes such as gnocchi, ravioli, and lasagna. Greens such as kale and collards are staples of Southern cooking. Surprising as it may seem, they're popular in Latin America too. When you're in a hurry, the filling alone, sprinkled with a little cheese, makes a succulent side dish. Impress your friends at your next potluck dinner or church supper with this exquisite dish.

4 tablespoons unsalted butter

1 cup minced Vidalia onion
(or other sweet onion)

½ cup finely chopped country ham
(or prosciutto or Serrano ham)

3 cups sliced cremini mushrooms

1 garlic clove, minced

½ teaspoon salt

¼ teaspoon freshly ground
black pepper

¼ teaspoon freshly ground nutmeg

8 cups thinly sliced kale
Thin Béchamel Sauce (page 16)
Basic Crepes (page 15) (see note
on page 186)

⅓ cup shredded Parmesan cheese

2 tablespoons unsalted butter,
cut into tiny pieces

Preheat the oven to 400°F. Butter a 9 × 13 × 2-inch baking dish. In a large skillet, melt the butter over medium-high heat; cook the onions for 2–3 minutes, or until soft. Add the ham and cook for 2 minutes. Add the mushrooms and cook, stirring, for 2–4 minutes, or until they begin to soften. Add the garlic, salt, pepper, and nutmeg and cook for 30 seconds. Add the kale and ¼ cup of water, stirring and scraping up any of the brown bits stuck to the bottom of the skillet. Reduce the heat to medium and cook until the kale has absorbed all of the liquid; remove from the heat and set aside to cool. (The filling can be made a day ahead and stored, covered, in the refrigerator for up to 2 days.)

Spread a heaping ¼ cup of filling on 12 crepes; roll and place seam side down in the prepared baking dish (see note). Ladle the béchamel sauce evenly over the crepes; top with the cheese and dot with the butter. Bake for 30–35 minutes, or until bubbly and golden. *Serves 4–6*

NOTE: You can substitute egg roll wrappers or fresh pasta squares for the crepes; just add ¼ cup of milk to your béchamel recipe and season with additional salt and pepper. The filled, unbaked canelones (without the sauce and cheese) can be refrigerated for up to 24 hours or frozen for up to 2 months. If frozen, there is no need to thaw; just cover in the sauce and cheese and bake, adjusting the time accordingly. For a vegetarian version, omit the ham.

new southern-latino cornbread dressing

Moist and custardy inside and crunchy on top, this comforting side-dish casserole tastes boldly of corn, spices, and smoked pork. Cajun tasso is pork shoulder seasoned with cayenne, garlic, and daring spices and then cured and expertly smoked. The addition of dried fruit adds sweetness that offsets the saltiness of the other ingredients, creating an interesting contrast of flavors that is pleasing to the palate. In the South, "stuffing" is what goes inside the bird and "dressing" is baked in a dish. The aromatic base of this dish, comprised of onion, celery, and bell pepper, is called the holy trinity of Creole and Cajun cuisines. Serve this with my New Southern-Latino Turkey (page 129).

5 cups day-old crusty bread cut into
   ½-inch cubes

3 cups cornbread cut into ½-inch
   cubes (page 22)

4 tablespoons unsalted butter,
   room temperature

1 cup finely chopped yellow onion

1 cup finely chopped celery

1 cup finely chopped red bell pepper

1 cup finely chopped cured
   pork tasso

1 teaspoon salt

1 teaspoon ground cumin

Preheat the oven to 350°F. Butter a 13 × 9 × 2-inch casserole dish. In a large bowl, combine the bread and cornbread; set aside. In a medium skillet, melt the butter over medium heat. Add the onion, celery, and bell pepper and cook for 4–5 minutes, or until soft. Add the tasso, salt, cumin, pepper, coriander, cinnamon, allspice, cloves, and nutmeg and cook for 2 minutes. Remove the pan from the heat. When the mixture is cool, add it to the bread; add the prunes, pecans, and parsley and stir until combined.

½ teaspoon freshly ground black pepper
½ teaspoon ground coriander
½ teaspoon ground cinnamon
¼ teaspoon ground allspice
½ teaspoon ground cloves
⅛ teaspoon freshly ground nutmeg
1 cup chopped prunes
1 cup pecan halves, toasted
¾ cup finely chopped flat-leaf parsley
2 eggs
1 cup chicken broth
½ cup white wine
½ cup heavy whipping cream

In a medium bowl, whisk together the eggs, broth, wine, and cream; pour the mixture over the bread base and stir well. Spread the bread mixture evenly in the prepared dish. Bake for 35–40 minutes, or until the casserole is set in the middle and the top is golden brown. *Serves 10*

pimiento and cheese chilaquiles

This warm and bubbly tortilla casserole is crunchy on the top and tender in the middle. Two worlds meld magically in this new rendition of a Mexican classic in which tortilla chips, drenched in sauce, bake slowly and soften to yield a texture similar to pasta. The dish is sure to please both children and adults alike. This is my new twist on pimiento cheese. The casserole, with its creamy, thick, and hearty richness, will enamor those who love the flavors of the Southern classic spread. You can serve this dish at any meal, for it makes a hearty side dish for brunches and buffet suppers. Double or triple it to feed large crowds. Add shredded chicken or cooked ground beef to the sauce and transform it into a complete meal. Tortilla chips are easy to make and well worth the effort. Serve this with a green salad.

12 corn tortillas, each cut into
       eight wedges
     Vegetable oil for frying
     Salt
1 tablespoon extra-virgin olive oil
1 (14-ounce) can crushed
       tomatoes
1 teaspoon salt

¼ teaspoon freshly ground black pepper
     Pimiento Sauce (page 36)
1½ cups shredded queso fresco
       (or Monterey Jack)
1¼ cups sour cream
2 Hass avocados
½ cup finely chopped cilantro
       (leaves and tender stems)

NOTE: The casserole can be assembled ahead of time (without the avocados and cilantro); bake it just before serving and then garnish with the avocados and cilantro.

Line two baking sheets with metal cooling racks. In a large skillet with high sides, heat 2–3 inches of oil to 360°F (or use a deep fryer according to the manufacturer's instructions). Working in batches, carefully add the tortillas, stirring constantly; fry them for 3–4 minutes, or until crispy and a light golden color (they darken as they cool, so don't let them get too dark). Using a slotted spoon, transfer the chips to the prepared cooling racks; immediately sprinkle with salt. (This step can be completed several hours ahead or the day before assembling the final dish.)

Preheat the oven to 400°F. In a medium skillet, heat the oil over medium-high heat. Add the tomatoes, salt, and pepper; bring to a simmer, cover, and cook for 10 minutes. Stir in the pimiento sauce and remove from heat.

Spread ⅓ of the sauce in the bottom of a 9 × 13 × 2-inch baking dish. Place half of the fried chips over the sauce. Spread ½ of the remaining sauce over the chips; spread half of the cheese over the sauce. Repeat layering, ending with the cheese; press down the tortillas with a wooden spoon (don't worry if some break). Drop the sour cream by dollops all over the top of the casserole; cover loosely with foil and bake for 30 minutes. Remove the foil.

Halve, pit, and peel the avocados and slice them thinly. Place the slices decoratively over the top of the casserole; sprinkle with cilantro and serve. *Serves 4–6*

squash casserole enchiladas

South meets south of the border in this comforting, creamy Southern squash casserole spiked with poblano peppers, wrapped in corn tortillas, and then bathed in a smoky and spicy sauce. A crown of golden and gooey melted cheese tops off this delicious vegetarian dish. Squash is ever-present in the cuisine of Mexico, where even the blossoms become culinary delights. In the South, squash is often transformed into casseroles and soufflés. Enchilada means "cooked in chile sauce." The sauce, made with dried chiles that are found in most supermarkets, is simple to prepare: just blend and cook. The hearty filling is made in a single skillet. Roll the enchiladas when the tortillas are warm. Assemble this casserole ahead of time and freeze it; it can go directly from the freezer to the oven. Once baked, it's easy to transport to your destination. It'll be the hit of any party.

FOR THE SAUCE

- 4 dried guajillo chiles
- 4 dried ancho chiles
- ½ cup roughly chopped onion
- 2 garlic cloves, peeled and left whole
- 3 large plum tomatoes, quartered
- 1 tablespoon unsulfured molasses
- 2 teaspoons salt
- 1 teaspoon ground cumin
- 2 tablespoons vegetable oil

Place the dried chiles in large bowl; cover them with 4 cups of boiling water and weigh them down with a plate to keep them submerged. Soak the chiles for 10 minutes, or until soft (don't let them soak for too long or they'll lose flavor). Drain the chiles, reserving 2 ½ cups of the soaking liquid. Remove the stems, seeds, and veins. In a blender, combine the chiles, onion, garlic, tomatoes, molasses, salt, cumin, and the reserved soaking liquid; blend until smooth. In a large skillet, heat the oil over medium-high heat; add the chile sauce (be careful; it will splatter briefly). Bring the sauce to a simmer and cook for 8–10 minutes, or until slightly thickened; set aside.

189

FOR THE ENCHILADAS

2	tablespoons unsalted butter
½	cup minced yellow onion
4	cups shredded yellow squash, packed
⅔	cup heavy whipping cream
1½	teaspoons salt
½	teaspoon ground cumin
⅛	teaspoon freshly ground black pepper
2	poblano chiles, roasted, peeled, seeded, deveined, and chopped into ¼-inch dice (see sidebar, page 116)
1	egg, lightly beaten
14	warm corn tortillas (see note on page 115)
2½	cups shredded Monterey Jack cheese
1	cup sour cream (for garnish)

NOTE: If you're short on time, make this dish like a lasagna by layering the filling and sauce between the tortillas; top with the sauce and cheese and bake as directed above.

In a large skillet, melt the butter over medium-high heat. Add the onions and cook for 2–3 minutes, or until soft. Add the squash and cook for 2–3 minutes, or until soft. Add the cream, salt, cumin, and pepper; cook for 4–5 minutes, or until the mixture is thickened. Stir in the poblanos. Remove from the heat and let cool for 10 minutes. Stir in the beaten egg and set aside.

Preheat the oven to 375°F. Butter a 13 × 9 × 2-inch baking dish. Place the tortillas in a damp kitchen towel and microwave on high for 2 minutes (or wrap in foil and heat in preheated oven for 10 minutes). Heat the sauce and pour 1 cup of it onto a shallow dish. Working with one tortilla at a time, dip the tortillas in the sauce; place a ¼ cup of the filling on each tortilla and roll tightly. Place the filled tortillas side by side in the prepared baking dish. Spread the remaining sauce evenly over the enchiladas; top with the shredded cheese. Bake for 20–25 minutes, or until the sauce is bubbly and the cheese is a golden brown. Serve with sour cream on the side. The assembled enchiladas can be frozen for up to 1 month. Bake, uncovered, until the filling is hot and the cheese has melted.

Serves 6

sweet potato and plantain casserole

Creamy, dense, and spice-laden, this casserole melds the lively flavors of the tropics with those of the South. Sweet potatoes, first domesticated around 2000 B.C. in Latin America, did not arrive in the Southern United States until the early 1800s, when they were introduced by Europeans. They have remained an integral ingredient of Southern cuisine ever since. Plantains, which are native to India, were introduced to the Americas in the 1500s, and they were widely adopted by the indigenous peoples and African slaves. Until very recently, they have been hard to come by in the South. Today, with the growth of the Latino population, you'll find plantains in virtually every supermarket south of the Mason-Dixon line. To get plantains to ripen faster, place them in a paper bag. This delightful recipe is a fun twist on a Southern classic that makes a yearly appearance at my Thanksgiving table.

4   plantains, ripened until skins are
      black and flesh is soft (3 cups flesh)
3   cups baked and mashed sweet
      potatoes
2   eggs, beaten
1   cup heavy whipping cream
1   cup brown sugar, packed
4   tablespoons unsalted butter, melted
¼   cup bourbon
1   teaspoon ground cinnamon
½   teaspoon salt
½   teaspoon allspice
¼   teaspoon freshly grated nutmeg
¼   teaspoon ground cloves

Preheat the oven to 350°F. Butter a 9×13×2-inch baking dish. Peel the plantains and cut them each into 4 chunks. In the bowl of a food processor, combine the plantains and sweet potatoes and pulse until smooth. Add the eggs, cream, brown sugar, butter, bourbon, cinnamon, salt, allspice, nutmeg, and cloves; pulse until combined. (Alternatively, in a large bowl, mash the plantains and sweet potatoes by hand until smooth. Add the remaining ingredients and blend well.) Spread the mixture into the prepared baking dish and bake for 40–45 minutes, or until center of the casserole is set and the edges have begun to brown. *Serves 10*

vegetables & side dishes

A common misconception about Southern and Latin cuisines is that they both lack fresh vegetables. Nothing could be further from the truth, and I hope to dispel such ideas in this chapter. In the South, macaroni and cheese isn't the only vegetable (and, yes, Southerners do consider it a vegetable!), just like beans are not the only vegetarian dishes served in Latin American homes.

Southerners and Latin Americans share a grand cornucopia of vegetables, from eggplant, corn, and tomatoes to squash, pole beans, and okra. Bell peppers, sweet potatoes, cucumbers, and fresh garden peas are common to both cuisines. North, Central, and South Americans eat quite a few varieties of edible gourds. What is known as the mirliton in New Orleans—the pale-green, pear-shaped gourd most often found in stores in the United States—is known as güisquil in Guatemala and chayote in Mexico. There are many other varieties of mirlitons grown in Central America, including some covered in needles and the white-skinned variety called perulero.

From acorn to zucchini, a wide array of squash and pumpkins (or calabazas, in Spanish) of many shapes and colors is grown in the Americas. Not surprisingly, Latin cuisine features them prepared in myriad ways. Southerners are partial to yellow squash, and here, I offer my rendition of Bacon and Squash Toss.

Traditionally, Southerners cook vegetables for a very long time, some until they're squishy and fall apart. The same is true for Latin Americans. In the South, this probably stems back to a time when issues of food safety and contaminated water required long cooking times for vegetables; that's the reason many Latinos still overcook vegetables today. To me, both Southern-style and Latin boiled vegetables have their place at the New Southern-Latino table. Properly seasoned they're deliciously comforting. Few vegetables, for example, are more scrumptious than boiled greens, particularly if a piece of ham or a smoked turkey wing has been added to the pot. But they're equally delicious sautéed briefly, the way you'll find them in South American countries, or when they're combined with other ingredients, as they are in the Swiss Chard Frittata recipe featured in this chapter.

The plantain is a very popular vegetable in Latin America. It has various uses depending on its stage of ripeness. When it's green, the plantain is starchy and can be fried, boiled, or baked and often serves as a substitute for potatoes. As it ripens, the starch turns to sugar, and when it's yellow it's often used in desserts (it tastes like a very ripe banana if allowed to ripen completely, that is, until its skin turns black). Almost every Latin American country has its version of beans, rice, and plantains to accompany its plato típico (national dish). Here, I've included my favorite rendition of sweet fried plantains called *maduros*. Although traditionally eaten as a side dish, these make an excellent dessert drenched in crema and sugar—which is the way I ate them in Guatemala. Yes, they, too, counted as a vegetable.

Side dishes are meant to play the supporting role to the main entrée and should not take a lot of effort to prepare. For the most part, the side dishes in this chapter can be made quickly and easily. All of them, of course, feature the marriage of Southern and Latin American flavors.

Carolina Fried Rice and Huancaína-Style Potatoes, for example, are inspired by Peruvian cuisine. And the flavors of Mexico infuse my Confetti Corn and Poblano Toss. My version of dirty rice, a traditional Cajun dish, is speckled with chorizo.

The supple and sweet Fresh Corn Tamales are similar to the ones I used to eat in my grandmother's house as a child. In the South, tamales are usually served as a main dish; but my grandmother served hers as a light snack in the middle of rainy afternoons to her guests. She always served them on her fine china, drenched in light cream. Mine were created to serve exclusively as a side dish; their sweetness makes a luscious contrast to spicy stews and braised dishes. Tamales are ubiquitous in Latin America, particularly during the holiday season. Here, I offer you a new version, Collard Green Tamales with Pimiento Sauce, which I created to incorporate Southern flavors and to showcase the traditional colors of Christmas.

My Croquetas de Arroz (Rice Fritters) are perfect for making ahead and freezing. They're so addictive that you'll want to double the recipe. These make a wonderful snack in the middle of the day, and since they go directly from freezer to oven, they're very convenient to have around for those nights when all you have time for is for grilling a steak or a chicken breast.

None of these side dishes requires learning new cooking techniques or spending long hours in the kitchen. It's my hope that at first bite, you recognize these recipes as something you've had before—with a twist— and feel compelled to make them again and again.

bacon and squash toss

This colorful fresh vegetable mélange speckled with crispy bacon and topped with a touch of cheese is a scrumptious and easy side dish fit for any night of the week. In Mexico, squash is cooked in a similar manner in a dish called calabacitas. You'll love this easy rendition that takes only minutes to prepare. I make this most often during the summer months, when yellow squash is most abundant. In fact, I like to keep all of the ingredients already chopped and at the ready so I can just toss them at the last minute. I suggest you pair this vibrant side dish with my Herb-Encrusted Pork Tenderloin (page 124) and my Coconut Rice (page 202). Any leftovers are great tossed into pasta, served as a topping for baked potato, or stuffed into an omelet. Omit the bacon and make it vegetarian.

4 slices bacon, chopped
½ cup finely chopped onion
4½ cups chopped yellow squash
¾ cup seeded and finely chopped plum tomatoes
½ teaspoon salt
¼ teaspoon freshly ground black pepper
1 cup shredded queso fresco (or Monterey Jack)

In a large skillet, cook the bacon over medium-high heat until it begins to turn golden (about 2 minutes). Add the onions and sauté for 2 minutes. Add the squash and tomatoes and sauté for 4–5 minutes, or until the squash is tender. Add the salt, pepper, and cheese; remove from the heat and toss until the cheese is melted. Serve immediately. *Serves 4–6*

carolina fried rice

This colorful dish, based on the chaufas—Chinese-style fried rice dishes—found in Peru, is speckled with vibrant, fresh vegetables and finished with a combination of herbs. It may surprise you to see a fried rice recipe in this book. However, the food of Peru has been greatly influenced by Asian cultures, and many Chinese dishes, such as this one, have been incorporated into Peruvian cuisine. My rendition incorporates the beloved ham of the South. I often serve this as a side dish to my Bacon-Wrapped Pork Tenderloin with Guava and Peanut Sauce (page 112). Chinese restaurants in Peru are called chifas, and there you'll find many versions of this simple and quick dish. Soy sauce is known as sillao by Peruvians. I'm partial to the low-sodium variety, but any will do. This recipe is perfectly suited for leftover rice. Because it goes together very quickly, be sure to have all the ingredients chopped and measured ahead of time. Once you begin cooking, the addition of these elements will go swiftly and the entire dish will be ready in a matter of minutes.

¼ cup vegetable oil
1 cup finely chopped carrots
1 cup finely chopped green bell pepper
¾ cup finely sliced green beans
½ cup finely chopped red onion
1 tablespoon minced serrano chiles
½ teaspoon minced garlic
1 cup finely chopped cooked ham
4 cups cooked white rice
2 tablespoons soy sauce
1 tablespoon Worcestershire sauce
½ cup chopped fresh parsley
    (leaves and tender stems)
¼ cup thinly sliced green onions

In a large skillet, heat the oil over high heat. Add the carrots, bell pepper, green beans, and onion and cook for 4 minutes, or until the vegetables begin to soften. Add the chiles and garlic and cook for 30 seconds. Add the ham and cook for 1 minute. Add the rice, soy sauce, and Worcestershire sauce and cook, stirring, for 2 minutes, or until the rice is hot and has taken on a uniform color. Stir in the parsley and green onions; serve immediately.

Serves 4–6

carolina mexican rice

In this tasty side dish, white rice is toasted and then "fried" in highly seasoned tomato sauce to yield a scrumptious pilaf. Long-grain rice is perfectly suited for this dish that originated with the Arabs and is popular in both Southern and Latin American cuisine. Depending on where you are in the South, similar rice dishes are called *pilau*, *purloo*, or *perloo*. In Mexico, this style of rice dish is called a *sopa seca* ("dry soup") since the liquid is fully absorbed by the rice. Here is a delectable marriage between that Mexican favorite and the Georgia Low Country classic: Savannah red rice. A fantastic party dish, it keeps well in a chafing dish. I often serve it alongside seafood or chicken dishes. It also pairs beautifully with Barbacoa de Carne with Vidalia Onion and Herb Salsa (page 113).

1 (14.5-ounce) can whole
    fire-roasted tomatoes
2 garlic cloves, peeled and left whole
½ teaspoon ground coriander
½ teaspoon ground cumin
1 serrano chile (seeded and deveined
    if less heat is desired)
1 teaspoon salt
¼ teaspoon freshly ground
    black pepper
2 tablespoons lard (or vegetable oil)
1 cup finely chopped yellow onion
1 cup finely chopped celery
1½ cups long-grain rice
2 poblano chiles, roasted, peeled,
    seeded, deveined, and chopped
    into ½-inch dice (see sidebar,
    page 116)
1 (2-ounce) jar diced
    pimientos, drained
1½ cups chicken broth
¼ cup sliced green onions

In a blender, combine the tomatoes, garlic, coriander, cumin, serrano, salt, and pepper; blend until smooth. In a medium saucepan, melt the lard over medium-high heat. Add the onion and celery and cook for 2–3 minutes, or until soft. Stir the rice into the vegetables and continue stirring and toasting for 2–3 minutes, or until the rice turns golden. Add the chiles and pimientos and the blended sauce (be careful; the sauce will splatter briefly). Cook, stirring, for 2 minutes, or until the sauce thickens slightly. Add the chicken broth and stir just until combined. Bring the liquid to a boil; cover, reduce the heat, and simmer for 20 minutes, undisturbed. Fluff the rice with a fork, transfer to a platter, and garnish with green onions; serve immediately. *Serves 6*

chorizo dirty rice

Rice is jazzed up in this version of Louisiana's classic side dish. Here, paprika-enhanced Mexican chorizo augments the flavor of chicken livers traditionally used in this dish, and chile powder replaces the more traditional cayenne pepper. The aromatic base of this luscious dish is imparted by the holy trinity of Cajun and Creole cuisine—onion, green bell pepper, and celery—and here it's enhanced by gutsy chiles. Dry sherry ties together the different elements. Every last bite of this dish showcases a mixture of succulent flavors. Side dishes deserve the same care and attention to detail often reserved for main dishes. This one demands equal billing alongside a roast duck, turkey, or chicken, such as my Lime and Chipotle Roast Chicken (page 128).

rice

Rice was introduced to Mexico and Central and South America by European traders and was quickly adapted into Latin cuisine. Today, it would be difficult to name a Latin American country that does not have its own version of the classic combination of beans and rice. Rice did not make its way into the South until the 1600s. As the story goes, the captain of a storm-battered ship arriving in Charles Towne from Madagascar paid the colonists who repaired his ship with a bag of golden rice. The low-lying marshes of South Carolina were ideal for growing rice, and soon Charleston became the main producer and the richest city in the South. At the end of the Civil War, most of the rice crops there had been destroyed, and so had the economic boom of this Southern port city. Although, historically, Latin Americans have favored short-grain rice—the key ingredient

2 teaspoons vegetable oil
1 cup finely chopped onion
½ cup finely chopped celery
½ cup finely chopped green bell pepper
¼ cup seeded and deveined jalapeño,
    finely chopped
1 cup (5 ounces) bulk Mexican chorizo
1½ cups (14 ounces) minced chicken livers
1 large garlic clove, finely chopped
1½ teaspoons guajillo chile powder
    (or 1 teaspoon cayenne pepper)
1 teaspoon salt, or to taste
¼ teaspoon freshly ground black pepper,
    or to taste
¼ cup dry sherry
4 cups cooked long-grain rice
¼ cup finely chopped flat-leaf parsley
    (leaves and tender stems)

In a large skillet with high sides, heat the oil over medium-high heat. Add the onion, celery, bell pepper, and jalapeño and cook for 4–5 minutes, or until soft. Add the chorizo and cook for 2 minutes, or until the fat is rendered. Add the chicken livers and cook for 3–4 minutes, or until they're no longer pink. Add the garlic, chile powder, salt, and pepper and cook, stirring well, for 2 minutes. Add the sherry and stir well, scraping up the brown bits at the bottom of the pan; cook for 2–3 minutes, or until most of the liquid has evaporated. Stir in the cooked rice and combine well—there should be no white grains of rice left. Transfer to a serving platter and garnish with parsley.

Serves 6

for creamy rice pudding—the twentieth century witnessed an increase in their consumption of long-grain rice, which has been long preferred in the South. Rice highlights the culinary similarities between Southern and Latino cuisines. Most of the cooking techniques used in preparing rice were introduced by the Spaniards and have roots in Arab culinary traditions. This is the case with rice pilaf (known in the South as purloos or pilaus), a Persian dish in which rice grains are slightly toasted in fat before liquid is added. Arroz con pollo, red rice, and jambalaya are prepared using the same technique. As with Latin American cuisine, the Creole cuisine of Louisiana was greatly influenced by Spain, which explains the prevalence of rice in dishes such as gumbo. Chaufas, the stir-fried rice dishes prepared in Peru, reveal Asian influences as well.

coconut rice

During the thirteen years I lived in Guatemala, I became well versed in the different culinary uses for coconuts. I recall visits to our family's summer home, where my grandmother kept half a cooler filled with fresh coconuts—the other half was filled with colas—so we could cool off with the refreshing coconut water. I learned to eat the meaty flesh right out of the shell, to shred it for use in desserts, and ultimately, to press it until it gave way to thick milk. Coconut and rice dishes such as *arroz con frijol*, coconut-rice puddings, and chowders are prepared throughout Latin America. This delicately aromatic rice provides the perfect base for dishes such as Beef Short Ribs with Roasted Tomato and Molasses Gravy (page 145). Luckily, you don't have to press coconuts for their milk; keep a can of it on hand in your pantry.

2 cups long-grain white rice

1 (14-ounce) can coconut milk
   (may use "light")

2 cups water

1 teaspoon salt

¼ teaspoon freshly ground
   black pepper

½ teaspoon ground coriander

¼ teaspoon ground cumin

1 bay leaf

¼ cup finely chopped flat-leaf parsley
   (leaves and tender stems)

¼ cup finely chopped fresh cilantro
   (leaves and tender stems)

¼ cup unsweetened coconut flakes,
   toasted (see note)

In a Dutch oven, combine the rice, coconut milk, water, salt, pepper, coriander, cumin, and bay leaf; stir well. Bring the liquid to a rolling boil over medium-high heat; cover, reduce the heat to low, and simmer, undisturbed, for 20 minutes, or until the rice is dry and fluffy. Remove the bay leaf and fluff with a fork. Sprinkle with parsley, cilantro, and coconut flakes and serve. *Serves 6*

NOTE: To toast the coconut flakes, place them in a dry skillet and stir over medium-low heat until golden (3-4 minutes). You can find unsweetened coconut in gourmet stores and in the frozen section of most supermarkets.

collard green tamales with pimiento sauce

These tamales, infused with garlicky intonations and enriched with greens, are drenched in a tangerine-colored sauce and then topped with crumbly cheese. Collard greens are as common in Latin American cuisine as they are in Southern cuisine. I've substituted them for the herbs found in the many varieties of traditional tamales. The colorful contrasts found here are as striking as the juxtaposition of flavors. Each bite offers the supple texture and earthy flavor of dumplings from ancient times and a refreshing take on a classic Southern ingredient. These morsels symbolize the merging of the New World with modern times. Tamales are considered a humble food, but here they're transformed into elegant fare fit for the Southern-Latino table. You can make tamales ahead of time and freeze them. Re-steam them until hot.

1 small bag dried corn husks (see note)
1 cup lard (or vegetable shortening), divided
½ cup finely chopped onion
2 teaspoons minced garlic
5 cups thinly sliced and roughly chopped collard greens, packed
1½ teaspoons salt, divided
Pinch freshly ground black pepper
3 cups masa harina
2¾ cups warm water (115°F)
Pimiento Sauce (page 36)
½ cup grated Cotija cheese or Parmesan (extra for garnish)

Submerge the husks in a large bowl of hot water for at least 1 hour, to soften. Keep them in the water until you assemble the tamales (for up to 24 hours). In a large skillet, melt 1 tablespoon of the lard over medium-high heat. Add the onion and cook for 2 minutes. Add the garlic and cook for 20 seconds. Add the collards and cook, stirring often, until they're wilted and soft, about 5 minutes. Season with ½ teaspoon of the salt and the pepper; remove from the heat and set aside.

In a large bowl, combine the masa harina and the remaining 1 teaspoon of salt. Gradually add the warm water, mixing the dough thoroughly with your hands after each addition, until the dough comes together into a smooth ball and is no longer sticky.

Using an electric mixer, beat the remaining lard until fluffy, about 2 minutes. With the motor running, gradually add the prepared masa, one small piece at a time, stopping to scrape the sides of the bowl every so often, until the lard is incorporated and the masa is the consistency of mashed potatoes. Add the collards and cheese and stir with a spatula until combined. Cover the masa and let it rest for 20 minutes.

NOTE: A small bag of corn husks contain about 50 husks. Sealed in a plastic bag, they'll keep for up to 2 years.

Tear 3 corn husks into long, thin strips (following the natural ridges of the husks) to make ties. Working with 1 corn husk at a time, spread ⅓ cup of masa onto the center with an offset spatula, leaving the bottom 3 inches and the top 2 inches of the husk exposed. Fold the long edges of the husk over the masa and then fold the two short ends over. Tie a husk strip around the tamale to secure it (but not too tight; it shouldn't have a "waist" or it will explode when steamed).

Fill a large stockpot or Dutch oven with 3 inches of water and fit it with a steamer basket. Line the basket with the remaining corn husks. Arrange the tamales in the basket (they can be laid flat in layers or placed side by side standing on end). Bring the water to a boil over medium-high heat; cover the pan and steam the tamales for 1 hour (replenishing the water periodically as needed); turn off the heat and steam for another 20 minutes. Place the cooked tamales in a casserole dish with a cover to keep warm before serving. Unwrap the tamales and serve each with a generous amount of warm pimiento sauce; sprinkle with cheese. *Makes 14 small tamales*

confetti corn and poblano toss

Sweet corn, spicy poblano peppers, and tender vegetables are enveloped in a creamy and smooth sauce in this dish that is a cinch to prepare and perfect for those evenings when time is of the essence and energy is low. Corn is a favorite vegetable in the South, sometimes simply dressed with butter. In Mexico and Central American countries, corn on the cob is often dipped into cream and sprinkled with cheese and chiles. My rendition combines both traditions into one dish. Lard is common to both Southern and Latin American cuisine, and it imparts a luscious flavor to this dish, but butter can be used instead. Cream cheese mimics the tanginess of real crema and provides body to the sauce. Cotija cheese—the Parmesan cheese of Mexico—is widely available in supermarkets across the South. This is like corn pudding, but with a kick.

1 tablespoon lard or butter

1 cup finely chopped onion

3 cups corn kernels (fresh or
   frozen and thawed)

2 poblano chiles, roasted, peeled,
   seeded, deveined, and sliced into
   strips (see sidebar, page 116)

1 (2-ounce) jar diced pimientos,
   drained

2 tablespoons finely chopped
   jalapeños

4 ounces cream cheese, softened

¼ cup grated Cotija cheese (or
   Parmesan or Pecorino)

½ teaspoon salt

¼ teaspoon freshly ground
   black pepper

In a medium skillet, melt the lard over medium-high heat. Add the onion and cook for 3 minutes, or until soft. Add the corn and cook for 5 minutes, or until it begins to brown. Add the poblanos, pimientos, and jalapeños and cook for 1 minute. Add the cream cheese and stir until it has melted; keep warm until ready to serve. Transfer to a serving platter and sprinkle generously with Cotija. *Serves 4*

NOTE: This recipe doubles and triples beautifully. If you're making it ahead, follow the recipe up until you have to add the cheese; refrigerate for up to 2 days. Warm it up and continue with the recipe as directed. If you want a thinner sauce, add a couple of tablespoons of half and half or heavy cream at the end.

croquetas de arroz (rice fritters)

From the sweet calas made in New Orleans to the spicy croquetas served in Guatemala, Southerners and Latinos share a love for rice fritters. In this mouth-watering rendition, short-grain rice is first embellished with pimientos, cheese, and achiote oil before it's shaped into balls; a quick sauté yields crispy morsels of cheesy, flavorful, and golden rice. Don't despair of all the steps that go into making these! They're really quite easy. You can prepare the rice mixture a day ahead and then, shape and fry the fritters whenever you plan to serve them. Once they're cooked, they freeze beautifully. Simply place them in a single layer on a baking sheet, freeze until solid, and transfer to zip-top bags. They can go straight from freezer to oven. Because these are not spicy-hot, they're very popular with kids and adults alike.

2 tablespoons achiote oil
  (page 14)

½ cup minced sweet onion,
  such as Vidalia

½ cup diced Roma tomatoes

1 (2-ounce) jar diced pimientos,
  drained

1 cup Arborio rice (or other
  short-grain rice)

¼ cup dry white wine
  (such as Chardonnay or
  Sauvignon Blanc)

2 cups chicken broth

½ teaspoon salt

1¼ cup grated Cotija or
  Parmesan cheese, divided

1 egg

¼ cup chopped cilantro
  (leaves and tender stems)

½ cup all-purpose flour
  (for dredging)

1½ cups dried bread crumbs, divided
  Egg wash made of 1 egg beaten
  with 1 tablespoon water

1 cup vegetable oil

In a medium saucepan, heat the achiote oil over medium-high heat. Add the onion and cook for 2 minutes, or until soft. Add the tomatoes and pimientos and cook for 4 minutes. Add the rice and cook, stirring, for 1 minute, or until the grains appear translucent. Add the wine and stir until it has evaporated. Add the broth and salt and stir well. Bring to a boil; reduce the heat, cover, and simmer for 18–20 minutes, or until all liquid has evaporated. Remove from the heat; stir in ¼ cup of the Cotija. Allow rice to cool completely.

In a large bowl, combine the rice mixture, egg, remaining 1 cup of Cotija, cilantro, and ¼ cup of the bread crumbs; blend until the mixture is smooth and holds together when pressed between your fingers. If the mixture is too moist to hold together, add more bread crumbs, one tablespoon at a time (but no more than ⅓ cup), until it's the proper consistency. Using your hands, shape the rice mixture, 2 tablespoons at a time, into balls; set them aside on a plate.

Fit a large baking sheet with a metal cooling rack. In a large skillet with high sides, heat the oil to 360°F (or use a deep fryer according to the manufacturer's instructions). Working in batches, lightly coat the croquetas with flour, shaking off any excess. Dip the croquetas in the egg wash and then roll them in the bread crumbs to coat. Carefully transfer them to the oil and cook for 2–3 minutes, or until they're golden on all sides (use two forks to turn them so they keep their round shape). Using a slotted spoon, transfer them to the prepared racks to drain before serving (or freezing).

Makes 18–20 croquetas

tamales: the first southern-latino recipe exchange

If you think the Southern-Latino movement is new, take a second look at the tamales prepared in the Mississippi Delta. Tamales were first made by the Mayans in Central America during the pre-Columbian era. Depending on where they're prepared, the filling base is made with corn, rice, potatoes, or starchy vegetables. They can be sweet or savory. The savory ones are made with beef, pork, or poultry and are sometimes flavored with fruits, olives, raisins, or pimientos, or a combination of these ingredients. Today, tamales connect the culinary foodways of Latin America and the United States. The Aztecs and Mayans introduced the Spanish *conquistadores* to these nutritious dumplings. Tamales then made their way into the American Southwest via Mexico. However, the Southwest is not the only area that enjoys tamales. There is a small area within the Mississippi Delta, where tamales are a long-standing tradition. Theories on how tamales reached the Deep South abound, but the most plausible one places this exchange in the early twentieth century, when there was a labor shortage in America and Mexican migrants were hired to harvest cotton. Mexican laborers introduced tamales to African American workers, who then substituted readily available ingredients for traditional Mexican ones. For example, they used cornmeal instead of masa, and for the most part, parchment paper replaced the corn husk wrappers. Delta-style tamales, which are longer and thinner than traditional Mexican dumplings are filled with highly seasoned pork, beef, or poultry. Rather than steamed, they're simmered in a broth seasoned with lots of cayenne pepper, which turns them bright red. Today, whether they're served drenched in the broth they were cooked in or with crackers and bottled hot sauce, "red hot tamales" are an African American tradition in the South.

fresh corn tamales

If you were to close your eyes and taste these soft, moist dumplings, the first thing you would recognize would be the unmistakable aroma of corn. Your first bite would bring the clear scent of sweet spice. After your palate welcomed the corn's sweetness it would meet the unexpected, albeit subtle, taste of cheese. The tamale's distinctive flavor is that of sweet, comforting corn pudding, and no matter where you live on either continent, you have most likely tasted it before in the form of Southern spoon bread laced with bacon, onion-speckled Uruguayan *humitas*, or Brazilian *pamonahs*, moist- ened with coconut milk. I think of this dish as embodying the spirit of the Americas, claiming all her children as her own.

30 large, fresh corn husks (see note)
6 cups fresh corn kernels (4–6 cobs)
1 cup lard or shortening
1¼ cups sugar
6 ounces grated Parmesan cheese
¼ teaspoon salt
1½ cups masa harina (or more, as needed)

Soak the corn husks in a large bowl of cold water for at least 1 hour. Place the corn in the bowl of a food processor fitted with a metal blade; pulse 8–10 times, for 5 seconds each, until the corn is mashed but still retains some texture (don't overprocess it or you'll end up with corn juice). Using an electric mixer, cream the lard; add the sugar and beat until fluffy, about 2 minutes. Add the corn, cheese, and salt; blend at low speed until they're incorporated. Gradually add the masa harina. The dough should hold together when pressed between your fingers (consistency will be similar to that of thick mashed potatoes); if the dough is too moist, gradually add more masa harina until it's the proper consistency. Cover the dough and let it rest for 20 minutes at room temperature.

Drain the corn husks and dry them between clean towels. Select the 6 longest husks and pull them apart into thin strips (following the natural ridges of the husks) to make ties. Working with one corn husk at a time, shape ¼ cup of the dough into a 4 × 1½-inch log and place it in the center of the husk, leaving the top ⅓ of the husk exposed.

NOTE: To remove the husks from the corncobs, slice off the very bottom of the cobs, then peel the husks away carefully. They roll up on their own, but that's okay; they'll "hug" the tamale dough and help it retain its shape. It's imperative that you soak fresh corn husks immediately after removing them from the ears of corn so they don't dry out. Keep them submerged in water until you're ready to assemble the tamales.

Fold the long edges of the husk over the dough and then fold the bottom part of the husk over, leaving one side open; tie a husk strip around the tamale to secure it (but not too tight; it should not have a "waist" or it will explode while steaming). Repeat until all tamales are assembled.

Fill a large stockpot or Dutch oven with 3 inches of water and fit it with a steamer basket. Line the basket with the remaining corn husks. Stand the tamales (open side up) in the prepared pan. Bring the water to a boil over medium-high heat; cover, reduce the heat to a simmer, and steam the tamales for 1 hour (replenishing the water periodically, if needed). Turn off the heat and steam for 30 more minutes. Unwrap the tamales before serving or allow guests to unwrap them at the table. Serve hot. Cooked and cooled tamales can be frozen for up to 3 months. To reheat, steam them over simmering water for 30 minutes. (Never reheat tamales in a microwave because they'll fall apart.) *Serves 8 (24 small tamales)*

fried okra with chipotle-lime mayonnaise

Fried okra is a classic Southern side dish and a popular one in Latin America. My version, featuring a perfectly crispy coating and a spicy remoulade for dipping, is a nod to both Southern and Latin American cultures. Okra is much maligned for its slimy texture, but it won't be slimy prepared this way. Use the freshest possible okra here. There is no better time to purchase okra than in the middle of summer, when roadside stands brim over with vibrantly green, firm pods. Choose smaller pods, which are the sweetest. The nontraditional combination of corn flours in the batter creates a light and crunchy crust.

FOR THE OKRA

¾ pound okra
⅔ cup milk
2 eggs, beaten
1 teaspoon hot sauce
   (such as Tabasco)
½ cup yellow cornmeal
½ cup masa harina
½ teaspoon salt
¼ teaspoon cayenne pepper,
   or to taste
   Vegetable oil for frying

FOR THE MAYONNAISE

1 cup mayonnaise
1 tablespoon lime juice
2 teaspoons minced chipotle chiles
   in adobo, or to taste (see note)
1 garlic clove, minced
   Salt and freshly ground black
      pepper, to taste

Fit a large baking sheet with a metal cooling rack; set aside. Cut the stems and tips off the okra and slice into ½-inch-thick pieces. In a medium bowl, whisk together the milk, eggs, and hot sauce. Add the okra to the milk mixture and chill for 10–20 minutes. In a wide, shallow bowl, combine the cornmeal, masa harina, salt, and cayenne; set aside.

In the meantime, make the mayonnaise: In a medium bowl, whisk together the mayonnaise, lime juice, chiles, and garlic; season with salt and pepper and chill until ready to use. (The mayonnaise can be prepared up to 24 hours ahead of time.)

In a large skillet with high sides, heat 2–3 inches of oil to 360°F (or use a deep fryer according to the manufacturer's directions). Working in batches, drain the okra and dredge it in the cornmeal mixture until well coated. Place the breaded okra in a colander and sift the excess coating back into the bowl. Repeat until all the okra has been dredged in the cornmeal. Working in batches, carefully add the okra to the hot oil; fry for 1–2 minutes, or until the coating is golden. Using a slotted spoon, transfer the fried okra to the prepared rack; immediately sprinkle with salt. Transfer the okra to a platter and serve with the prepared mayonnaise. *Serves 4-6*

NOTE: The heat of chipotles can vary greatly and the flavor of commercial adobo varies by brand, so adjust the amount of chiles judiciously.

huancaína-style potatoes

Smoky, creamy, and rich, this luxurious side dish offers an interesting new take on papas a la *Huancaína*, a traditional Peruvian salad served cold, often accompanied by hard-boiled eggs. My rendition is served hot. The potatoes can be cooked ahead of time, and the sauce takes only a couple of minutes to assemble. Best of all, it's all cooked in the same pan, making for easy cleanup. Any good melting cheese will work, but I prefer the combination of queso fresco and domestic Muenster. Smoked Spanish paprika takes these to a new level of goodness. Ají amarillo is a spicy, fruity yellow pepper from Peru, available whole in jars or in a paste; you can substitute minced jalapeños in a pinch. Adjust the heat to your taste.

2 pounds Yukon Gold potatoes, scrubbed
6 ounces queso fresco, cut into ½-inch cubes
5 ounces Muenster cheese, cut into ½-inch cubes
1 cup heavy whipping cream
2 tablespoons unsalted butter
1½ teaspoons salt
1½ teaspoons ají amarillo paste
½ teaspoon smoked Spanish paprika
¼ teaspoon freshly ground black pepper
¼ cup finely chopped chives

In a large pan, place the potatoes and enough cold water to cover them over high heat. Boil the potatoes, covered, for 30–35 minutes, or until they're fork tender. Drain the potatoes and cut each into quarters; set aside. In the same pan, combine the cheese, cream, butter, salt, ají, paprika, and pepper. Cook, stirring constantly, over medium-high heat until the cheeses are melted (4–5 minutes). Return the potatoes to the pan and stir them into the sauce. Cook, stirring occasionally, for 2–3 minutes, or until the sauce thickens slightly. Transfer the potatoes to a serving platter, garnish with chives, and serve immediately. *Serves 8*

macaroni con queso

This spicy and colorful concoction is both creamy and crunchy. Cheese and chiles are a classic combination, and nowhere is it more successful than in this scrumptious dish that juxtaposes the flavors of the Deep South with those of Mexico. This dish, technically a casserole, is in this chapter because in the South it's considered a vegetable (which my children won't let me forget). Cheese-laden pasta dishes, such as *tallarines con crema*, are common in South American countries like Argentina, and this one could easily be compared to the *sopas secas* found in Mexican cuisine. This comforting dish will feed a crowd; it's luscious and filling. Make it a main course by doubling the amount of ham.

1 pound macaroni, cooked according to package directions

5 tablespoons unsalted butter

1 cup finely chopped yellow onion

3 garlic cloves, minced

¼ cup all-purpose flour

2½ cups warm milk

1 teaspoon salt

8 ounces Monterey Jack cheese, grated

2 poblano chiles, roasted, peeled, seeded, deveined, and chopped into ½-inch dice (see sidebar, page 116)

¾ cup chopped country ham

1 (4-ounce) jar diced pimientos, drained

1¼ cups dried bread crumbs

½ cup finely chopped flat-leaf parsley (leaves and tender stems)

4 tablespoons unsalted butter, melted

½ teaspoon cayenne pepper (or pasilla chile powder)

Preheat the oven to 375°F. Butter a 9 × 13 × 2-inch baking dish. In a medium saucepan, melt the butter over medium-high heat. Add the onions and cook for 2 minutes, or until soft. Add the garlic and cook for 30 seconds. Add the flour and cook, stirring well, for 1 minute. Remove the pan from the heat and add the warm milk all at once and stir until smooth. Return the pan to the stove and cook the sauce over medium-high heat, stirring until thickened (2–3 minutes). Reduce the heat to low; add the salt and cook, stirring, for 3–4 minutes. Add the cheese and stir until melted (4–5 minutes). When the cheese has melted, add the chiles, ham, and pimientos. In a large bowl, combine the cooked macaroni and the sauce. Spread the macaroni and cheese evenly into the prepared baking dish.

In a small bowl, combine the bread crumbs, parsley, melted butter, and cayenne; mix well. Spread the breadcrumb mixture evenly over the macaroni. Bake for 35–40 minutes, or until the topping is golden and the casserole is bubbly. Let stand at room temperature for 10 minutes before serving. *Serves 12*

maduros (fried sweet plantains)

Sweet and soft with caramelized exteriors and a slight chewy flesh, fried sweet plantains are prepared throughout Latin America and the Caribbean. When plantains ripen—first turning yellow and then a deep black—their starch content converts into sugar, yielding sweet flesh with the consistency of bananas. Purchase green plantains for this recipe and allow them to ripen on your kitchen counter; quicken this process by storing them in paper bags until they blacken. Cook ripe plantains at a moderately low temperature, until golden brown, turning them only when they have begun to caramelize. The combination of plantains, beans, and rice is very popular in Latin American countries.

3 very ripe plantains
   (skins should be black)
   Vegetable oil for frying

Fit a baking pan with a metal cooling rack. Using a sharp knife, peel the plantains. Cut them on the bias into ½-inch slices. In a large skillet with high sides, heat ½ inch of oil over medium-low heat. Add the plantains and fry them slowly, letting them get golden on the first side before turning them onto the other side (about 4 minutes per side). Don't let the oil get too hot, or the plantains will burn and blacken; reduce the heat if necessary. Using a slotted spoon, transfer the fried plantains to the prepared cooling rack to drain. Serve immediately or keep them warm in a 250°F oven for up to 1 hour. *Serves* 6

potato and yuca cakes with chile honey

These delightful cakes have a crispy surface and a creamy interior that makes them irresistible. Yuca (also called *cassava* or *manioc*) is a starchy tuber popular in Latin cuisine. It's often consumed as a vegetable and cooks like a potato. Yuca is also converted into flour for breads, cakes, and tapioca beads. This recipe brings to mind a scene in To Kill a Mockingbird, when Scout gets in trouble for asking Walter Cunningham "what in Sam Hill" he was doing by pouring sweet syrup all over his dinner. I say pour all the sweetness you want! This is a popular recipe for children. Since the honey may be too spicy for kids, serve these with plain honey or molasses.

FOR THE CAKES

2 cups white potatoes, cooked, peeled, and cubed

3 cups cooked yuca, drained and cubed (canned yuca works here)

1 egg yolk

1 whole egg, lightly beaten

¼ cup minced Vidalia onion

¼ cup minced flat-leaf parsley (leaves and tender stems)

½ cup grated Cotija cheese (or Pecorino)

½ teaspoon salt

¼ teaspoon freshly ground black pepper, or to taste

½ cup lard (or vegetable oil) for frying

FOR THE CHILE HONEY

2 tablespoons apple cider vinegar

½ teaspoon ground cinnamon

¼ teaspoon allspice

¼ teaspoon ancho chile powder

⅓ cup honey

¼ teaspoon hot sauce

Preheat the oven to 250°F. Fit a baking pan with a metal cooling rack. In a large bowl, mash the potatoes and yuca very well (or, if you have one, put them through a potato ricer or food mill). Add the egg yolk, whole egg, onion, parsley, cheese, salt, and pepper; stir to combine well. Let this mixture rest for 10 minutes at room temperature before proceeding. With damp hands (to prevent mixture from sticking to your hands), pat ⅓ cupfuls of mixture into round cakes (about ½ inch thick). In a cast iron skillet or heavy-bottomed pan, heat ¼ cup of the lard over medium-high heat. Working in batches, carefully add the cakes to the pan. Cook for 2–3 minutes on the first side, or until golden and crispy and then carefully turn them over with a spatula; cook for 2–3 minutes on the second side, or until golden and crispy. Transfer the cooked cakes to the prepared cooling rack. Repeat with the rest of the cakes, adding more lard to the pan as needed. Keep the cakes warm in the oven (up to 1 hour) while you make the chile honey.

In a small bowl, whisk together the vinegar, cinnamon, allspice, chile powder, and honey. Add the hot sauce and stir well. Covered, the honey will keep in the refrigerator for up to 1 week. *Serves 4-6*

potato and poblano bake

This richly spiced dish is quickly assembled but tastes as if it took hours to prepare. These addictive tubers develop a crispy exterior while they roast, and their centers remain soft and creamy. Melted butter encourages caramelization and helps them develop their naturally sweet taste; it also grabs onto spices, which infuse the potatoes with aromatic flavor. Chiles lend a healthy kick that does not overpower. This dish represents the union between the Old and New Worlds. Spaniards introduced myriad spices from the Far East to the countries they colonized and left an indelible mark on their cuisines. Latin Americans domesticated potatoes and chiles, among them the tiny pepper that is dried and ground to produce paprika. Sweet potatoes are beloved in the South, and here they take on new character, lending color and sweetness to this savory dish. Serve it alongside Rib Eyes with Pimiento Cheese Butter and Chimichurri (page 134).

2½ pounds yellow potatoes (such as Yukon Gold), peeled and cut into 1-inch cubes

1 pound sweet potatoes, peeled and cut into 1-inch cubes

2 poblano chiles, roasted, peeled, seeded, deveined, and chopped into ½-inch dice (see sidebar, page 116)

3 tablespoons unsalted butter, melted

1½ teaspoons salt

1 teaspoon ground cumin

½ teaspoon garlic powder

½ teaspoon smoked Spanish paprika

Preheat the oven to 400°F. Butter a 9 × 13 × 2-inch baking pan. In a large bowl, combine the potatoes, sweet potatoes, and chiles. Drizzle with the butter and stir together well. In a small bowl, combine the salt, cumin, garlic powder, and paprika; add the mixture to the potatoes and stir until well distributed. Spread the potatoes in the prepared baking dish and bake, uncovered, for 40–45 minutes, or until the potatoes are golden and fork tender. Remove the potatoes from the oven and let them cool for 5 minutes before serving (this will prevent the potatoes from sticking to the bottom of the dish and breaking). *Serves 4–6*

three-cheese grits with loroco

If you like cheese, you'll love this stick-to-your-ribs dish, which showcases a combination of tangy goat cheese, nutty Cotija, and sharp cheddar. Here, smooth grits serve as the perfect background to tender loroco, an edible vine flower found in Central America, akin to the caper berries of the Mediterranean. Visually, it resembles asparagus tips, with a flavor reminiscent of broccoli and chard. Central Americans use it in tamales and to stuff Salvadorian *masa* cakes called *pupusas*. Like capers, lorocos are found pickled, frozen, or preserved in brine and are widely available in Latin tiendas. Substitute equal parts of cooked asparagus tips and chopped Swiss chard if you can't find loroco. Pair with Country Fried Steaks with Cilantro-Lime Gravy (page 119) or with Caramelized Chicken (page 117).

the african diaspora and food

Mentioning in a cookbook the terrible history of Atlantic World slavery, a legacy shared by U.S. Americans and Latin Americans alike, may seem strange—but the fact is that the forced movement of enslaved Africans throughout the Americas over the course of centuries, from the 1400s to the 1800s, fundamentally influenced our shared foodways.

In the Caribbean and in Latin America, indigenous peoples were at the mercy of the *conquistadores*. Subjugated by violence, fear, disease, and forced labor, native populations collapsed and disappeared from large swaths of territories. European colonists brutally began to carry enslaved Africans to colonies throughout the Americas to work for them. Eager to expand the lucrative cultivation of sugar, the Portuguese, Spanish, British, and other European powers brought huge numbers of Africans to labor in the fields of the sugar plantations in Brazil, Venezuela, Colombia, Peru, Belize, Nicaragua, Cuba, the Dominican Republic, Panama, and many other countries.

In Latin America and the American South, enslaved Africans were often put in charge of the farm and plantation kitchens. As historians have now shown, the Africans who labored in food production

2 cups water

2 cups whole milk

1 cup stone-milled grits

1 cup lorocos, drained and rinsed

1 cup shredded sharp cheddar cheese

¼ cup grated Cotija cheese
   (or Parmesan)

¼ cup crumbled goat cheese

¾ teaspoon salt, or to taste

¼ teaspoon freshly ground black
   pepper, or to taste

In a large saucepan, bring the water and milk to a boil over medium-high heat (watch it carefully so it doesn't boil over). Slowly add the grits to the boiling liquid in a thin stream while whisking vigorously; when the grits begin to thicken, reduce the heat to low and continue cooking, stirring often, for 20 minutes, or until the grits are soft and creamy. Add the lorocos and cook for 5 more minutes, just to warm them through. Remove from the heat and add the cheese, salt, and pepper; stir until the cheese is melted and the grits are smooth. Serve immediately. *Serves 4–6*

and preparation contributed greatly in shaping the regional cuisines that developed. As Jessica B. Harris writes in *The Encyclopedia of Southern Culture*, "The result of this Africanizing of the taste of the South is a predilection for okra, both fried and cooked in a variety of soupy stews often called gumbo; the tradition of eating black-eyed peas and rice on New Year's Day for luck; a taste for spicier food than is favored in most other regions of the country; and a consumption of leafy greens, be they mustards, collards, turnips, or gumbo z'herbes." Modern Latin cuisines, too, continue to showcase strong elements of African influence. Over time, as peoples of different ethnicities lived together throughout Latin America, a Creole culture and fused culinary history—called *cocina mestiza*—took shape. Time has fortified these blended foodways, today enjoyed in a multiplicity of ways throughout the Americas. Here is a just a partial list of ingredients contributed by Africans to the New World: millet, sorghum, yams, cowpeas (black-eyed peas), sesame seeds, garlic, onion, cucumbers, eggplant, tamarind, melons, watermelons, figs, dates, honey, collard greens, mustard greens, plantains, okra, and palm oil (*dendé*).

torta de acelga (swiss chard frittata)

This tender, smoky, and hearty egg dish is a great way to eat your greens. It comes together with very little effort and is the ideal dish for a weekday supper or light luncheon. Green, leafy vegetables—kales, collards, and chards—are mainstays of both Southern and Latino cuisine, a direct result of the African influence in both culinary cultures. In Spanish, the word torta means cake, and here it refers to the round shape of the frittata. Serve this frittata warm or at room temperature. I like to serve it with my Lime and Chipotle Roast Chicken (page 128) or with Rib Eyes with Pimiento Cheese and Chimichurri (page 134). Cut into bite-size pieces, it makes a great appetizer as well. If you prefer, you can substitute spinach for the chard.

5   slices of bacon

½   cup finely chopped white onion

2   large garlic cloves, minced

6   cups thinly shredded Swiss chard, packed

5   eggs

¼   cup heavy whipping cream

½   teaspoon freshly ground nutmeg

⅛   teaspoon salt

⅛   teaspoon freshly ground black pepper

Place the bacon slices in an 8-inch, dry skillet with high sides. Cook the bacon over medium-high heat until all the fat is rendered and the bacon is crispy (about 1½ minutes on each side). Remove the bacon and set it on paper towels to drain; when cool enough to handle, chop coarsely and set aside. Add the onions to the skillet and cook for 2–3 minutes, or until golden. Add the garlic and cook, stirring, for 30 seconds. Add the Swiss chard in batches (it won't all fit into the skillet at once, but as it cooks down it will reduce in volume) and cook, stirring, for 3 minutes, or until the chard has wilted; set aside.

In a medium bowl, whisk together the eggs, cream, nutmeg, salt, and pepper. Return the bacon to the skillet with the chard and stir well to combine; set the skillet over medium-low heat. Add the egg mixture and stir briefly to distribute well. With a wooden spoon, pull the eggs away from the sides of the pan as they cook in order to form a round, tall edge. Cook for 4–6 minutes, or until the bottom and sides of the frittata are set and the top is beginning to set. To flip the frittata, place a large plate (larger than skillet), face-down, over the top of the skillet. Place the palm of your hand on the plate and quickly flip the skillet over so that the frittata is transferred to the plate. Slide it back into the skillet and cook on the second side for 4 minutes, or until fully set. Transfer the frittata to a platter and serve.

Serves 4-6

desserts

Your cooking is only as good as your last course because it's what your guests will remember most when they leave your house.

Here is where desserts come in. If you visit other continents, you'll most likely find that desserts are not as sweet as the ones you'll find throughout the Americas. I believe that this is because we are part of a sugar culture. In colonial times, the New World was prime territory for cultivating sugarcane. The introduction of sugar to the Americas changed the landscape and history of these continents. Initially only available to the wealthy, by the 1800s, sugar had made its way into most kitchens. Try to imagine desserts without sugar today!

I love to bake. Baking cakes for weddings and birthday parties was my first business venture. Cakes have a festive air, and I love presenting a cake at the end of a meal. They make even the most informal gatherings feel like celebrations. Some of the cakes in this chapter are classics, such as the Magdalena, a Latin American pound cake fragrant with oranges; others are twists on classics, such as the moist and ultra-rich Peach and Bourbon Tres Leches Cake. Others, like my Pecan Rum Cake with Figs is perfect when all you want is just a little something to go with your afternoon cup of tea. In general, the cakes here are so easy to make that all you have to do is combine all of the ingredients in a bowl and stir. My Squash and Chile Cake with Cayenne and Ancho Chile Icing is a good example. After one bite, your guests will be convinced that you spent hours baking for them. (Don't worry! I won't tell if you don't!) My cake repertoire would not be complete without at least one layer cake to represent this Southern baking tradition. My Guava

Cake with Cream Cheese Icing is the perfect cake to take to a bake sale or potluck dinner.

I would be remiss not to include something for the chocolate lover here. My dense and rich New World Chocolate Cake will satisfy even the fiercest of chocolate cravings. The Chocolate-Chile Brownies are meant for those occasions when you feel a bit more adventurous; they feature a deliciously unexpected kick of heat.

Pies and cobblers are favorite year-round desserts in the South, and I had fun creating a couple of new variations on Southern classics. For instance, my Mango, Peach, and Tequila Cobbler is a unique and tropical interpretation, but it still retains the comforting quality that characterizes these fruit-laden desserts. My Apple Pie with Rum-Soaked Cherries is one of my husband's favorites. He likes this one served warm and topped with a scoop of Buttermilk Ice Cream and a cup of Huehuetenango coffee. My tart and creamy New Southern-Latino Lime Pie is refreshingly delicious.

Dulce de leche took North America by storm in the nineties. However, this Latin American caramel sauce (also called *arequipe* and *manjar*) has been part of the Latin dessert tradition for several centuries. I've used it in two very different but exquisitely rich desserts: easy-to-make Cajeta Bread Pudding and Dulce de Leche and Bourbon Crepes, an elegant twist on the traditional Appalachian stack cake.

I love going to the fair, whether it's the state fair at the Raleigh fairgrounds or the Feria de Jocotenango in Guatemala. Not surprisingly, my favorite part of these festivals is the food. Luckily, we don't have to wait until then to eat our favorites. Here, I've taken a few liberties with some beloved desserts of both cultures. For instance, I've translated caramel corn into a sumptuous Corn Ice Cream with Hot Praline Sauce and re-produced a traditional Mayan candy in a recipe for Pumpkin Seed Brit-tle. It would not be a fair without at least one kind of fried dough con-coction, so I've included my Sweet Potato Churros, which, dipped into luxurious chocolate sauce, are to die for.

Who doesn't love the velvety texture of a flan, the ultimate custard? Try my Coconut Flan, which takes only minutes to prepare.

This chapter would not be complete without a recipe for the ultimate Southern dessert: strawberry shortcake. My Anise and Rum Strawberry Shortcake features some unique flavors that turn a classic into some-thing even better.

Whether it's a simple flan served in plain ramekins or a fancied-up cake decorated with fluffy frosting, the memories of these desserts will linger in your guest's mind for longer than just a sweet, fleeting moment.

anise and rum strawberry shortcakes

The sweet, flaky biscuits in this version of a Southern favorite are scented with aromatic licorice, making them an ideal backdrop for delicate berries macerated in tropical syrup. Topped with smooth and fluffy whipped cream, tender biscuits make the most luxurious shortcakes imaginable. The anise seed, introduced to Latin America by the Spaniards during the *Conquista*, is used to flavor baked goods, buñuelos, alfajores, and some tamales. The term "shortcake" comes from the crumbly, or "short," texture yielded when lard or butter is cut into flour. The origin of this sweet biscuit remains unclear, but it likely derived from the British scone; the addition of strawberries is all-American.

2 pints strawberries, washed, hulled, and thinly sliced
2 tablespoons dark rum
¼ cup confectioners' sugar (or to taste), sifted
2 cups self-rising flour
2 tablespoons sugar
1 teaspoon anise seeds
¼ cup chilled lard or vegetable shortening
1¼ cups plus 2 tablespoons heavy whipping cream, divided
½ teaspoon anise extract
2 tablespoons unsalted butter, melted
8 mint sprigs

NOTE: If you prefer, cut the biscuits using a round cutter. I like to make the biscuits square so I don't have to overwork the dough.

Preheat the oven to 450°F. In a large, nonreactive bowl, combine the strawberries, rum, and confectioners' sugar; stir well and set aside while you make the biscuits (or chill for up to 2 hours).

In a large bowl, whisk together the flour, sugar, and anise seeds. Using a pastry cutter (or two knives), cut the lard into the dry ingredients, until the mixture resembles coarse sand. In a small bowl, combine ¾ cup of the cream and the anise extract and add it to the flour mixture. Using your hands (or a wooden spoon), stir in the liquid just until the dough holds together. Turn the dough out onto a lightly floured surface and knead it gently a couple of times. Pat it into a 1-inch-thick square. Using a sharp knife (or square biscuit cutter), cut out 8 biscuits. Place the biscuits on an ungreased baking sheet (sides touching for soft edges; separated for crusty edges). Brush the tops of the biscuits with the melted butter and bake for 12–15 minutes, or until golden.

Using an electric mixer or a whisk, beat the remaining cream until soft peaks form, about 3–4 minutes. Split the biscuits in half, spoon strawberries over the bottom halves, add a dollop of whipped cream, and top with the remaining halves. Garnish with mint. *Serves 8*

apple pie with rum-soaked cherries

Nothing is more American than apple pie. This one features a flaky crust that envelops layers of sweetened fruit embellished with rum. Rum, made from fermented sugarcane by-products like molasses, is a frequent ingredient in desserts throughout Latin America. The darker the rum, the richer its flavor; use the darkest rum you can find in this recipe. I'm partial to both Ron Botrán and Bacardi. I generally make pastry in a food processor because it saves time, but you can also make it by hand (see sidebar, page 173). Let this pie cool a bit before slicing so that the filling has time to firm up. Serve it plain or with a scoop of your favorite vanilla ice cream.

½ cup dried cherries

2 tablespoons dark rum

3¼ cups all-purpose flour, divided

1 teaspoon salt

1 cup (2 sticks) unsalted butter, chilled and cut into ½-inch cubes

2 teaspoons white vinegar

4–6 tablespoons iced water

In a small bowl, combine the cherries and the rum; set aside for at least 2 hours, stirring occasionally. In the bowl of a food processor fitted with a metal blade, combine 3 cups of the flour and the salt; pulse for 20 seconds. Add the butter and pulse until the mixture resembles coarse sand. Add the vinegar and pulse for 10 seconds. Gradually add the iced water through the feed tube, pulsing briefly between additions, until the dough begins to hold together. (Press some of the dough between your fingers; if it holds together, it's ready. If it doesn't, add a bit more water and pulse a few more seconds.) Turn the dough out onto a clean surface and divide it in half. Press each half into a disk and wrap tightly in plastic wrap; chill for at least 30 minutes (up to overnight, or freeze for up to 2 months).

6   large Granny Smith apples
      (or other firm apples), peeled,
      cored, and sliced very thinly
⅓   cup white sugar
⅓   cup brown sugar, packed
½   teaspoon ground cinnamon
¼   teaspoon ground cloves
⅛   teaspoon salt
      Grated zest of 1 lemon
1   tablespoon lemon juice
1½ tablespoons unsalted butter,
      cut into tiny pieces

Preheat the oven to 425°F. Let the dough stand at room temperature for 10 minutes, or until it's warm enough to roll. In a large bowl, combine the apples, the remaining ¼ cup flour, the sugar, brown sugar, cinnamon, cloves, and salt. Stir in the lemon zest, lemon juice, and cherries; toss to combine.

On a lightly floured surface, roll out the bottom pastry to a circle 12 inches in diameter. Fit the dough into a 9-inch pie plate and trim the edges to leave a 1-inch overhang. Place the apple mixture in the pastry, mounding it slightly in the center. Dot the filling with butter. Roll out the top pastry, drape it over the filling, and trim the overhang to remove the uneven edges. Fold the top pastry under the bottom one and crimp the edges decoratively. Using a sharp knife, cut steam vents in the top pastry.

Place the pie on a baking sheet and bake for 20 minutes. Reduce the heat to 375°F and bake for 50–60 minutes, or until the filling is bubbly and the crust is golden (if the edges are browning too quickly, cover them loosely with aluminum foil). Transfer the pie to a cooling rack. Cool 45 minutes to 1 hour before serving. *Serves 6-8*

buttermilk ice cream

Buttermilk ice cream is tart, creamy, and absolutely decadent. Lemon zest lends a clean citrus flavor while honey embellishes it with luscious sweetness. You'll need an ice cream maker for this dessert, but it's easy to make. Buttermilk is the liquid left after butter is churned from milk or cream. Today, most commercial buttermilk is made by adding lactic acid to skim milk. Because there is no butter in buttermilk (don't be confused by its name!), this iced dessert is low in fat. In the South, however, it's still possible to find buttermilk with small specks of butter solids—a few escapees—floating in the milky liquid. Buttermilk ice cream is great on its own, but it's particularly delightful when paired with berries.

southern biscuits

The word "biscuit" comes from the Latin *bis* (twice) and *coctus* (cooked), an origin reflected in similar terms in several languages. Italian *biscotti*, for instance, are cookies that are baked, sliced, and then toasted. In modern-day England, a biscuit is a cracker or a cookie; in Spanish, the term *biscocho* means cookie or small cake.

The ancient Romans carried crackerlike biscuits on their expeditions and called them stone bread because of their long shelf life; Prussians ate something similar called *zwieback*. Southern-style biscuits likely originated in Europe.

In colonial times, before leavening agents were available, Southerners made beaten biscuits, which got their name from the fact that the dough (made of flour, butter, and milk or water) had to be beaten for a long time with a mallet until malleable enough to be rolled thinly and cut. The biscuits are hard and flat—like crackers and last a good while before getting stale They're served cold

3 cups buttermilk
½ cup honey
1 teaspoon vanilla extract
  Grated zest of 1 lemon

In a large, nonreactive bowl, combine the buttermilk, honey, vanilla extract, and lemon zest. Stir well, cover, and chill for 1 hour. Transfer the buttermilk mixture to an ice cream maker and freeze, according the manufacturer's directions, for 20–30 minutes, or to soft-serve consistency. Transfer to a freezer-safe container; cover and freeze for at least 2 hours before serving. *Serves 8*

with thin slices of ham. Beaten biscuits are no longer easy to find in the South; very few people make them, perhaps because they require so much work.

The accessibility of leavening agents in the nineteenth century transformed Southern biscuits into the light and flaky breads we have come to recognize today. Southerners make two kinds: raised biscuits and angel biscuits. The raised kind are made with flour, salt, baking powder, fat (lard, shortening or butter, or a mixture of the three) and milk or buttermilk; they're flaky, tender, and light. Angel biscuits are made with baking powder and yeast, which makes them fluffy. The flour of the South, which is planted in the fall and harvested in winter, is naturally low in protein (*gluten*) and produces softer, lighter biscuits than those made with all-purpose flour. Southern cooks often use self-rising flour, which is all-purpose flour mixed with baking powder and salt.

cajeta bread pudding

There is no denying that Southerners and Latinos share a penchant for sweets, and if there is any dessert worth saving room for, it's this warm, comforting bread pudding. Rich, luxurious custard soaks humble day-old bread, transforming it as it bakes into a spongy, creamy, and sweet dessert. Its crowning glory is a topping of thick caramel and crunchy pecans that take this pudding over the edge. Decadent, yet easy to re-create, it's made with inexpensive ingredients. Cajeta is the sweet caramel sauce of Mexico that is made by cooking sweetened goat's milk until it's gooey, sticky, and absolutely irresistible. It's easy to find in supermarkets and Latin tiendas. Dulce de leche, which is made of sweetened cow's milk, can be substituted in this recipe. Serve this with a cup of cafecito or tea.

1 day-old French baguette, cut into 1-inch pieces (about 7 cups)
4 eggs, at room temperature
3½ cups heavy whipping cream
⅓ cup cajeta *quemada* or cajeta *vainilla* (see note)
¼ cup dark brown sugar, packed
1 teaspoon ground Mexican cinnamon (canela)
1 teaspoon vanilla extract
¼ teaspoon salt
2 tablespoons unsalted butter
1 cup cajeta (for topping)
1½ cups toasted pecan halves
Powdered sugar (for garnish)

Place the cubed bread in a large bowl. In a separate bowl, whisk together the eggs, cream, cajeta, brown sugar, cinnamon, vanilla, and salt until the sugar has dissolved and the mixture is smooth. Pour the custard over the bread and press the bread down with a spatula so that all of it's coated. Cover with plastic wrap and chill for 1½ to 2 hours, or until all of the liquid has been absorbed by the bread.

Preheat the oven to 350°F. Butter a 13 × 9 × 2-inch baking dish. Pour the bread into the prepared baking dish; dot with butter. Bake for 45–50 minutes, or until a toothpick inserted in the center of the pudding comes out clean. Remove it from the oven and immediately drizzle with the remaining cajeta and top with the pecans. Cool for 15 minutes before cutting into squares. Sprinkle with powdered sugar and serve. *Serves 10*

NOTE: Cajeta comes in different flavors, and any of them will work in this recipe; I prefer to use the quemada ("burnt"), which has the deepest color and caramel flavor or the vainilla (vanilla) flavor.

chile-chocolate brownies

These decadent bars have a rich, moist, and dense texture. The luxurious taste of choc-olate will meet your taste buds and the sweetness will seduce your senses. Then slowly the slight heat of chiles will spread across your tongue and surprise you with a tingling sensation. The combination of chocolate and chiles gives the well-known mole poblano of Mexico and the mole de plátano of Guatemala their distinctive flavor. And here, fruity ancho chiles are a perfect match for rich, dark chocolate. The meaty pecans lend an unmistakable Southern touch. These are "grown-up" goodies. Make a batch without chiles for the kids.

1 cup (2 sticks) unsalted butter
6 ounces unsweetened chocolate
2 cups sugar
4 eggs, at room temperature
1½ teaspoons vanilla
¾ cup all-purpose flour
1¼ teaspoons ancho chile powder
½ teaspoon salt
1 cup chopped and toasted pecans (optional)

FOR THE GLAZE
¼ cup confectioners' sugar, sifted
2 tablespoons cocoa powder
2 tablespoons unsalted butter, melted
1 tablespoon coffee-flavored liqueur
½ teaspoon vanilla
¼ teaspoon chipotle chile powder

Preheat the oven to 350°F. Butter a 13 × 9 × 2-inch baking pan. Place the butter and chocolate in the top of a double boiler and heat over low heat, stirring occasionally, until they have melted and are well combined. Lift the bowl carefully from the pan so no water droplets come into contact with the chocolate mixture; let cool for 5 minutes and transfer to a large bowl. Stir in the sugar; add the eggs one at a time, beating well after each addition; stir in the vanilla. In a medium bowl, whisk together the flour, ancho chile powder, and salt; gradually add the dry ingre-dients to the chocolate mixture, beating well until fully combined. Add the pecans. Pour the batter into the pre-pared pan and bake for 30–35 minutes, or until the center is set and the brownies begin to pull back from the sides of the pan. Cool brownies for 1 hour in the pan.

To make the glaze: In a medium bowl, combine the confectioners' sugar, cocoa powder, butter, liqueur, vanil-la, and chile powder; blend until smooth. Place the glaze in a pastry bag (or zip-top bag with a snipped corner), and drizzle back and forth over the brownies. Cut them into 20 bars. *Makes 20 brownies*

buttermilk: southerners' secret ingredient

Buttermilk is an important staple in Southern cuisine. It gives biscuits and cornbread their delicious tang, tenderizes fried chicken, and adds creaminess to dressings. European settlers brought cattle and the ability to produce dairy products to North America. However, before refrigeration, the natural sugars in milk (lactose) caused it to sour quickly. This meant that only a few Americans could enjoy it, particularly so in the South where the climate is often warm. Buttermilk, however, lasted a few days, which made it very popular, predominantly during colonial times and up to the beginning of the twentieth century.

Natural buttermilk is the watery residue that results after cream is churned into butter. Contrary to what many believe—and perhaps the confusion is due to its name—buttermilk does not contain any butter and in fact, has less than 2 percent fat content. Cultured buttermilk, which is what we find in grocery stores today, is made by adding lactic acid to skim or low-fat milk, which produces its tangy flavor. Commercial buttermilk consists mainly of water—a whopping 90–92 percent—and only a small percent of lactose, which makes it easier for lactose intolerant people to digest. Cultured buttermilk also happens to be thicker than natural buttermilk and can be used in baking as a substitute for milk. Not only does it add depth of flavor to baked goods; it also reacts with batters that contain baking soda, acting as a leavening and helping them to rise properly. It also acts as an emulsifier, a stabilizer that helps join two seemingly incompatible solutions—like water and oil—that don't combine naturally. It's an ideal ingredient for creamy salad dressings, particularly since it does not add any fat content to the formula, and yields a smooth, luxurious texture. If you don't have buttermilk on hand for a recipe, substitute an equal amount of low-fat yogurt.

coconut flan

This smooth and creamy custard drenched in caramel sauce is one of the most ambrosial desserts in the Latin repertoire. Fragrant with the aroma of vanilla, it's infused with rich, silky, coconut milk. This is the first flan I learned to make, and my never-fail recipe is simple to follow. Although there are many ways to make caramel, this easy method is perhaps the safest. It's vital to keep a close watch on the sugar as it melts, since the process occurs quite rapidly. Once the melted sugar turns a caramel color, you'll need to move swiftly—and carefully—to pour it into the prepared dishes because it sets quickly, hardening in a matter of minutes. As if by magic, once the flan is chilled, the caramel is transformed into a supple sauce. Perfectly chilled, this flan is the ideal end to any meal.

1 cup sugar
1 (14-ounce) can sweetened condensed milk
1 (13.5-ounce) can unsweetened coconut milk
5 eggs
1 teaspoon vanilla
Pinch salt

Preheat the oven to 350°F. Line a large, deep roasting pan with a clean, damp kitchen towel. In a large stainless steel skillet, heat the sugar over medium heat. When the sugar has begun to melt and turn a light amber color (about 5–7 minutes), stir with a wooden spoon until it has liquefied and is smooth (about 2–4 minutes). As soon as it reaches a copper (toffee) color, remove it from the heat. Divide the caramel evenly among 8 ramekin dishes and quickly (being careful not to burn yourself with the caramel), swivel each ramekin to cover the base with caramel. Place the ramekins in the prepared pan.

In a blender, combine the condensed milk, coconut milk, eggs, vanilla, and salt; blend on high speed until thoroughly combined (or whisk together in a large bowl until smooth). Pour the custard through a sieve into the ramekins, filling them almost to the top. Set the pan on the middle rack of the oven. Pour boiling water into the pan until the water reaches ¾ of the way up the sides of the ramekins. Bake for 30–35 minutes, or until the flan is almost set at the center of the ramekins (it will still wiggle) and the tops are lightly golden; cool at room temperature for 30 minutes. Remove the ramekins from the pan, cover with plastic wrap, and chill completely, at least 2 hours or for up to 3 days.

To serve, use a knife to release the sides of each flan. Invert the ramekins onto individual plates; slide the flat side of the knife under each ramekin and lift gently to break the air seal. The flan should plop into place and the caramel should form a sauce. *Serves 8*

dulce de leche and bourbon crepes

This is the ultimate luxury: tender crepes drenched in bubbly, sweet, and sticky sauce. When milk and sugar are cooked together over very low heat, they're transformed into thick, amber-colored, and gooey caramel. Here, store-bought dulce de leche meets Kentucky bourbon, resulting in a sweet and decadent caramel sauce with attitude. The addition of pecans to this dessert lends a meaty succulence and crunch. During the short-lived empire of Maximilian I, French chefs left indelible marks on Mexican cuisine; among them was the use of crepes in desserts. Throughout the twentieth century, European cultures also shaped the dessert scene of South American countries. Not surprisingly, the pairing of caramel sauces (such as cajeta and dulce de leche) with crepes has become a classic in Latin cuisine. Here, all of these elements come together to produce a delightful dessert.

FOR THE CREPES
Batter for Basic Crepes (page 15)
Grated zest of 1 lemon (optional)
¼ cup unsalted butter, melted

Preheat the oven to 350°F. Butter a 10 × 13 × 2-inch baking pan. If using, add the lemon zest to the crepe batter. Cover the batter and let it sit, undisturbed, for 10 minutes at room temperature.

Heat a shallow, 9-inch nonstick pan (or crepe pan) over medium-high heat; brush lightly with the butter. Ladle ¼ cup of the batter into the hot pan and tilt the pan in a circular motion so the batter covers the base of the pan. Cook for 1 minute on the first side, or until the edges of the crepe start to pull away from the pan. To flip the crepe, tilt the pan so ½ inch of the crepe slides over the side of the pan; with your fingers, hold the edge and carefully turn the crepe over; cook for 15–20 seconds and slide

FOR THE SAUCE

- 2 cups dulce de leche
- ½ cup heavy whipping cream
- ⅓ cup bourbon
- 1 cup roughly chopped pecans, toasted

it onto a plate. Stack the rest of the crepes on the plate and cover loosely with aluminum foil while you make the sauce.

In a medium saucepan, heat the dulce de leche and cream over medium heat. Heat, stirring, until smooth; remove the pan from the heat and add the bourbon, stirring well. Return the pan to the heat and stir for 2 minutes; remove from heat. Transfer ½ of the sauce to a large, deep plate; cool slightly.

Working with one crepe at a time, dip the crepe into the dulce de leche sauce on the plate; fold it in half, then in half again to form a wedge shape. Place the crepes, slightly overlapping, in the prepared baking dish (add more sauce to the plate, as needed). When all of the crepes are folded and in the dish, pour any remaining sauce (in the plate and the saucepan) over the top of the crepes and sprinkle with the toasted pecans; bake for 20–25 minutes, or until the sauce is bubbly; cool for 5 minutes before serving. Serve them plain or with a scoop of vanilla ice cream. *Serves 6*

empanadas de viento (sweet vidalia pies)

Many Latin American countries prepare a version of delectable baked or fried turnovers. This version is traditional to Ecuador. Elegant morsels, crumbly and delicate, they're said to be made of air (*viento*). Vidalia onions, which are native to Georgia, are grown in sandy, low-sulfur soil that allows them to develop honeyed layers of flavor. Here, a generous coating of crunchy sugar on the pastries enhances the onion's natural sweetness, turning these little pies into crispy and sweet delights. Why include a recipe with onions in the dessert chapter? Try them and you'll understand. Too sugary to serve as appetizers, I like to serve them as part of a dessert cheese tray composed of seasonal fruit, a mix of creamy, blue, and sharp cheeses, and quince or guava paste. Paired with an ice (dessert) wine or with champagne, they make an elegant end to any meal. But be careful! They're addictive.

2 cups all-purpose flour
¼ teaspoon salt
1 (8-ounce) package cream
   cheese, cubed and chilled
½ cup (1 stick) unsalted butter,
   cubed and chilled
1 teaspoon apple cider vinegar
2¾ cups grated queso fresco
   (or Monterey Jack)
¾ cup minced Vidalia onion
   Egg wash made with 1 beaten
      egg and 1 tablespoon water
   Vegetable oil for frying
2 cups sugar

NOTE: When re-rolling pastry, shape it into a disk and let it rest 10 minutes before rolling out. These freeze beautifully. Freeze the uncooked empanadas on a baking sheet in a single layer until solid and then transfer them to freezer bags; store in the freezer for up to 1 month. They can go directly from freezer to fryer without thawing. Roll in sugar as directed after frying. Make these larger, if you wish; adjust the frying time accordingly.

In the bowl of a food processor fitted with a metal blade, combine the flour and salt and pulse 2–3 times. Add the cream cheese, butter, and vinegar and pulse until the dough comes together to form a ball (about 2–3 minutes). Turn the dough onto a clean surface and divide it in half. Press each half into a disk and wrap tightly in plastic wrap; chill for at least 1 hour or up to 24 hours. (You can freeze the dough for up to 2 months; thaw it in the refrigerator before proceeding with the recipe.)

In a medium bowl, combine the cheese and onion and blend well; set aside in the refrigerator.

On a lightly floured surface, roll out the pastry to ⅛-inch thickness (as you would a pie crust). Using a 2½-inch round cookie cutter, cut out pastry rounds; keep the rounds covered with a clean kitchen towel as you work to prevent them from drying out. Re-roll the dough as necessary to make more rounds until you have 48 (see note). Working with a few pastry rounds at a time, moisten the edges with the egg wash; place 1 teaspoon of filling in the center of each round and fold the pastry in half over the filling. Seal the joined edges well by pressing them together with the tines of a fork and transfer to a baking sheet (keeping them covered with a clean kitchen towel as you work); when completed, refrigerate, uncovered, for 1 hour.

Fit a large baking sheet with a metal cooling rack. Place the sugar in a shallow bowl; set aside. In a large skillet with high sides, heat 2–3 inches of oil to 360°F (or use a deep fryer according to the manufacturer's instructions). Working in batches, carefully slide the empanadas into the oil and fry for 2–3 minutes, or until golden brown, turning them over halfway through. Using a slotted spoon, transfer the empanadas to the prepared cooling rack; cool for 1 minute. While still warm, roll them in the sugar (use a gentle touch—they're fragile), coating all sides. Return them to the rack and cool slightly before serving. These are best eaten fresh, but they will keep in an airtight container for up to 24 hours. *Makes 48 empanadas (4–6 per person)*

guava layer cake with cream cheese frosting

Fluffy and sweet icing tops this soft cake filled with tropical fruit jam. From caramel cakes and jam cakes, to chocolate cakes and apple stack cakes, layered cakes have long been a tradition in the South. Church bake sales and fund-raising dinners are sure to feature at least a handful of meticulously frosted and delicately layered cakes. My own version features flavors I know well: the classic marriage of guava and cream cheese, so beloved by Cubans and widely popular in South Miami. Guavas, or *guayabas*, which are grown throughout the Latin tropics, taste a lot like strawberries. Candied guava shells are traditionally served with cream cheese, which tempers the sweetness of the fruit. Here, I use guava jelly, available in most grocery stores. The cake base is a snap to make, so it's ideal for novice bakers.

FOR THE CAKE

- 2¼ cups self-rising flour
- 1 teaspoon baking powder
- 1 cup (2 sticks) unsalted butter, at room temperature
- 1 cup sugar
- 4 eggs, at room temperature
- 1 teaspoon vanilla extract
- 1¼ cups guava jelly

FOR THE FROSTING

- 1 (8-ounce) package cream cheese, at room temperature
- ½ cup (1 stick) unsalted butter, at room temperature
- 2½ cups confectioners' sugar, sifted
- 1 teaspoon vanilla extract

Preheat the oven to 350°F. Butter two 8-inch round cake pans; line the bottom of the pans with parchment paper and butter the parchment. Sift together the flour and baking powder into the bowl of an electric mixer; add the butter, sugar, eggs, and vanilla. Beat on low speed until combined. Increase the speed to medium and beat for 3 minutes, or until the batter is light, fluffy, and very pale yellow (or beat for 5 minutes by hand). Divide the batter into the prepared pans and bake for 35–40 minutes, or until a toothpick inserted in the center of the cakes comes out clean. Cool the cakes in the pans for 5 minutes. Loosen the cakes from the sides of the pans with a knife, then invert them onto cooling racks; peel off the parchment paper and turn them right side up to cool completely.

In the meantime, make the frosting: In a large bowl of an electric mixer, beat the cream cheese and butter together until smooth, about 1–2 minutes (or beat by hand using a wooden spatula for about 2–3 minutes). Gradually add the confectioner's sugar, beating until smooth; stir in the vanilla, cover, and set aside.

COOK'S TIP: To slice cakes into layers easily, freeze them for about 25 minutes beforehand.

Using a serrated knife, carefully slice each cake into 2 even layers. Place the top half of a cake, top side down, on a platter. Spread ⅓ of the guava jelly evenly over it. Put the bottom half of the cake, cut side down on top of the bottom layer and spread on the second ⅓ of the jelly. Place the bottom half of the other cake on the second layer, cut side up, and spread on the remaining jelly. Top with the remaining layer, top side up. Ice the sides and top of the cake with the cream cheese frosting; chill the cake for 1 hour or up to 24 hours before serving. *Serves 8–10*

magdalena

Practicality is vital to simple entertaining, and this Latin American pound cake, called a Magdalena, is an ideal treat to serve to unexpected guests along with a cafecito or a glass of iced tea. It has a fine and buttery crumb with comforting hints of orange and vanilla. Its name derives from French madeleines, the dainty cakes shaped like seashells. Typically made with citrus and dried fruit (usually raisins), this cake is ideal for dunking into steamy café con leche or pairing with fruit sorbet. My version freezes beautifully and thaws quickly on the kitchen counter. In keeping with Southern tradition, I serve it with fresh strawberries and cream.

FOR THE CAKE

- 3 cups all-purpose flour
- 2½ teaspoons baking powder
- ¼ teaspoon salt
- 1 cup (2 sticks) unsalted butter, at room temperature
- 1½ cups sugar
- 3 eggs, at room temperature
- Grated zest of 1 orange (about 3½ teaspoons)
- 2 tablespoons orange juice
- 1½ teaspoons vanilla extract
- 1 cup whole milk
- 1 pint strawberries, washed and sliced
- 2 tablespoons sugar
- 2 tablespoons orange liqueur

FOR ORANGE WHIPPED CREAM

- 1 cup chilled heavy whipping cream
- 2 tablespoons confectioners' sugar
- 1 tablespoon grated orange zest

Preheat the oven to 350°F. Butter and flour a Bundt cake pan or a 9-inch springform pan. Sift together the flour, baking powder, and salt into a large bowl; set aside. With an electric mixer, beat the butter and sugar on medium speed until light and fluffy (3–4 minutes), stopping to scrape down the sides of the bowl occasionally. Add the eggs, one at a time, beating well after each addition; add the orange zest, orange juice, and vanilla; beat well. With the mixer on low speed, add a third of the flour mixture and beat until combined; blend in half of the milk. Add another third of the flour mixture and half of the milk and blend well. Add the rest of the flour mixture and blend just until combined (don't overmix). Pour the batter into the prepared pan and bake for 45–50 minutes, or until a toothpick inserted in the center of the cake comes out clean. Transfer the cake to a cooling rack. Cool for 10 minutes; unmold and cool completely.

In a medium bowl, combine the strawberries, sugar, and liqueur; set aside for 10 minutes. In a large bowl, using an electric mixer or a whisk, whip the cream while gradually adding the confectioners' sugar until soft peaks form; fold in the orange zest. Serve the cake with the berries and whipped cream. *Serves 10–12*

mango, peach, and tequila cobbler

Ask a Southerner what the ultimate summer dessert is and the answer is likely to be peach or blueberry cobbler. Here, I merge the tropical flavor of mangoes with sweet freestone peaches. (When the summer heat reaches its peak, freestone peaches, as the name implies, loosen their stones, which makes them much easier to slice neatly.) I add a splash of bold tequila and sweeten the cobbler with piloncillo (unrefined whole cane sugar). The result is a sweet, juicy, and bubbly dessert. Southerners can have very passionate debates about what kind of crust is best. It usually boils down to what their mothers made. Some are made with a rolled-dough crust that allows the fruit juices to break through, but I fancy a dropped biscuit topping that resembles cobblestones. In the South, peaches are in season from June through September. Avoid using overly ripened mangoes in this recipe. Look for mangoes that yield to the touch but are not mushy. Serve with a scoop of Buttermilk Ice Cream (page 226).

FOR THE FILLING

5 cups peeled, pitted, and sliced
   peaches (fresh or frozen and
   thawed) (see cook's tip, page 33)
4 cups peeled, seeded, and cubed
   mango (see cook's tip, page 32)
2 tablespoons white sugar
2 tablespoons grated piloncillo
   or packed brown sugar
2 tablespoons tequila
   (Reposado preferred)
2 tablespoons cornstarch
   Grated zest of 1 lime
2 teaspoons lime juice
¼ teaspoon allspice

FOR THE TOPPING

2½ cups self-rising flour
2 tablespoons sugar
½ teaspoon salt
¼ cup lard or shortening
1¼ cups cold buttermilk
1 tablespoon unsalted butter,
   melted
1 tablespoon coarse, sparkling
   sugar (optional)

Preheat the oven to 450°F. In a large bowl, toss together the peaches, mango, white sugar, piloncillo, tequila, cornstarch, lime zest, lime juice, and allspice. Spread the fruit in a 13 × 9 × 2-inch baking dish and set aside.

In a large bowl, whisk together the flour, sugar, and salt. Using a pastry blender (or 2 knives), cut the lard into the flour mixture until it resembles coarse sand (a few slightly larger lumps are okay). Add the buttermilk and stir until well combined (the dough will be sticky and loose). Using an ice cream scoop or spoon, drop the dough over the filling. Brush the dough with melted butter and sprinkle with sparkling sugar. Bake for 35–40 minutes, or until the filling is bubbly and the topping is golden brown. *Serves 8–10*

new southern-latino lime pie

A blanket of sweet, tart custard sits over buttery, crumb crust in this creamy dessert featuring the lively flavors of citrus. Spanish conquerors introduced citrus fruits to the Americas (including oranges into Florida, which proved to be an ideal habitat for their cultivation). Although the highly acidic key lime is found throughout Latin America, the Persian lime, which is most commonly found in the grocery store, and other varieties are featured more prominently in Latin cuisine. The lemon is virtually unknown in Latin America. Based on the Florida key lime pie, this dessert combines the mild acidity of lemons with the gutsy tanginess of limes. Egg whites add an airy consistency to the custard. This refreshing pie needs to chill fully before it can be served. Plan to make it early on the day or even the night before you serve it.

1½ cups graham cracker crumbs
¼ cup sugar
1 cup unsalted butter, melted
1 (14-ounce) can sweetened condensed milk
Grated zest of 3 lemons
Grated zest of 3 limes
¼ cup lemon juice
¼ cup lime juice
2 eggs, at room temperature, separated
1 cup heavy whipping cream
1 tablespoon confectioners' sugar
Thin slices of lemon and lime, for garnish

Preheat the oven to 325°F. In a small bowl, combine the graham cracker crumbs, sugar, and butter. Press the crumb mixture into the bottom and up the sides of a 9-inch pie plate. In a medium bowl, combine the condensed milk, lemon zest, lime zest, lemon juice, lime juice, and egg yolks; blend until the mixture has thickened slightly. In a separate bowl, with an electric mixer or a whisk, whip the egg whites until stiff peaks form. Using a rubber spatula, gently fold one-third of the yolk mixture (custard base) into the egg whites. Fold in the rest of the custard base. Pour the filling into the prepared pie crust and smooth the top. Bake for 15 minutes, or until the filling is barely firm (it will still jiggle a bit in the center; it will firm up as it cools). Cool completely on a wire rack. Chill, uncovered, for at least 3 hours (or up to overnight) before serving.

Up to 1 hour before serving, whip the cream. In a large bowl, using an electric mixer or a whisk, whip the cream while gradually adding the confectioners' sugar until soft peaks form. Place the cream in a pastry bag and pipe it decoratively around the rim of the pie; garnish with alternate slices of lemon and lime. *Serves 6-8*

new world chocolate cake

It's hard to resist a slice of this moist, dark, and dense cake, particularly when served with a glass of milk or a cup of coffee brewed from beans from the highlands of Antigua, Guatemala. The importance of cacao to the Mayan and Aztec civilizations has been widely documented. Lauded for its nutritional value, a bitter chocolate drink made with chiles was heralded for its aphrodisiac powers. Cacao beans were the first currency of the New World, so valuable that edible chocolate concoctions were often reserved for royalty. Its bitter taste made it a hard sell in Europe until sugar was added. Oaxacan nuns are credited with adding cinnamon and vanilla, flavorings still used to make Mexican drinking chocolate today. The intoxicating amalgamation of chocolate and spices is delicious here. This richly aromatic cake will keep for a few days—if you can bear it.

5 ounces unsweetened chocolate, chopped
¼ cup coffee liqueur
1¾ cups warm tap water (not boiling)
2 cups all-purpose flour
¼ cup finely ground almonds
1 teaspoon baking soda
½ teaspoon ground cinnamon
¼ teaspoon salt

Preheat the oven to 350°F. Butter the bottom and sides of a 10-inch springform pan, line the bottom with parchment paper, and butter the paper. Combine the chocolate, coffee liqueur, and water in the top of a double boiler and heat over low heat, stirring often, until the chocolate is melted; set aside to cool for 8 minutes. In a medium bowl, combine the flour, almonds, baking soda, cinnamon, and salt; set aside. Using an electric mixer, cream the butter and the sugars until fluffy, about 2 minutes. Add the

1 cup (2 sticks) unsalted butter,
    at room temperature
1 cup sugar
1 cup brown sugar
2 eggs, at room temperature
1 teaspoon vanilla extract
    Confectioners' sugar
    (for garnish)

eggs, one at a time, beating well after each addition; add the vanilla and beat on low to combine. Alternately add the dry ingredients and the chocolate mixture to the egg mixture (beginning and ending with the dry ingredients), beating well after each addition. Pour the batter into the prepared pan. Bake for 60–65 minutes, or until a toothpick inserted in the center of the cake comes out clean and the cake begins to pull away from the sides of the pan. Cool on a wire rack for 10 minutes; remove the sides of the pan and cool completely. Invert the cake to remove the bottom of the pan and the parchment and transfer it, right side up, to a platter; sprinkle liberally with confectioners' sugar. *Serves 8–10*

NOTE: This freezes beautifully for up to 3 months; thaw at room temperature for 1 hour before serving.

peach and bourbon tres leches cake

This dense cake is drowned in a sugary, creamy sauce and is topped with turrón, a gooey, sticky meringue. This newfangled rendition of the Nicaraguan favorite leaves nothing to the imagination. It's composed of three parts: the cake base, the liquid syrup, and the fluffy frosting. The high sugar-to-flour ratio in the cake produces a porous base that absorbs the sauce made with three different milk products (hence the name "three milks cake"). Bourbon and peaches provide the Southern touch. Make this a day ahead so the cake has ample time to soak up the sauce. For Latinos and Southerners, the sweeter the dessert the better, and this one more than fits the bill.

FOR THE CAKE

2½ cups all-purpose flour
1 cup sugar
1 teaspoon baking powder
6 eggs, beaten
¾ cup whole milk
1 teaspoon vanilla

FOR THE THREE MILKS

1 (14-ounce) can sweetened condensed milk
1 (12-ounce) can evaporated milk
¾ cup heavy whipping cream
¼ cup bourbon

FOR THE FROSTING

6 egg whites, at room temperature
Pinch salt
¼ teaspoon cream of tartar
1½ cups sugar
¾ cup water
3½ cups peeled and diced peaches

Preheat the oven to 350°F. Grease a 13 × 9 × 2-inch baking pan. In a large bowl, combine the flour, sugar, and baking powder. In a medium bowl, whisk together the eggs, milk, and vanilla. Add the wet ingredients to the dry ingredients and blend well. Pour the batter into the prepared pan and bake for 40–45 minutes, or until the cake is set in the middle and a toothpick inserted in the center comes out clean (it will be a bit golden around the edges). Cool completely. Using a fork or a skewer, poke holes all over the top of the cake. In a medium bowl, whisk together the condensed milk, evaporated milk, cream, and bourbon. Slowly pour this mixture over the cake—it will eventually absorb all of it. Cover the cake with plastic wrap and chill for at least 4 hours, or until most of the liquid has been absorbed (overnight works best).

To make the *turrón*: Using an electric mixer, beat the egg whites, salt, and cream of tartar on high speed until soft peaks form (about 3 minutes); set aside.

In a medium heavy-bottomed saucepan, combine the sugar and water; cook over medium-high heat for 15–20 minutes, or until it reaches the soft-ball stage, or 238°F on a candy thermometer. To prevent the sugar from crystallizing, as the sugar melts, use a pastry brush to brush the inside of the pan with additional water (keep a small bowl of water next to the stove as you work) but don't stir or the mixture will crystallize, forcing you to start again. Watch it carefully: this sugar mixture can go from the soft-ball stage to the hard-ball stage in no time. Remove the pan from the heat.

Begin beating the egg whites again on high speed and, slowly, add the hot sugar syrup in a thin stream until all is incorporated. Continue beating until the mixture is cool, stiff, and shiny (about 6 minutes).

To assemble the cake, layer the diced peaches all over the top and frost generously with the *turrón*. Chill well, for up to 4 days, until ready to serve. *Serves 10-12*

pecan rum cake with figs

Every bite of this rich, sweet cake—a cross between the rum cake I enjoyed as a child and the famous fig cake made on Okracoke Island, North Carolina—delivers the exotic taste of figs and spices and a satisfying crunch of pecans. If you don't want to make your own fig preserves, use store-bought ones instead (see note). Since cake flour, which produces a lighter crumb, is not readily available in Latin America, it's common to use cornstarch in cakes. Most of the rum will evaporate during baking, leaving only its rich essence behind; be sure to use the darkest rum that you can find. The addition of mayonnaise—a favorite ingredient in the South—keeps the cake moist as it bakes. If you love figs as much as I do, you may want to serve the cake topped with extra preserves.

1½ cups all-purpose flour
1 cup cornstarch
2 teaspoons baking powder
½ teaspoon allspice
¼ teaspoon salt
1 cup (2 sticks) unsalted butter, at room temperature
1 cup sugar
6 eggs, at room temperature
⅓ cup dark rum
1 teaspoon vanilla extract
2 tablespoons mayonnaise
½ cup chopped pecans
1¼ cup fig preserves (page 29)
¼ cup confectioners' sugar

Preheat the oven to 350°F. Butter the bottom and sides of a 10-inch springform pan, line the bottom with parchment paper, and butter the paper. Sift the flour, cornstarch, baking powder, allspice, and salt into a large bowl; set aside. Using an electric mixer, beat the butter and sugar on high speed for 2–3 minutes, or until light and fluffy. Add the eggs, one at a time, beating well after each addition, stopping to scrape the sides of the bowl. Turn the mixer to low and add the dry ingredients; blend until well incorporated, stopping occasionally to scrape the sides of the bowl. Add the rum and vanilla and mix until combined. Add the mayonnaise and beat for 30 seconds, or until the mixture is smooth. Stir in the pecans and preserves. Pour the batter into the prepared pan and bake for 50–55 minutes, or until a toothpick inserted in the center of the cake comes out clean and the cake begins to pull away from the sides of the pan. Remove from the oven and cool on a wire rack for 10 minutes; remove the sides of the pan and cool completely. Invert the cake to remove the bottom of the pan and the parchment and transfer it, right side up, onto a platter; sprinkle liberally with confectioners' sugar. *Makes 1 cake (10-12 servings)*

NOTE: You can substitute 1 cup of store-bought preserves for the homemade ones (which are thicker than most you can buy). You can make this cake entirely by hand by beating the batter with a sturdy spatula. If wrapped well, this cake will freeze perfectly for up to 3 months.

pumpkin seed brittle

This traditional Mayan treat popular in Guatemala is sugary and crunchy with a nutty taste that will please anyone with a sweet tooth. In August, Guatemalans celebrate the Feast of the Assumption with enormous fairs (the most famous is held in Jocotenango). My childhood memories of going to la feria include watching the giant procession of the Virgin Mary make its way to the cathedral. I'd sample the typical candies found only at that time of the year, including milk candies, giant, colorful rosaries made out of sugar, and these delightful treats called pepitoria. The addition of sugar is actually a modern touch; the Mayans used only honey to sweeten it.

2 cups raw pumpkin seeds
1¾ cups sugar
¼ cup honey (raw preferred)

Butter a large metal baking pan. Place the pumpkin seeds in a large skillet over medium heat; toast, stirring, until they're golden and puffy, 5–7 minutes. Remove to a plate and cool. In a medium saucepan, combine the sugar and honey and cook, stirring, over medium-high heat until the sugar melts. Reduce the heat to medium and cook, stirring for 8–9 minutes, or until it turns a dark amber color; it should register between 300°F and 310°F on a candy thermometer (or a little of the mixture dropped into iced water will turn hard as glass). Remove from the heat and stir in the seeds. Spread the mixture carefully onto the prepared pan (it will be very hot). Cool completely (about 25 minutes) and break it into pieces. *Serves 6–8*

a brief history of sugar and candy in latin america

Sugar, native to Asia, was introduced to Europeans by the Arabs. Before the colonization of America, sugar was very expensive in Europe and was available only to the rich. It was often used by apothecaries to make bitter medicines more palatable. On his second voyage to the New World in 1493, Christopher Columbus introduced sugar to the Americas via Santo Domingo (then known as La Española), which he discovered was an ideal place for the production of sugarcane. Hernán Cortés would later do the same in Mexico, and Pizarro in Peru. Before the New World was discovered, Genovese and Venetian traders controlled most of the sugar market in Europe and the distribution channels from the Far East. Spaniards coveted the control of the routes from the New World. The Portuguese, who had gained power of the territories of present-day Brazil, ultimately took over the route into Europe through Lisbon. Europeans' consumption of sugar reached new heights when sugar began to be used as a sweetener for coffee and chocolate. Expanding the production of sugar and controlling the market became the ultimate goal for Europeans, who, after decimating the indigenous peoples, brought slave laborers to work their plantations from Africa, continuing what had been a bitter period of bloodshed and violence. Sugar quickly captivated the palates of the Novo-Hispanic and the indigenous alike, all of whom began producing everything from rum to desserts and candies. Spaniards inherited techniques necessary for the confection of candy from the Moors. During the colonial period in Latin America, nuns were often put in charge of producing candy (*dulces típicos y confecciones*). For a long time they held on to the secrets of candy making and kept the art of confections within convent walls, where it was passed down for generations.

squash and chile cake
with cayenne and ancho chile icing

This unusual cake is moist, spongy, speckled with delicious spice, and suitable for a special occasion. The addition of chiles to desserts is not as far-fetched as you may think, and here they add a peppery bite but not too much of a kick. Ancho chiles, which are dried poblano peppers, are among the sweetest dried chile varieties used in Latin America. To me, they taste like a mixture of chocolate and raisins. I often use butternut squash, known as zapallo in many South American countries, in place of pumpkin in recipes for soups, muffins, and casseroles, but my favorite use is in this unique cake. If you're a novice baker, you'll love this recipe that comes together quickly. It's easy, impressive, and different.

FOR THE CAKE

1 small butternut squash
    (1–1½ pounds)
2¼ cups all-purpose flour
½ cup sugar
¼ cup brown sugar, packed
2 teaspoons baking powder
½ teaspoon baking soda
1 teaspoon ancho chile powder
¼ teaspoon salt
½ cup (1 stick) butter, melted
2 eggs, at room temperature
1 cup whole milk

FOR THE ICING

⅓ cup brown sugar, packed
1 teaspoon ancho chile powder
¼ teaspoon cayenne pepper
¼ cup heavy whipping cream

Preheat the oven to 400°F. Line a baking sheet with parchment paper. Cut the butternut squash in half lengthwise, remove the seeds, and place it cut side down on the baking sheet; bake for 40–45 minutes, or until soft. Scoop out the flesh into a small bowl and mash until smooth; set aside.

Butter the bottom and sides of a 10-inch springform pan, line the bottom with parchment paper, and butter the paper. In a large bowl, whisk together the flour, sugar, brown sugar, baking powder, baking soda, ancho chile powder, and salt. In a separate bowl, combine the butter, eggs, milk, and squash. Add the wet ingredients to the dry ingredients and blend until there are no lumps in the batter; don't overmix. Pour the batter into the prepared pan and bake for 35–40 minutes, or until a toothpick inserted in the center of the cake comes out clean. Remove from the oven and cool on a wire rack for 15 minutes; remove the sides of the pan and cool completely. Invert the cake to remove the bottom of the pan and the parchment and transfer the cake, right side up, to a platter.

For the icing, in a small bowl, combine the brown sugar, chile powder, cayenne, and cream; drizzle over the cake.

Serves 8-10

sweet corn ice cream with hot praline sauce

If you like caramel corn, you'll love this creamy, cool summer dessert. The ice cream is delicate and lightly sweetened and a praline sauce gives it a delightful crunch. Fresh corn is shucked off the cobs and churned with creamy custard until thickened. The result is a lightly textured ice cream that melts sensuously in your mouth. Latinos are known for making ice cream out of everything from avocados to papaya, and it's not uncommon to find corn ice cream in coastal towns throughout Mesoamerica. The French introduced pralines to Louisiana. Pecans, native to the South, took the place of almonds traditionally used by Europeans. Corn syrup and brown sugar make the sauce gooey, sweet, and deliciously sticky. Serve it for your next Fourth of July celebration or Latin Heritage Month Fiesta.

FOR THE ICE CREAM

- 3 cups fresh corn kernels
- 1 cup heavy whipping cream
- 1½ cups whole milk
- 1 (14-ounce) can sweetened condensed milk
-   3-inch piece Mexican cinnamon stick (canela)
- ¾ cup sugar
- 5 egg yolks
- 1 teaspoon vanilla extract

FOR THE SAUCE

- 1 cup heavy whipping cream
- 1 cup dark brown sugar, packed
- 1 cup light corn syrup
- ⅓ cup unsalted butter
- 1 teaspoon vanilla
- ⅛ teaspoon salt
- ¾ cup toasted pecans

Begin the ice cream a day before you plan to serve it or early in the day. In the bowl of a food processor (or in a blender), combine the corn, cream, and milk; process for 3–4 minutes, or until smooth. In a large saucepan, heat the mixture over medium heat; stir in the condensed milk and cinnamon. Cook, stirring occasionally, until it comes to a simmer, about 8–10 minutes. In the meantime, in a large bowl, whisk together the sugar and egg yolks until thickened and a pale yellow color, about 2 minutes (or use an electric mixer and beat for 1 minute). Remove the pan from the heat. While whisking vigorously (or with the electric mixer running), ladle ½ cup of the hot corn mixture in a thin stream into the eggs. Add another ½ cup of the corn mixture to the eggs whisking continuously, then add an additional cup. Whisk the egg and corn mixture into the remaining corn mixture in the pan. Return the pan to the stove and cook the mixture over low heat, stirring constantly, until the custard thickens (it should coat the back of a spoon), about 12–14 minutes. Discard the cinnamon stick. Remove the pan from the heat and stir in the vanilla; pour the custard into a large bowl and

247

cool for 10 minutes. Place a sheet of parchment paper directly over the custard to prevent it from forming a skin; cover the bowl with plastic wrap and chill for at least 4 hours (or overnight).

Transfer the custard to an ice cream maker and freeze, according to the manufacturer's directions, for 20–30 minutes, or to soft-serve consistency. Transfer the ice cream to a freezer-safe container, cover, and freeze for at least 4 hours or up to 1 week.

For the sauce, in a large saucepan, combine the cream, brown sugar, corn syrup, butter, vanilla, and salt and cook over medium heat until it comes to a boil. Cook for 10 minutes (it will bubble madly), stirring constantly. Remove the pan from the heat and stir in the pecans; cool slightly.

Scoop the ice cream into bowls, top with warm sauce, and serve immediately. *Serves 10*

sweet potato churros

Light and fluffy, these deliciously tempting bits of fried dough embellished with cinnamon are the perfect pastry to enjoy for breakfast, whether they're simply sprinkled with powdered sugar or dipped into thick chocolate sauce. Churros were introduced to the Americas by the Spaniards. Unlike the beignets New Orleans is famous for, which are traditionally made with yeast, churros are made with choux pastry (used to make éclairs and cream puffs). Churros are sold throughout Latin America, usually wrapped in paper bags to help absorb excess fat and to keep them crunchy. Here, sweet potato puree adds both succulence and a beautiful, golden color without making them heavy. For this recipe, you'll need a good-quality cookie press (or sturdy pastry bag) fitted with a large star tip.

FOR THE CHURROS

2 cups all-purpose flour

¾ teaspoons salt

1 tablespoon plus ½ teaspoon
   ground cinnamon, divided

¼ cup vegetable oil

3 eggs, at room temperature

¾ cup mashed sweet potato

2 cups superfine sugar

FOR THE CHOCOLATE SAUCE

1 cup heavy whipping cream

12 ounces chopped semisweet
   chocolate

Fit a large baking sheet with a metal cooling rack. In a medium bowl, whisk together the flour, salt, and ½ teaspoon cinnamon; put the mixture through a sifter 3 times. Bring 2 cups of water to a boil in a medium saucepan; add the ¼ cup of oil and the flour mixture, stirring quickly with a wooden spoon until the dough is smooth. Transfer the dough to the bowl of an electric mixer and beat for 1 minute on high (or transfer the dough to a large bowl and beat for 3 minutes by hand) to cool it slightly (this is so that the eggs don't scramble). Add the eggs, one at a time, beating well after each addition (the dough will break apart with each addition, then will re-emulsify when it's ready to take another egg). Add the mashed sweet potato and blend well. Cover the dough and let it rest for 10 minutes, or until cool enough to handle.

In a large baking pan, combine the superfine sugar and remaining cinnamon; set aside. In a large skillet with high sides, heat 3 inches of oil to 360°F (or use a deep fryer according to the manufacturer's directions). Working in batches, fill a cookie press (or sturdy pastry bag) fitted with a large star tip with the dough and pipe it directly into the oil in strips 7–8 inches long. Fry the churros, a few at a time (it's important not to crowd them) until golden brown (about 2–3 minutes total) turning once or twice. Using a slotted spoon, transfer the churros to the prepared cooling rack to drain. While still hot, roll them in the cinnamon-sugar mixture. (See sidebar, page 25, for how to keep fried foods warm.)

To make the chocolate sauce: In a small saucepan, bring the cream to a gentle boil; stir in the chocolate and remove from heat. Let it rest for 5 minutes and then stir until smooth. Serve the churros warm or at room temperature with the chocolate sauce on the side. *Serves 8-10*

the love apple of the americas

Contrary to what many think, the tomato is not native to Italy. A native to the Andes in South America, it was first domesticated by the Mayans in Central America in pre-Columbian times. How it traveled that far before it became a comestible fruit is not known; it's believed to have traveled with prehistoric natives from Peru. By the time Spanish *conquistadores* reached Mexico and Guatemala, they found that tomatoes were already part of the Aztec and Mayan diets. They were used to make salsas called *moli* (or mixture) featuring chiles and ground pepitas (pumpkin seeds). Spanish colonizers took the tomato, which is a member of the nightshade family, back to Europe, where it was believed to be poisonous. The first records of tomatoes indicate that they were used only for ornamental purposes. The French named them *pommes d'amour*: love apples. Although there are records that date tomato consumption in Italy back to the fourteenth century, it took several centuries before tomatoes were consumed in England. By 1550, tomatoes were widely grown in southern Italy, where they became a staple of the region's cuisine. Spanish colonists introduced tomatoes to the Southern United States via Florida, and English settlers brought them to North and South Carolina. By 1780, Thomas Jefferson was cultivating tomatoes in Virginia.

Culinary uses of tomatoes vary greatly. In the South they're often stuffed with cold salads and served as appetizers or main courses; transformed into jams, relishes, and chutneys; or used as fillings for pies and tarts and as the base of red rice. Most famously, they're eaten between two slices of white bread slathered in mayonnaise. In Latin America they're used most famously in pico de gallo (chunky tomato salsa), as well as in stews, called *guisos*, and refreshing salads. In the 1980s, tomato salsa began outselling tomato ketchup in the United States.

sweet tomato cobbler

This gooey dessert made with grape tomatoes and unrefined sugar, known as panela or piloncillo, is sublime. Southern cobblers are often made with peaches or blueberries. Tomatoes, which technically are fruits, are surprisingly well suited for this comforting dessert. Tomatoes develop an intoxicating sweetness when they're cooked in sugary syrup. Your guests will be hard-pressed to figure out what they are, since they look and taste like plump cherries. You can make the filling up to one week in advance. The pastry can also be prepared ahead of time and chilled (or frozen), until ready to use.

2 pounds grape tomatoes
1 cup granulated sugar
1 cup grated piloncillo (or brown sugar), packed
1 cup finely diced Vidalia onion
1 stick Mexican cinnamon (canela)
2 tablespoons grated lemon zest
¼ teaspoon ground cloves
¼ teaspoon ground allspice
 Pinch of salt
2 cups all-purpose flour
1 teaspoon salt
½ cup (1 stick) unsalted butter, cut into ½-inch dice and chilled
1 teaspoon white vinegar
4–6 tablespoons iced water
2 tablespoons heavy whipping cream

In a 2-quart, heavy-bottomed nonreactive saucepan, combine the tomatoes, sugar, and piloncillo. Cook over medium-high heat for 15 minutes, stirring occasionally, until the sugars have melted. Add the onions, cinnamon, lemon zest, cloves, allspice, and salt and cook for another 15 minutes (it should bubble madly). Reduce the heat to medium-low and cook for 20–25 minutes, or until it has thickened to the consistency of jam (the time will depend on how juicy the tomatoes are); set aside to cool.

In the bowl of a food processor fitted with a metal blade, combine the flour and salt; pulse for 10 seconds. Add the butter and pulse until the mixture resembles coarse sand. Add the vinegar and pulse to incorporate; add the water, 1 tablespoon at a time, pulsing after each addition, until the dough holds together. (Press some of the dough between your fingers; if it holds together, it's ready; if it doesn't, add a bit more water and pulse a few more seconds.) Turn the dough out onto a clean surface and press it into a disk. Wrap it tightly in plastic wrap and chill for 1 hour (or freeze for up to 3 months).

Preheat the oven to 375°F. Butter the bottom of an 8-inch pie plate. Roll out the dough into a 12-inch circle; using a pastry wheel or a sharp paring knife, cut the dough widthwise into ½-inch strips. Transfer the tomato mixture to the prepared pan. Lay half of the strips of dough across the top of the filling in one direction, then turn the pan and place the remaining strips across the others. Trim off the excess dough with scissors, crimp the edges, and brush the dough with the cream. Place the cobbler on a baking sheet and bake for 30–35 minutes, or until the crust is golden and the filling is bubbly. *Serves 6–8*

glossary

Acarajés Brazilian black-eyed pea fritters.

Achiote seeds from the annatto tree; used to add color and flavor to Latin dishes.

Adobar to marinate.

Adobo tomato sauce with garlic, onions, and vinegar used to preserve chiles; also the name of a spice mixture used in Puerto Rico and the Latin Caribbean.

Ají(es) South American term for chile.

Ají amarillo South American long, yellow chile used in the cuisines of Peru, Chile, and Ecuador; found fresh, dried, or preserved in jars.

Ají panca Peruvian dark red pepper with fruity and smoky flavors; found dried or in paste form.

Ancho chile a poblano chile that has been ripened and dried; it's red and acidic with a fruity taste with hints of prunes.

Arepa fried, sautéed, or griddled flat-bread traditional to Venezuela and Colombia made from precooked corn flour, with a crispy exterior and soft interior and a texture like polenta or grits.

Arepa flour precooked cornmeal used to make arepas.

Arroz con leche rice pudding.

Buñuelos Latin sweet or savory fritters.

Cafecito term of endearment that implies sharing time over a cup of coffee.

Cajeta Mexican caramel sauce, tradition-ally made with goat's milk and sugar.

Canela Mexican cinnamon; also known as Ceylon cinnamon; widely used in Latin America for desserts and savory cooking, it's sweeter than the cassia variety commonly used in the United States.

Capsaicin the heat-producing compound in chiles that creates a burning sensation on the mouth or skin.

Ceviche fish marinated in citrus juices (traditionally lime, but other citrus may be used).

Chayote a type of squash with mild flavor and native to Mesoamerica; also known as vegetable pears (or mirlitons in Louisiana).

Chiles de árbol small, long, and very hot red chiles; also known as Thai chiles; cayenne can be substituted.

Chiltepín a small, round, very spicy green or red chile, also known as "birds-eye"; find it dried or preserved in jars.

Chipotles smoked jalapeños that can be found dried and sold in bulk or canned and preserved in adobo.

Churros fried strips of dough.

Dulce de leche South American caramel sauce made with cow's milk and sugar.

Escabeche a technique in which vegetables, meat, fish, or fruit are sautéed briefly in oil before an acid (vinegar or citrus) and sweetener are added.

Fiambre Guatemalan composed salad of charcuterie, pickled vegetables, cheese, beans, eggs, and cooked meats, served on the Day of the Dead (November 1); refers to deli meats in South America.

Gremolata a parsley, garlic, and lemon zest condiment.

Guajillo a long, narrow, reddish chile (also known as Mexican chile), commonly used in powder form in sauces, marinades, pastes, and stews.

Huevos rancheros fried eggs topped with spicy tomato sauce.

Loroco an herbaceous, edible flower native to Guatemala, Honduras, and El Salvador. It's usually brined and preserved in jars.

Masa harina the flour that results from nixtamalization (the process in which corn is soaked in lime, then dried and crushed into flour); used to make tortillas, tamales, pupusas, and other Mexican and Central American foods.

Mexican chorizo ground pork seasoned with paprika, garlic, cumin, and other spices, sold raw, sometimes shaped as sausage links or in bulk; not to be confused with Spanish chorizo, which is sold already cooked and cured.

Milanesas breaded cutlets (veal, beef, chicken, pork, or fish).

Mote the term for nixtamalized corn in Peru and other South American countries.

Mulato chile similar to a poblano pepper but darker in color with a spicy flavor that hints of sweetness and chocolate.

Nixtamalization the process in which corn is soaked in lime, then dried and crushed into flour.

Panela unrefined whole cane sugar, typically shaped into cones or disks (also known as papelón, chancaca, rapadura, or piloncillo).

Panes con frijol black bean sandwiches.

Papalinas fried potato chips.

Pasilla pepper a dried chilaca chile; mildly hot to hot, it's frequently used in sauces or rehydrated, stuffed, and fried.

Pastel de choclo Chilean casserole made of layers of spiced beef and chicken and topped with savory corn pudding.

Pepitas pumpkin seeds.

Pico de gallo the classic salsa made with tomatoes, onions, cilantro, and lime juice.

Piloncillo (see Panela)

Pimiento the Spanish term for sweet bell pepper, regardless of color; in the United States, it refers to a boiled, peeled, and brined red bell pepper.

Pino Chilean mixture of ground beef, olives, raisins, and hard-boiled eggs, traditionally used to stuff empanadas.

Piquillo pepper a small, sweet red pepper traditionally grown in northern Spain that has been roasted, peeled, and pre-served in water; similar to the pimiento but is bought whole (not chopped or diced).

Plantain a starchy vegetable resembling a large, green banana that is used for different cooking purposes depending on its stage of ripeness.

Plataninas fried green plantain chips. (also known as *mariquitas*, *chifles*, or *patacones*).

Posole Mexican hominy stew.

Queso fresco fresh, whole-milk cheese that is mild, creamy, and white.

Queso seco a Mexican dried cheese, similar in flavor to Parmesan.

Rocotó a red Peruvian chile with black seeds and a texture similar to that of a pimiento; it's very spicy and available whole in jars or in paste form.

Sofrito base of flavor for Latin dishes; recipes vary but may include onion, garlic, peppers, and tomatoes.

Tamales Latin sweet or savory dumplings wrapped in leaves (banana, corn, or other) and steamed.

Tasso Cajun specialty consisting of lean pork shoulder that is cured and seasoned with spices such as cayenne, chiles, garlic, and filé before being smoked.

Tomatillo a pale green fruit enveloped in a papery, inedible husk, frequently used in salsas and sauces; it's a member of the gooseberry family and a relative of the tomato.

navigating a latin tienda

When I moved to the South in the 1980s, grocery stores offered me a wide variety of quality ingredients. However, when it came to satisfying my cravings for Latin flavors, I was at a loss. Holiday trips to Miami afforded me the opportunity to stock up on some Latin ingredients (particularly Cuban, Venezuelan, and Central American foods). Every few months, I would fly down to visit family in Florida and replenish my low provisions. I carefully planned shopping excursions so that the last thing I did before boarding the plane was to pack up a box of goodies and mail it to my home in North Carolina. By the time I got back, dried beans, annatto seeds, cured chorizo, spices, masa harina, corn husks, coffee, and dulce de leche would welcome me home.

Family members traveling to the United States knew to bring us boxes of canned beans, ground coffee from Antigua, and a bottle (or two) of Guatemala's premium rum, Ron Botrán. Occasional treks to Durham's Wellspring store on Ninth Street allowed me the only opportunity to purchase small Hass avocados, fresh jalapeños, and black beans. Around this time, salsa had become popular and tortilla chips had become as ubiquitous as popcorn. But a Latina girl does not live on chips and salsa alone.

By the time the twentieth century came to a close, Southern supermarkets had already been transformed by the public's demand for international ingredients. Nevertheless, when it came to Latin items, there was still a lot left to be desired. The

one aisle to which Latin food was relegated held mostly processed Tex-Mex concoctions and the stereotypical fare: taco kits, refried beans, pickled chiles, yellow cheese dips, tinned tamales, and enchilada sauces. Thankfully, dried beans, lentils, short-grain rice, and tortillas soon appeared.

In the last decade, Southerners have witnessed the arrival of immigrants from all over Latin America. One of the most dramatic changes can be seen in the commercial landscape of Southern towns and sprawling cities, where countless Latin tiendas have popped up. Latin entrepreneurs are feeding the need of entire communities and opening everything from small, free-standing retail establishments to midsize neighborhood stores and massive superstores filled with all kinds of foods from south of the border.

Interestingly, the stock in these stores varies greatly depending on the nationality of their owners and clientele. The majority of tiendas in the South are owned by and cater to Mexican nationals. A vast number of these, however, supply the legions of Central and South American Latinos who have begun to settle in the South with their traditional foods.

This chapter is a guide to help you find your way around a Latin grocery store. Of course, not all stores will be set up the same way, but some general patterns exist, and these make it possible to shop more efficiently.

Since not all stores are created equal, the first thing you'll have to determine is whether or not the establishment you select has enough traffic to ensure the food is fresh. This is particularly important when dealing with the smaller tiendas. Generally speaking, if a store is often crowded, it's likely that products are restocked regularly. A restaurant attached to a small store is pretty much a guarantee that the products are fresh.

Regardless of size, the second thing you'll need to determine is whether or not the place is clean. If a store is unkempt, smells of insecticide, or is in disarray, it's best to choose another establishment.

Like typical American supermarkets, in addition to food, tiendas carry everything from housewares to paper goods and cleaning supplies, but my focus is on the food sections of the store: produce, meat, bulk, dry goods, bakery, freezer, snacks, preserved foods, and condiments.

Produce section: The quality of a store's produce will indisputably reveal the quality of the store. If it's fresh and abundant, you have hit a gold mine. Most of the time you will be pleasantly surprised by how much lower the price of produce is in a tienda compared to grocery stores. Here you'll find herbs such as cilantro, epazote, and parsley. Tiendas that cater to Caribbean Latinos will also carry *culantro* (the key ingredient in some sofritos). Latin tiendas usually carry several different kinds of squash, tomatoes, tomatillos, bulbous green onions, beets, potatoes, and corn. You will also find lots of fresh chiles such as poblanos, serranos, jalapeños, and habaneros, in addition to fresh banana leaves to wrap tamales, cactus paddles (called *nopales*) for salads, and fresh tamarind pods to infuse drinks. Tropical fruits such as papaya, mangos, avocados, fresh coconut, chico-zapote, passion fruits, yautía, nances, malanga, breadfruit, and plantains are a common sight.

The meat department: This section, for many, makes or breaks the experience of shopping at a Latin tienda, and it's an experience in and of itself, one definitely not for the faint-hearted. Like Southerners, Latinos are used to cooking all parts of an animal—whether chicken, pork, beef, or goat. Packaging and presentation in American supermarkets has long been cleaned up for public consumption. Not so in Latin stores. Don't be taken aback when in place of the typical cuts of meat you find in your local grocery stores, you encounter chicken feet, pig's hooves, cow's liver, kidneys, hearts, pig's ears, oxtail, tripe, whole tongues, sweetbreads, and sometimes the entire head of a hog. These all have an important place in the Latin kitchen. Chicken feet, for instance, are delicious when added to soups; they have a high collagen content that produces thick, gelatinous stock. Pig's ears and snout are traditional ingredients in Brazilian *feiojada*, and beef hearts are a key component of Peruvian *anticuchos* (kabobs).

Latin cuts of meat will also be different from typical American cuts. Among them will be pounded beef cutlets for milanesas and thinly sliced short ribs for asados. Here you will also find fresh chorizos, sometimes more than one variety representing different countries, as well as fatback and precious lard. If you're lucky, you'll also find vats of toasted lard, rendered from fresh *chicharrones* (pork rinds), which are usually deep fried on the premises.

The majority of Latin tiendas won't have a fish department, but some of the larger establishments do. It's always best to inspect seafood before purchasing. I make it a rule to purchase it only as long as the establishment is clean and the owner is willing to let me smell the seafood to ensure freshness. If the product you're looking for is in trays and tightly wrapped in plastic, look elsewhere.

The dairy section has a wide variety of cheeses to offer, usually from different Latin countries. This is where you'll find grating cheeses such as Cotija and queso seco, as well as great melting cheeses like panela, Chihuahua, quesadilla, and asadero. You will probably find different kinds of queso fresco (fresh cheese similar to feta), including queso de capas wrapped in banana leaves. Look out for myriad kinds of crema (similar to crème fraiche), which range from very thick to light; some are tangy, some have a sweet aftertaste, and others are tinged with a golden color because they have additional butterfat. Here is where you'll also find a collection of tortillas (fresh, corn, flour, thick, and thin).

The frozen section of most tiendas offers a huge array of products, from fruit pulps (guava, papaya, tamarind) to frozen sofrito bases. If you can't find fresh banana leaves, you'll find them frozen here. Go to this section if you're looking for black-eyed peas, tamales of all varieties, okra, empanada disks, yuca, *tostones* (plantain chips), and premade arepas and empanadas. You'll be impressed by the variety of processed foods that cater to the Latino palate. If you're really lucky, you'll also find Mexican *paletas*, or frozen pops.

The bulk section is where you want to head to when you're in need of dried chiles such as ancho, chiles de árbol, chipotles, guajillos, and mulatos. The spices you'll find here, such as Mexican oregano, canela, annatto (in all its forms), anise seeds, coriander seeds, cumin, star anise, allspice, cloves, and ground chile powders will jazz up any pantry. I never leave a tienda without bags filled with natural teas such as chamomile (manzanilla), anise, and Rosa de Jamaica (hibiscus flowers).

Chances are that near this section you'll also find a wall stocked with prepackaged bags of the items you will find in the bulk section, but I prefer to select my own, not only because I'm able to inspect the items for freshness but also because it's less expensive to purchase them in bulk than in the little packages. While you're there, add these to your basket: dried corn husks, sesame seeds, pepitas (pumpkin seeds), piloncillo or panela, and Mexican chocolate.

The dry section will be in an aisle in the middle of the store, and here you'll find rice (both long grain and short grain) used for dishes such as asopao and chaufas. Here, too, will be the different kinds of meal and flour you'll need for recipes in this book, including precooked corn flour called harina pan for arepas, masa harina for tortillas, yuca flour for *pão de queijo*, rice flour, cornstarch, and sometimes purple corn flour used to make Peruvian desserts. Oils, condiments, coffee, dried beans, and legumes, and hydrogenated lard are in this section as well.

The preserves section is where you'll find guava, quince, tamarind, mango, and other fruit jellies and fruit pastes. You'll also find myriad varieties of canned chiles here. If the store is frequented by Latin nationals, these will include everything from jars of Mexican chipotles in adobo and escabeches (made with jalapeños, car-

rots, and onions) to Peruvian favorites such as ají amarillo, rocotó, and ají panca, in addition to Guatemalan chiltepines. Salsas, beans, dried soups, grains such as quinoa, and other unusual items such as *chuño* (Andean freeze-dried potatoes), lorocos, and chipilín will also be in this section, in addition to Latin caramel sauces, including cajeta and dulce de leche.

The bakery usually offers Latin cakes, breads, and fresh cookies, most of which are made with lard. Among my favorite breads are Mexican *conchas* (sweet breads shaped like seashells), *mantecados* (lard-based sweet breads ideal to dunk into a cup of coffee), and *pan de huevo* (similar to challah). You may also find *tortas* (great for making sandwiches), *cuernitos* (similar to croissants), all kinds of empanadas, and churros. Depending of the clientele, you may find Cuban bread, *champurradas* (Guatemalan cookies), *bolillos* and *teleras* (sandwich buns), and *pan de agua* (similar to French bread). Cookies may include *alfajores* sandwiched with dulce de leche, Mexican wedding cakes, and *polvorones*. If you happen to be hungry when you visit a tienda, you'll probably have a hard time resisting the bakery section. The same goes for the snacks section, where you'll find all sorts of crackers, chips, and candies. *Arequipes* (rice paper stuffed with dulce de leche) and *maní japonés* (chile encrusted peanuts) are particularly delicious.

I hope that this virtual tour of a Latin tienda makes your trip more enjoyable and makes shopping for ingredients easy and fun.

sources for ingredients

Most of the ingredients that you will need to make the recipes featured in this book are widely available and can be easily found in grocery stores around the country or in the many Latin tiendas that have opened in many neighborhoods around the United States. However, there will be times when you may find it easier to order products online or through mail order. The following are some of my favorite sources and some of the products and ingredients that they are best known for.

Bob's Red Mill
5209 Southeast International Way
Milwaukie, OR 97222
(800) 349-2173
www.bobsredmill.com

Organic quinoa, pepitas, assorted rice, sesame seeds, masa harina, cornmeal, yuca flour (which they call tapioca flour).

Dean & DeLuca
www.deandeluca.com

Spices, herbs, ground chile powders, dulce de leche, Mexican oregano, annatto seeds.

Frieda's
4465 Corporate Center Drive
Los Alamitos, CA 90720
(800) 241-1771
www.friedas.com

Dried chiles (guajillo, ancho, de árbol, pasilla, etc.), plantains, pepitas, banana leaves, corn husks, Mexican cinnamon (canela), piloncillo (or panela).

GOYA Foods

www.goya.com

Mexican, Central, and South American ingredients and condiments, such as masarepa or arepa-harina, canned and frozen yuca, chiltepe, loroco, rocotó peppers, ají amarillo (whole and paste), refried black beans, hominy, sour orange (*naranja agria*), capers, olives, annatto seeds and powders, tamarind frozen concentrate, piloncillo, chipotle chiles in adobo sauce, tortillas, empanada disks, and guava jelly.

La Tienda

Williamsburg, Virginia
(800) 710-4304
www.tienda.com

Although they specialize in products from Spain, they have a great line of what they call "New World products" that includes ají amarillo (whole and paste), rocotó pepper (paste), ají panca (paste), quinoa, and smoked paprika.

Melissa's Produce

www.melissas.com

Dried chiles, including ancho, guajillo, chipotle, chiles de árbol, and pasilla; Mexican cinnamon (canela) and vanilla beans; banana leaves and chayote squash; corn husks; pepitas; piloncillo (or panela); tamarind; and yuca root.

Ocracoke Fish & Seafood Co.

(252) 928-3811

Fig preserves.

Pearson Farms

1102 Highway 341
Fort Valley, Georgia 31030
(888) 423-2374
www.pearsonfarm.com

Georgia pecans, peanuts, peaches, and Vidalia onions.

Penzeys Spices

www.penzeys.com

Great source for spices, including ancho chiles (whole and ground), anise seeds, annatto seeds, chiles de árbol, cayenne pepper, Mexican canela (they call theirs Ceylon soft-stick cinnamon), chipotle, guajillo peppers, coriander, and cumin; also carries vanilla and almond extract.

A Southern Season

University Mall
201 South Estes Drive
Chapel Hill, NC 27514
www.southernseason.com

Grits, self-rising flour, dried chiles, ground chiles, dulce de leche, coconut milk, masa harina, and any and all Southern ingredients you can imagine, including tasso and country ham.

selected reading

The following are some of my favorite books that I've consulted over the years.

Anderson, Jean. *The American Century Cookbook: The Most Popular Recipes of the 20th Century*. New York: Clarkson Potter, 1997.

———. *A Love Affair with Southern Cooking*. New York: HarperCollins, 2007.

Atlanta Cooknotes. [Atlanta]: Junior League of Atlanta, 1982.

Belk, Sarah. *Around the Southern Table*. New York: Simon & Schuster, 1991.

Brooks, Shirley Lomax. *Argentina Cooks! Treasured Recipes from the Nine Regions of Argentina*. New York: Hippocrene Books, 2001.

Conway, Linda G., ed. *Party Receipts from the Charleston Junior League*. Chapel Hill: Algonquin Books, 1993.

Dupree, Nathalie. *Southern Memories: Recipes and Reminiscences*. New York: Potter, 1993.

Egerton, John. *Southern Food: At Home on the Road in History*. Chapel Hill: University of North Carolina Press, 1993.

Fowler, Damon Lee. *Classical Southern Cooking*. Layton, Utah: Gibbs Smith, 2008.

Hamilton, Cherie Y. *Brazil: A Culinary Journey*. New York: Hippocrene Books, 2005.

Henry, Linda. *Heritage of America Cookbook*. Des Moines, Iowa: Better Homes and Garden Books, 1993.

Joachim, David, and Andrew Schloss. *The Science of Good Food*. Toronto: Robert Rose, 2008.

Kennedy, Diana. *The Art of Mexican Cooking*. New York: Clarkson Potter, 1989, 2008.

Kijac, Maria Baez. *The South American Table: The Flavor and Soul of Authentic Home Cooking from Patagonia to Rio de Janeiro, with 450 Recipes*. New York: Harvard Common Press, 2003.

Laurd, Elisabeth. *The Latin American Kitchen: A Book of Essential Ingredients with over 200 Authentic Recipes*. New York: Kyle Books, 2006.

Lovera, Jose E. Rafael. *Food Culture in South America*. New York: Greenwood Press, 2005.

Mintz, Sidney W. *Sweetness and Power: The Place of Sugar in Modern History*. New York: Penguin Press, 1985.

Neal, Bill. *Bill Neal's Southern Cooking*. Chapel Hill: University of North Carolina Press, 1989.

Osteen, Louis. *Louis Osteen's Charleston Cuisine*. New York: Algonquin Books, 1999.

Quintana, Patricia. *Las Fiestas de la Vida en la Cocina Mexicana*. Madrid: Editorial Limusa S.A. De C.V., 1999.

Ramos, Jorge. *The Latino Wave: How Hispanics Will Elect the Next American President*. New York: HarperCollins, 2004.

Rogers, Mara R., Jim Auchmutey, and Susan Puckett. *South the Beautiful Cookbook: Authentic Recipes from the American South*. San Francisco: Collins, 1996.

Sánchez-H., José. *My Mother's Bolivian Kitchen: Recipes and Recollections*. New York: Hippocrene Books, 2005.

Schulz, Phillip S. *America the Beautiful Cookbook*. Alexandria, Va.: Stonehenge Press, 1992.

Smith, Andrew F., ed. *The Oxford Companion to American Food and Drink*. New York: Oxford University Press, 2007.

Toussaint-Samat, Maguelonne. *The History of Food*. Cambridge, Mass.: Blackwell, 1994.

Index

Acarajés (Brazilian fritters), 49
Achiote, 135, 158
   in citrus marinade, 63
   in Yucatán Fish Cartuchos with Maque Choux,
      139–40
Achiote oil, 14
   in Croquetas de Arroz (Rice Fritters), 206
   in Shrimp 'n' Grits, 136
   in Sweet Potato Soup, 163
Adobo, 11–12, 116
   in Latin Smoky Ketchup, 127
   spice-crusted tuna with, 136–37
African cuisine, 216–17
   adobo, 136–37
   benne seeds, 49, 91
   black-eyed peas, 49, 84, 144
   Creole fusion with, 217
   greens, 217, 218
   okra, 158, 162
Agridulce (sweet and sour), 97
Ají amarillo, 12, 88, 211
   heat level index of, 98
Ají panca, 12
Ají rocotó, 12
Ajonjolí (sesame seeds), 91
Albóndigas with Sweet Fire-Roasted Tomato
      Chutney, 110–11

Alfajores (caramel cookies), 223
Allspice, 11
Ancho chile, 11
   Ancho Chile–Cheese Wafers, 44–45
   Cayenne and Ancho Chile Icing, 246
   in Chile-Chocolate Brownies, 229
Anderson, Jean: *The American Century Cookbook*, 71
Andouille sausage
   in Creole Black Bean Soup with Rum, 155–56
   in Nuevo Red Beans and Rice with
      Chiltepín Gremolata, 157
Angel biscuits, 227
Anise, 11
Anise and Rum Strawberry Shortcakes, 222, 223
Annatto
   coloring of, 62
   powder, 61, 62
   seeds, 11, 14, 158
   see also Achiote
Antojitos/Aperitivos. See Appetizers
Appalachian stack cake, 221
Appetizers
   advance preparation and presentation of,
      41, 42–43
   Ancho Chile–Cheese Wafers, 44–45
   Arepitas with Goat Cheese and Green Tomato
      Chutney, 46–47

Avocado and Pimiento Cheese Terrine, 47–48
Black-Eyed Pea Croquettes with Chimichurri-
    Benne Mayonnaise, 49–50
Carrot Escabeche, 50–51
Cheese and Fig Thumbprints, 51–52
Cocktail Chiles Rellenos with Latin Pimiento
    Cheese, 53–54
Crab Croquetas with Latin Tartar Sauce, 55
Crab Dip, 56
Hamburger Sliders with Latin Pimiento Cheese
    and Pico de Gallo, 58
Jalapeño Deviled Eggs, 59
Masa-Encrusted Fried Green Tomatoes with
    Cilantro Crema, 60
Miami Guava and Cream Cheese Empanaditas,
    61–62
Mini Pibil Barbecue Sandwiches, 62–63
Mushroom and Leek Empanaditas, 64–65
New Year's Collard Green Empanadas, 66
Pickled Mushrooms, 67
Pickled Shrimp, 68
Rolled Ham Salad Cake (Pionono), 69–70
Shrimp and Cilantro Mousse, 71
Shrimp Ceviche with Plataninas, 72–73
Spiced Pepitas, 75
Sweet Potato Chips with Spicy Honey, 76
Two-Potato Cakes with Green Butter, 77
Warm Pimiento Cheese Logs, 78
Apple Pie with Rum-Soaked Cherries, 221, 224–25
Arab cuisine
    escabeche, 30, 50, 67, 82, 97
    rice, 199, 201
    sugar, 245
    sweet spices and tomatoes, 145
Arepa (Venezuelan/Colombian flatbread),
    22, 45, 46
Arepa flour, 12, 45, 46, 253
    working with, 47
Arepitas with Goat Cheese and Green Tomato
    Chutney, 46–47
Arequipe (caramel sauce), 221
Argentinian cuisine
    beef, 134

chimichurri, 26, 135
    Italian influence on, 185
Artichoke Fritters, 153–54
Asparagus, Vidalia, and Poblano Soup, 164
Atole (Mayan drink), 159
Avocado
    Avocado and Pimiento Cheese Terrine, 47–48
    Avocado Butter, 21, 77
    Chilled Avocado-Buttermilk Soup with
        Crab Salad Nacho, 150–51
    cutting technique for, 77
    paste (guasacaca), 134
    in Pimiento and Cheese Chilaquiles, 187–88
    purchase/ripening of, 37
    in Romaine, Orange, and Pepita Salad with
        Creamy Serrano Vinaigrette, 99
    Sandra's Ultimate Guacamole, 37
    in Two-Potato Cakes with Green Butter, 77
Aztecs
    cacao, 240
    charred vegetables, 145
    chiles, 145
    mole, 133
    pigs, 126
    tamales, 207
    tomatoes, 250

Bacalao a la vizcaína (Basque dried cod dish), 135
Bacon
    Bacon and Squash Toss, 197
    Bacon, Vidalia, and Chayote Pie, 170–71
    Bacon-Wrapped Pork Tenderloin with Guava and
        Peanut Sauce, 112–13
        Carolina Fried Rice paired with, 198
    in Broccoli Salad with Pepitas and Tamarind-
        Buttermilk Dressing, 85
    Butternut Squash Soup with Chipotle and
        Bacon, 147
    chopping method, 171
    in New Year's Collard Green Empanadas, 66
    in Shrimp 'n' Grits, 135–36
    in Torta de Acelga (Swiss Chard Frittata), 218
    in Yucatán Fish Cartuchos with Maque Choux, 139

Baez Kijac, Maria: *The South American Table*, 18
Baked goods
    buttermilk leavening in, 230
    parchment paper uses for, 78
    Southern biscuits, 20
    see also Breads; Cakes; Cookies; Pastry; Pies
Baking pans, 12
    dark or nonstick vs. light, 224
Baking sheets, 12
Banana leaves
    in pibil barbecue, 62, 63, 64
    working with, 64
Barbacoa. *See* Grilling
Barbecue
    derivation of word, 113, 127
    Mini Pibil Barbecue Sandwiches, 62-64
Basic Crepes, 15
    for Butternut Squash Canelones with Coconut Sauce and Praline Powder, 174-75
    for Dulce de Leche and Bourbon Crepes, 232-33
    for Kale Canelones with Country Ham and Mushrooms, 185-86
Basic Grits, 16
    Shrimp 'n' Grits, 135-36
Basics, 10-37
    Béchamel Sauce, 16-17
    biscuits, 20, 226-27
    buttermilk, 20, 230
    compound butters, 28
    equipment, 12, 13, 25
    pimiento cheese, 35
    pan sizes, 13
    staple ingredients, 11-12
Batata (sweet potato), 76, 163
Batidos (smoothies), 74
Bay leaves, 11
Beans (canned), 12
Beans (dried), presoaking of, 155, 156
Beans and legumes, 143-44
    Braised Lentils, 146
    Creole Black Bean Soup with Rum, 155-56

Green Bean Casserole, 180
    Nuevo Red Beans and Rice with Chiltepín Gremolata, 157
    with rice, 200
    See also Black-eyed peas
Beaten biscuits, 226-27
Béchamel Sauce (Salsa Blanca), 16-17
    in Butternut Squash Canelones with Coconut Sauce and Praline Powder, 174-75
    in Crab Croquetas with Latin Tartar Sauce, 55
    in Kale Canelones with Country Ham and Mushrooms, 185, 186
Beef
    Barbacoa de Carne with Vidalia Onion and Herb Salsa, 113-14
    Beef Carnitas Soft Tacos, 114-15
    Beef Short Ribs with Roasted Tomato and Molasses Gravy, 145
        Coconut Rice paired with, 202
    Cola Brisket with Dried-Chile Gravy, 151-52
    Country Fried Steaks with Cilantro-Lime Gravy, 119-20
    Grits and Pino Casserole, 182-83
    Hamburger Sliders with Latin Pimiento Cheese and Pico de Gallo, 58
    history of, 107, 134
    Latin American specialties, 107, 134
    Rib Eyes with Pimiento Cheese Butter and Chimichurri, 134-35
Beer, 74
Benne seeds (sesame seeds), 49
    Green Mango Salad with Pepita and Benne-Dusted Shrimp, 91-92
    tahini substitute, 49, 50
    toasting method, 92
Best Potato Casserole, 171-72
Beverages, 74
Biscuits
    authentic Southern, 20, 226-27
    Buttermilk and Pork Rind (Chicharrón) Biscuits, 18-19
        Compound Butter paired with, 28
    Chile-Cheese Biscuits, 21

as Mango, Peach, and Tequila Cobbler
        topping, 238
    origin of word, 226
    Anise and Rum Strawberry Shortcakes, 223
Bistecs de palomilla (cube steaks), 119
Black beans, 144
    Creole Black Bean Soup with Rum, 155–56
Black-eyed peas, 144
    Black-Eyed Pea Croquetas with Chimichurri-
        Benne Mayonnaise, 49–50
    Black-Eyed Pea Salad, 84
    rice paired with, 217
Blueberry and Corn Salsa, 131, 132
Boquitas/Botanas. See Appetizers
Bourbon
    Bourbon Gravy, 129, 131
    Dulce de Leche and Bourbon Crepes, 232–33
    Peach and Bourbon Tres Leches Cake,
        241–42
    Pork Tenderloin with Cocoa, Chile, and
        Bourbon Mole, 133–34
Braised dishes
    Beef Short Ribs with Roasted Tomato and
        Molasses Gravy, 144–45
    Braised Lentils, 146
    Chicken and Mango Braise, 149–50
    Cola Brisket with Dried-Chile Gravy, 144, 151–52
    Nuevo Red Beans and Rice with Chiltepín
        Gremolata, 157
    technique, 144
Brazilian cuisine
    adobo, 136–37
    black beans, 144
    cheese bread, 18
    cold drink, 74
    flatbread, 45
    fritters, 49, 253
    grilled beef, 134
Brazilian-Style Cheese and Pimiento Buns, 18
Brazos gitanos (sweet rolled cakes), 69
Breaded cutlets (milanesas)
    Pecan Milanesas with Corn and Blueberry
        Salsa, 131–32

Bread pudding
    Cajeta Bread Pudding, 228
Breads
    Brazilian-style Cheese and Pimiento Buns, 18
    Chile Cornbread, 22
    Latin American flatbreads, 45, 46
    see also Biscuits
Brisket
    Beef Carnitas Soft Tacos, 114–15
    Cola Brisket with Dried-Chile Gravy, 151–52
Broccoli Salad with Pepitas and Tamarind-
        Buttermilk Dressing, 85
Broth
    giblet, 130
    low-sodium (canned), 12
Browning meat, 115
Buñuelos (savory/sweet fritters), 23, 223
Butter
    Chile-Cheese Biscuits with Avocado Butter, 21, 77
    Compound Butter, 28
        Chipotle-Honey Butter, 28
        Pimiento Cheese Butter, 28
    Two-Potato Cakes with Green Butter, 77
    unsalted, 13
Buttermilk, 230
    baking with, 20, 230
    Broccoli Salad with Pepitas and Tamarind-
        Buttermilk Dressing, 85
    Buttermilk and Pork Rind (Chicharrón) Biscuits,
        18–19
        Butternut Squash Soup with Chipotle and Bacon
            paired with, 147
        Compound Butter paired with, 28
    Buttermilk Ice Cream, 226–27
        Fig Preserves paired with, 29
        Mango, Peach, and Tequila Cobbler paired
            with, 238
    in Catfish Soft Tacos with Mango Salsa, 118
    Chilled Avocado-Buttermilk Soup with Crab Salad
        Nacho, 150–51
    history of, 230
    in Latin Fried Chicken with Smoky Ketchup, 125, 126
    types of, 230

Butternut Squash
  Butternut Squash Canelones with Coconut
    Sauce and Praline Powder, 174–75
  Butternut Squash Soup with Chipotle and
    Bacon, 147
  Squash and Chile Cake with Cayenne and
    Ancho Chile Icing, 246

Cacao beans, 240
Caesar salad, 95–96
Cajeta (Mexican caramel sauce), 12, 228, 232
  Cajeta Bread Pudding, 228
Cajun cuisine
  corn stew, 139
  dirty rice, 196
  red beans and rice, 157
  tasso, 186, 256
  trinity (onions, green bell peppers, celery),
    186, 200
Cake pans, 12
Cakes, 220–21
  Guava Layer Cake with Cream Cheese Frosting,
    235–36
  Magdalena (pound cake), 236–37
  New World Chocolate Cake, 240–41
  Peach and Bourbon Tres Leches Cake, 241–42
  Pecan Rum Cake with Figs, 243–44
  Rolled Ham Salad Cake (Pionono), 69–70
  slicing into layers method, 236
  Squash and Chile Cake with Cayenne and
    Ancho Chile Icing, 246
Calabacitas (Mexican squash dish), 197
Calabaza (pumpkin), 194
Camote (sweet potato), 76, 163
Campbell's Soup Company, 165
Candy, 222, 244
  history of, 245
  Pumpkin Seed Brittle, 244
Canela. See Mexican cinnamon
Canelones
  Basic Crepes as basis for, 15
  Butternut Squash Canelones with Coconut Sauce
    and Praline Powder, 174–75

  Kale Canelones with Country Ham and
    Mushrooms, 185–86
Capirinha (Brazilian drink), 74
Capsaicin (chile compound), 98
Caramel corn, 222, 247
Caramelization, 115
Caramelized Chicken, 117–18
  Three-Cheese Grits with Loroco paired with, 216
Caramel Sauce
  in Coconut Flan, 231
  see also Cajeta; Dulce de leche
Cardini, Caesar, 95
Carnitas ("little meats"), 114
  Beef Carnitas with Soft Tacos, 114–15
Carolina Fried Rice, 198
Carolina Inn (Chapel Hill, N.C.), 58
Carolina Mexican Rice, 199
Carrot Escabeche, 50–51
Cartuchos (packages), 139–40
Cassava. See Yuca
Casseroles, 165–91
  Best Potato Casserole, 171–72
  Butternut Squash Canelones with Coconut Sauce
    and Praline Powder, 174–75
  Chicken Enchiladas with Tomatillo Sauce, 176–77
  Coconut, Chayote, and Corn Bake, 178
  containers for, 12
  definition of, 165
  Green Bean Casserole, 180
  Green Rice and Corn Casserole, 181–82
  Grits and Pino Casserole, 182–83
  Hearts of Palm and Rice Casserole, 184
  Kale Canelones with Country Ham and Mushrooms,
    185–86
  Macaroni con Queso, 212
  New Southern-Latino Cornbread Dressing, 186–87
  Pimiento and Cheese Chilaquiles, 187–88
  Squash Enchiladas, 189–90
  Sweet Potato and Plantain Casserole, 191
Catfish Soft Tacos with Mango Salsa, 118–19
Causas (layered potato salads), 81, 93, 94
  Causa Vegetariana (Layered Potato and
    Egg Salad), 94–95

Cayenne
    in Braised Lentils, 146
    heat level index of, 98
    Squash and Chile Cake with Ancho Chile and
        Cayenne Icing, 246
Celery seed, 11
Central American *chirmol*, 134
Central American tortillas, 45
Ceviche
    Shrimp Ceviche with Plataninas, 72–73
Chaufa (Chinese-style fried rice), 198, 201
Chayote, 194, 254
    Bacon, Vidalia, and Chayote Pie, 170–71
    Coconut, Chayote, and Corn Bake, 178
Cheese, 256
    Ancho Chile–Cheese Wafers, 44–45
    in Bacon and Squash Toss, 197
    in Best Potato Casserole, 172
    Brazilian-style Cheese and Pimiento, 18
    Cheese and Fig Thumbprints, 51–52
    in Chicken Enchiladas with Tomatillo Sauce,
        176–77
    Chile-Cheese Biscuits, 21
    in Confetti Corn and Poblano Toss, 204–5
    in Crab Dip, 56
    in Croquetas de Arroz (Rice Fritters), 206
    in Empanadas de Viento (Sweet Vidalia Pies),
        233
    in Fresh Corn Tamales, 208
    in Green Rice and Corn Casserole, 181
    in Grits and Pino Casserole, 183
    in Hearts of Palm and Rice Casserole, 184
    in Huancaína-Style Potatoes, 211
    in Kale Canelones with Country Ham and
        Mushrooms, 185
    Macaroni con Queso, 212
    Pimiento and Cheese Chilaquiles, 187–88
    in Squash Casserole Enchiladas, 189–90
    Three-Cheese Grits with Loroco, 216–17
    tray assortment of, 43
    see also Classic Pimiento Cheese; Cotija
        Cheese; Cream cheese; Goat cheese;
        Latin Pimiento Cheese

Cherries
    Apple Pie with Rum-Soaked Cherries, 224–25
Chicharrón/chicharrones (pork mince/fried
        pork rind), 45
    Buttermilk and Pork Rind (Chicharrón) Biscuits,
        18–19
        Compound Butter paired with, 28
        Creole Black Bean Soup with Rum paired with,
        155
Chicken, 107–8
    Caramelized Chicken, 117–18
    Chicken and Dumplings, 148
    Chicken and Mango Braise, 149–50
    Chicken Enchiladas with Tomatillo Sauce, 176–77
    Chicken livers, in chorizo dirty rice, 200–201
    Drunken Chicken with Muscadine Grapes and
        White Wine, 122–23
    Latin Fried Chicken with Smoky Ketchup, 125–27
    Lime and Chipotle Roast Chicken, 128
    Pecan Milanesas with Corn and Blueberry Salsa,
        131–32
Child, Julia, 121
Chilean cuisine
    palta reina (avocado stuffed with salad), 150
    pastel de choclo (casserole), 182
    pebre (spicy tomato sauce), 134
    pino (ground meat mixture), 182
    wines, 122
Chile paste, 12
Chile powder, 11, 44, 116, 127
    in spicy honey, 76, 214
Chiles, 11–12, 254
    in Caramelized Chicken, 117–18
    Chile-Cheese Biscuits with Avocado Butter, 21
        Sweet Potato Soup paired with, 163
    Chile-Chocolate Brownies, 229
    Chile Cornbread, 22
    Chile Hushpuppies, 23
    Chile Sauce, 189–90
    in Chorizo Dirty Rice, 200–201
    Cocktail Chiles Rellenos with Latin Pimiento
        Cheese, 53–54
    cooking with, 116

dried, 116, 117, 189
  in gravy, 151–52
  pectin in, 116, 117, 151
  reconstituting, 116, 117, 189
  seeding, 116
  toasting, 116
guajillo, 11, 98
guajillo sauce, 189
handling caution, 24, 98, 116
heat adjustment, 211
heat level index of, 98
incremental adding of, 136
in Macaroni con Queso, 212
origin/history of, 98, 102
pickled, 97
Pork Tenderloin with Cocoa, Chile, and
  Bourbon Mole, 133–34
Potato and Yuca Cakes with Chile Honey, 214
planted in garden, 179
preserved, 12, 116
Squash Cake with Cayenne and Ancho Chile
  Icing, 246
Tomatillo Sauce, 176
varieties, 11–12, 98, 116
see also Ancho chile; Chipotle chiles in adobo;
  Jalapeños; Poblanos
Chiles de árbol, 11, 254
  in Shrimp 'n' Grits, 136
Chilled Avocado-Buttermilk Soup with Crab Salad
  Nacho, 150–51
Chiltepín, 12, 254
  handling caution, 24
  heat level index, 98
  Chiltepín Gremolata, 11
  Nuevo Red Beans and Rice with Chiltepín
    Gremolata, 24, 157
Chimichurri
  Chimichurri-Benne Mayonnaise, 49, 50
  Classic Argentinian Chimichurri, 26, 135
  Creamy Potato-Leek Soup with Chimichurri and
    Country Ham, 154–55
  Rib Eyes with Pimiento Cheese Butter and
    Chimichurri, 134, 135

Chinese parsley. *See* Cilantro
Chinese-style fried rice, 198, 201
Chipotle chiles in adobo (canned), 11–12, 116, 254
  Butternut Squash Soup with Chipotle and
    Bacon, 147
  Chipotle Honey Butter, 28
  Chipotle-Lime Mayonnaise, 210–11
  in Latin Smoky Ketchup, 127
  in Latin Tartar Sauce, 31
  Lime and Chipotle Roast Chicken, 128
Chirmol (charred tomato salsa), 134
Chitlins, 107
Chocolate
  Chile-Chocolate Brownies, 229
  chocolate sauce, 249
  history of, 240
  in mole poblano, 133, 229
  New World Chocolate Cake, 240–41
Chorizo Dirty Rice, 200–201
  Lime and Chipotle Roast Chicken paired with, 128
Chowders. *See* Soups
Christmas Wreath Salad, 86–87
Churrasco (Brazilian grilled beef), 134
Churros (fried dough strips)
  Sweet Potato Churros, 248–49
Chutney
  Green Tomato Chutney, 30
  Sweet Fire-Roasted Tomato Chutney, 110–11
Cilantro, 121
  Cilantro Crema, 60
  Cilantro-Lime Gravy, 119, 120
  parsley vs., 121
  planted in gardens, 179
  Shrimp and Cilantro Mousse, 71–72
Cinnamon Hushpuppies, 159, 160
Cinnamon stick. *See* Mexican cinnamon
Citrus
  and achiote marinade, 63, 139–40
  ceviches, 72, 254
  drinks infused with, 74
  garlic combination, 180
  introduction into Americas, 239
  see also Limes; Oranges

Classic Argentinean Chimichurri, 26, 135
Classic Pimiento Cheese, 35
   Avocado and Pimiento Cheese Terrine, 47–48
   Pimiento Cheese Butter, 28
   Rib Eyes with Pimiento Cheese Butter and
      Chimichurri with, 35, 134–35
Cobbler, 221
   Mango, Peach, and Tequila Cobbler, 237–38
   Sweet Tomato Cobbler, 251–52
Coca-Cola, 152
Cochinita pibil, 62
Cocina mestiza (Creole fused cuisine), 217
Cocktail Chiles Rellenos with Latin Pimiento
      Cheese, 53–54
Coconut
   Butternut Squash Canelones with Coconut
      Sauce and Praline Powder, 174–75
   Coconut, Chayote, and Corn Bake, 178
   coconut flakes, toasting method, 202
   Coconut Flan, 231–32
   coconut milk (canned), 153, 174, 178, 202, 231
   Coconut Rice, 202
      Bacon and Squash Toss paired with, 197
Cola Brisket with Dried-Chile Gravy, 151–52
Cold drinks, 74
Cold foods, seasoning of, 84
Coleslaw, 27
   Mini Pibil Barbecue Sandwiches paired with,
      62, 63
Collard greens
   Collard Greens, Oranges, and Pepita Salad with
      Buttermilk Dressing, 87
   Butternut Squash Soup with Chipotle and
      Bacon paired with, 147
   Collard Green Tamales with Pimiento Sauce,
      203–4
   Pork Tenderloin with Cocoa, Chile, and
      Bourbon Mole paired with, 133
   New Year's Collard Green Empanadas, 66
Columbus, Christopher, 80, 106, 107, 126, 245
Compound Butters, 28
Confetti Corn and Poblano Toss, 204–5
Conquistadores. See Spanish conquistadores

Cookies
   Cheese and Fig Thumbprints, 51–52
   Chile-Chocolate Brownies, 229
Coquito (Puerto Rican eggnog), 74
Coriander, 11, 121
   by-products, 121
   see also Cilantro
Corn, 104
   in Christmas Wreath Salad, 86–87
   Coconut, Chayote, and Corn Bake, 178
   Corn and Poblano Toss, 204–5
   Corn and Blueberry Salsa, 131, 132
   Fresh Corn Tamales, 208–9
   Green Rice and Corn Casserole, 181–82
   history of, 104
   nixtamalization of, 45, 103, 104, 254, 255
   Sweet Corn Ice Cream with Hot Praline Sauce,
      247–48
   Sweet Corn Soup with Cinnamon Hushpuppies,
      159–60
   Two-Corn Salad, 103
   in Yucatán Fish Cartuchos with Maque Choux,
      139–40
Cornbread
   Chile Cornbread, 22
   New Southern-Latino Cornbread Dressing, 186–87
Corn husks, 203, 204, 208–9
   removing/soaking of, 209
Cornmeal, 12
   in Arepitas with Goat Cheese and Green Tomato
      Chutney, 46–47
   as breading, 118, 119–20, 210
   in Chile Hushpuppies, 23, 160
   in Coconut, Chayote, and Corn Bake, 178
   precooked, 22, 45, 46, 47
   see also Hominy; Masa harina
Corn tortillas. See Tortillas
Cortés, Hernán, 106, 107, 126, 245
Cotija cheese
   in Best Potato Casserole, 172
   in Christmas Wreath Salad, 86–87
   in Collard Green Tamales with Pimiento Sauce,
      203–4

in Confetti Corn and Poblano Toss, 204–5

in Croquetas de Arroz (Rice Fritters), 206

in Green Bean Casserole, 180

in Green Rice and Corn Casserole, 181

in Hearts of Palm and Rice Casserole, 184

in Potato and Yuca Cakes with Chile Honey, 214

in Three-Cheese Grits with Loroco, 216–17

Country Fried Steaks with Cilantro-Lime Gravy, 119–20

Three-Cheese Grits with Loroco paired with, 216

Country ham. *See* Ham

Covered dishes. *See* Casseroles

Crab

Crab Cakes Salad with Peaches and Tamarind Vinaigrette, 88–89

Crab Croquetas with Latin Tartar Sauce, 55

Crab Dip, 56

Crab Salad Nacho, 150, 151

Crab Soup with Artichoke Fritters, 153–54

Cream, boiling of, 183

Cream cheese

in New Year's Collard Green Empanadas, 66

Guava Layer Cake with Cream Cheese Frosting, 235–36

Miami Guava and Cream Cheese Empanaditas, 61–62

Creamy Potato-Leek Soup with Chimichurri and Country Ham, 154–55

Creole Black Bean Soup with Rum, 155–56

Creole cuisine

as culinary fusion, 217

flavored gravy, 129

rice dishes, 201

trinity (onions, green bell peppers, celery), 135, 146, 186, 200

Creole mustard, 112

Crepes. *See* Basic Crepes; Canelones

Crook's Corner (Chapel Hill, N.C.), 58

Croquetas. *See* Fritters

Croutons, 95

Crudités platter, 43

Cuban cuisine

guava and cream cheese combination, 235

mojo, 119, 138

Cube steaks, 107

Country Fried Steak with Cilantro-Lime Gravy, 119–20

Cucumbers

Cucumber Pico de Gallo Salad, 89–90

moisture removal from, 89–90

Culinary global exchanges, 102

adobo, 136–37

beef, 107, 134

breaded cutlets, 131

cacao and chocolate, 240

candy, 245

chiles, 98, 102

chutney, 30

citrus fruits, 239

corn, 104

Creole fusion, 201, 217

crepes, 174, 232

escabeches, 30, 50, 67

lentils, 146

molasses, 174

okra, 158, 162, 217

pork, 106–7, 126–27

potatoes, 81, 90, 93

rice, 199, 200, 201

sugar, 245

sweet potatoes, 191

tamales, 207

tomatoes, 250

turkey, 129

Cumin, 11

Cuñapes (Bolivian buns), 18

Curry, Jimmy, 26

Cutlets. *See* Milanesas

Deep fryer, 12. *See also* Frying technique

Desserts

Anise and Rum Strawberry Shortcakes, 223

Apple Pie with Rum-Soaked Cherries, 224–25

Buttermilk Ice Cream, 226–27

Cajeta Bread Pudding, 228

Chile-Chocolate Brownies, 229

Coconut Flan, 231–32

Dulce de Leche and Bourbon Crepes, 232–33
Empanadas de Viento (Sweet Vidalia Pies),
    233–34
Guava Layer Cake with Cream Cheese Frosting,
    235–36
Magdalena, 236–37
Mango, Peach, and Tequila Cobbler, 237–38
New Southern-Latino Lime Pie, 239
New World Chocolate Cake, 240–41
Peach and Bourbon Tres Leches Cake, 241–42
Pecan Rum Cake with Figs, 243–44
Pumpkin Seed Brittle, 244
Squash and Chile Cake with Cayenne and
    Ancho Chile Icing, 246
Sweet Corn Ice Cream with Hot Praline Sauce,
    247–48
Sweet Potato Churros, 248–49
Sweet Tomato Cobbler, 251–52
Dip, crab, 56
Dressing
    New Southern-Latino Cornbread Dressing, 186–87
    stuffing vs., 186
Duke's mayonnaise (brand), 57, 90
Dulce de leche (caramel sauce), 12, 221, 228
    Dulce de Leche and Bourbon Crepes,
        232–33
Dumplings, 143
    Yuca, 148–49
Dutch oven, 13, 25

Ecuadoran empanadas de viento, 233–34
Eggnog, 74
Egg roll wrappers
    as crepe substitute, 186
    as empanada dough substitute, 66
Eggs
    bringing to room temperature, 172
    egg whites
        beating technique, 172, 240
        meringue (turrón) frosting, 242
    Jalapeño Deviled Eggs, 59
    Layered Potato and Egg Salad (Causa
        Vegetariana), 94–95
    peeling hard-boiled, 59
    Torta de Acelga (Swiss Chard Frittata), 218
Ellis, Belinda, 20
El Salvadoran cuisine, 45
Empanadas
    Empanadas de Viento (Sweet Vidalia Pies),
        233–34
    Miami Guava and Cream Cheese Empanaditas,
        61–62
    Mushroom and Leek Empanaditas, 64–65
    New Year's Collard Green Empanadas, 66
    prepackaged dough for, 66
Enchiladas
    Chicken Enchiladas with Tomatillo Sauce, 176–77
    definition of, 189
    Squash Casserole Enchiladas, 189–90
English cucumbers, 89
Ensalada Rusa (Russian Salad), 90–91
Escabeche, 82
    Carrot Escabeche, 50–51
    history/uses of, 30
    Pickled Chiles, 97
    Pickled Mushrooms, 67
    pickled pig's feet, 107
    Pickled Shrimp, 68
    pickling technique, 67, 68
Estofados, 122

Figs
    Cheese and Fig Thumbprints, 51–52
    Fig Preserves, 29
    Pecan Rum Cake with Figs, 243–44
Fish. See Seafood
Flan, 222
    Coconut Flan, 231–32
Flatbreads, 45, 46
Flat iron steak, 113
Flat-leaf parsley. See Parsley, flat-leaf
Flour
    for biscuits, 20
    measuring of, 20
    pre-chilling, 20
    self-rising, 12, 19, 20, 21

types of, 12
  yuca, 12, 18, 45
Franklin, Benjamin, 108
French cuisine, 93, 232
  Béchamel Sauce, 16–17
French fries, 93
French green lentils, 146
Fricassees, 122, 143
Fried Okra with Chipotle-Lime Mayonnaise, 210–11
Fried rice, 198, 201
Fried Sweet Plantains (Maduros), 213
Fried yuca, 136, 137
Frittata, 45
  Torta de Acelga (Swiss Chard Frittata), 218
Fritters
  Artichoke Fritters, 153–54
  Black-Eyed Pea Croquetas with Chimichurri-Benne Mayonnaise, 49–50, 49–50
  Chile Hushpuppies, 23
  Cinnamon Hushpuppies, 159, 160
  Crab Croquetas with Latin Tartar Sauce, 55
  Croquetas de Arroz (Rice Fritters), 205–6
Frosting
  Cayenne and Ancho Chile Icing, 246
  cream cheese, 235, 236
  meringue (turrón), 242
Fruits. See specific types
Frying technique, 25
  temperature adjustment, 76

Gandúles (black-eyed peas), 49
Gardens, Southern-Latino, 179
Garlic-citrus combination, 180
Garlic-Studded Pork, 123–24
Garnishes
  for chicken enchiladas, 177
  for soups, 143, 153, 154
Gelatin molds. See Molded salads
German cuisine
  breaded cutlets, 131
  crepes, 174
  potato salad, 81

Giblet broth, 130
Glaze
  for Chile-Chocolate Brownies, 229
  Whiskey and Tamarind–Glazed Baby Back Ribs, 138
Goat cheese
  Arepitas with Goat Cheese and Green Tomato Chutney, 46, 47
  in Three-Cheese Grits with Loroco, 216, 217
Graham cracker crust, 239
Grapes. See Muscadine grapes
Gravy
  Bourbon Gravy, 129, 131
  Cilantro-Lime Gravy, 119, 120
  Dried-Chile Gravy, 151–52
  Roasted Tomato and Molasses Gravy, 145
  see also Sauces
Green Bean Casserole, 180
  New Southern-Latino Turkey paired with, 129
Green Mango Salad with Pepita and Benne-Dusted Shrimp, 91–92
Green Rice and Corn Casserole, 181–82
Greens, 195, 217, 218
  Kale Canelones with Country ham and Mushrooms, 185–86
  planted in vegetable garden, 179
  shredding method, 66
  Torta de Acelga (Swiss Chard Frittata), 218
  types/cuisine uses of, 162
  see also Collard greens
Gremolata, 254
  chiltepín, 24
Grilling
  Barbacoa de Carne with Vidalia Onion and Herb Salsa, 113–14
    Carolina Fried Rice paired with, 198
  Rib Eyes with Pimiento Cheese Butter and Chimichurri, 134–35
  Spice-Crusted Tuna with Peach Salsa and Yuca Fries, 137
  Whiskey and Tamarind–Glazed Baby Back Ribs, 138

Grits, 12, 104
Basic Grits, 16
Grits and Pino Casserole, 182–83
Shrimp 'n' Grits, 135–36
Three-Cheese Grits with Loroco, 216–17
Ground meat
Albóndigas (meatballs) with Sweet Fire-
Roasted Tomato Chutney, 110–11
Grits and Pino Casserole, 182–83
Hamburger Sliders, 58
Guacamole, 37
Guasacaca (Venezuelan avocado paste), 134
Guatemalan cuisine
candies, 244
coconut, 202
composed salad, 254
tortillas, 45
Guava jelly, 12
Guava and Peanut Sauce, 112–13
Guava Layer Cake with Cream Cheese
Frosting, 235
Miami Guava and Cream Cheese Empanaditas,
61–62
Southern-Latino turkey brushed with, 130
Guisos (stews), 250
Güisquil (chayote), 194
Gumbos, 142, 143, 217

Ham
Creamy Potato-Leek Soup with Chimichurri
and Ham, 154–55
Kale Canelones with Country Ham and
Mushrooms, 185–86
in Macaroni con Queso, 212
Rolled Ham Salad Cake (Pionono), 69–70
Hamburger Sliders with Latin Pimiento Cheese
and Pico de Gallo, 58
Harina pan (precooked cornmeal), 46
Harris, Jessica B.: The Encyclopedia of
Southern Culture, 217
Hearts of Palm and Rice Casserole, 184
Herb-Encrusted Pork Tenderloin, 124–25
Bacon and Squash Toss paired with, 197

Herbs, 11
planted in garden, 179
Vidalia Onion and Herb Salsa, 113–14
see also specific herbs
Hominy, 12, 104
dried or canned, 103
in Sweet Potato Posole, 161
in Two-Corn Summer Salad, 103
see also Grits
Honey
in Buttermilk Ice Cream, 226, 227
Chile Honey, 214
Chipotle-Honey Butter, 28
in Pumpkin Seed Brittle, 244
Spicy Honey, 76
Horchata (beverage), 74
Huancaína-Style Potatoes, 211
Hushpuppies. See Fritters

Ice cream
Buttermilk Ice Cream, 226–27
Sweet Corn Ice Cream with Hot Praline
Sauce, 247–48
Iced tea, 74
Icing. See Frosting
Incas
chiles, 98
potatoes, 93, 94
Irish potato blight, 93
Italian cuisine
as Argentinian influence, 185
milanesas, 131, 255
tomatoes, 250
Italian parsley, cilantro vs., 121

Jalapeños
in Chile Cornbread, 22
in Chile Hushpuppies, 23
in Cilantro-Lime Gravy, 120
heat level index, 98
Jalapeño Deviled Eggs, 59
in Vidalia Onion and Herb Salsa, 114

in Yucatán Fish Cartuchos with Maque
    Choux, 139–40
Jefferson, Thomas, 93, 250
Jelly rolls, 69
Jewish cuisine, 77

Kale Canelones with Country Ham and
    Mushrooms, 185–86
Kennedy, Diana, 37
Ketchup, 125, 126, 127
Key limes, 95, 239

Lard, 62, 107, 114
    in biscuit dough, 20, 223, 227
    in Confetti Corn and Poblano Toss, 204
    pork-fat rendering, 18–19
Latin Fried Chicken with Smoky Ketchup, 125–27
    Black-Eyed Pea Salad paired with, 84
    Coleslaw paired with, 27
    Layered Potato and Egg Salad paired with, 94
Latin Pimiento Cheese, 35
    Cocktail Chiles Rellenos with Latin Pimiento
        Cheese, 53–54
    Hamburger Sliders with Latin Pimiento Cheese
        and Pico de Gallo, 58
    leftover fried green tomato sandwiches with, 60
Latin Tartar Sauce, 31
    Crab Croquetas with, 55
Latkes, 77
Layered Potato and Egg Salad (Causa
    Vegetariana), 94–95
Leeks
    cleaning method, 65
    Creamy Potato-Leek Soup with Chimichurri
        and Country Ham, 154–55
    Mushroom and Leek Empanaditas, 64–65
Lentils
    Braised Lentils, 146
Lettuce, 80, 95–96
Limeade, 74
Limes
    in ceviches, 254
    Chipotle-Lime Mayonnaise, 210–11

Cilantro-Lime Gravy, 119, 120
Lime and Chipotle Roast Chicken, 128
    Chorizo Dirty Rice paired with, 200
    Torta de Acelga paired with, 218
New Southern-Latino Lime Pie, 239–40
Loroco
    Three-Cheese Grits with Loroco, 216–17
Louisiana cuisine
    andouille sausage, 157
    chayote (mirliton), 178, 194
    dirty rice, 196, 200
    gumbos, 142, 143, 217
    see also Cajun cuisine; Creole cuisine

Macaroni con Queso, 212
Maduros (Fried Sweet Plantains), 213
Magdalena (pound cake), 236–37
Main dishes, 106–40. See also Casseroles; Stews
    Albóndigas with Sweet Fire-Roasted Tomato
        Chutney, 110–11
    Bacon-Wrapped Pork Tenderloin with Guava
        and Peanut Sauce, 112–13
    Barbacoa de Carne with Vidalia Onion and
        Herb Salsa, 113–14
    Beef Carnitas Soft Tacos, 114–15
    Caramelized Chicken, 117–18
    Catfish Soft Tacos with Mango Salsa, 118–19
    Country Fried Steaks with Cilantro-Lime Gravy,
        119–20
    Drunken Chicken with Muscadine Grapes and
        White Wine, 122–23
    Garlic-Studded Pork, 123–24
    Herb-Encrusted Pork Tenderloin, 124–25
    Latin Fried Chicken with Smoky Ketchup, 125–27
    Lime and Chipotle Roast Chicken, 128
    New Southern-Latino Turkey with Bourbon Gravy,
        129–31
    Pecan Milanesas with Corn and Blueberry Salsa,
        131–32
    Pork Tenderloin with Cocoa, Chile, and Bourbon
        Mole, 133–34
    Rib Eyes with Pimiento Cheese Butter and
        Chimichurri, 134–35

Shrimp 'n' Grits, 135–36
Spice-Crusted Tuna with Peach Salsa and
    Yuca Fries, 136–37
Whiskey and Tamarind–Glazed Baby Back
    Ribs, 138
Yucatán Fish Cartuchos with Maque Choux,
    139–40
Maize. *See* Corn
Mangoes
    Chicken and Mango Braise, 149–50
    Green Mango Salad with Pepita and Benne-
        Dusted Shrimp, 91–92
    Mango, Peach, and Tequila Cobbler, 237–38
    Mango Salsa, 32
        Catfish Soft Tacos paired with, 118–19
    selection/preparation of, 32, 91, 238
Manioc. *See* Yuca
Marinades
    Chimichurri as, 26
    citrus and achiote, 63, 139–40
    citrus and garlic, 119, 138
    container/procedure for, 63, 123, 125
    garlic and herbs, 125
    for Garlic-Studded Pork, 123
    for Pickled Chiles, 97
Masa-Encrusted Fried Green Tomatoes with
    Cilantro Crema, 60
Masa harina, 12, 254
    in Chile Cornbread, 22
    in Collard Green Tamales, 203, 204
    in Fresh Corn Tamales, 208, 209
Maximilian I, emperor of Mexico, 232
Mayans
    atole drink, 159
    cacao, 240
    candy, 222
    charred vegetables, 145
    chiles, 98
    corn domestication, 104
    pumpkin seed brittle, 244
    tamales, 207
    tomatoes, 250

Meat
    braising method, 144
    browning method, 115
    resting period before cutting, 113
    See also specific cuts and types
Meatballs (Albóndigas) with Sweet Fire-Roasted
    Tomato Chutney, 110–11
Meatloaf, 111
Meringue Frosting (*turrón*), 242
Mexican chile. *See* Guajillo
Mexican cinnamon (canela), 11, 254
    grinding method for, 134
Mexican cuisine, 196
    cajeta (caramel sauce), 228, 232, 253
    calabacitas (squash dish), 197
    chocolate drinks, 240
    Mini Pibil Barbecue Sandwiches, 62–64
    Mod-Mex Caesar Salad with Pecans, 95
    mole poblano, 133, 229
    Pico de Gallo, 34, 250, 255
    posole (stew), 160, 256
    sopas secas (rice or pasta), 199, 212
    tamales, 207
    tortillas, 45
Miami Guava and Cream Cheese Empanaditas,
    61–62
Milanesas (breaded cutlets), 255
    Pecan Milanesas with Corn and Blueberry
        Salsa, 131–32
Mini Pibil Barbecue Sandwiches, 62–64
    Coleslaw paired with, 27
Mint juleps, 74
Mirliton. *See* Chayote
Mississippi Delta tamales, 207
Mod-Mex Caesar Salad with Pecans, 95–96
Mojitos, 74
Mojo, citrus and garlic, 119, 138
Molasses Gravy, 145
Molcajete (mortar and pestle), 37
Molded salads, 80
    Avocado and Pimiento Cheese, 47–48
    Shrimp and Cilantro Mousse, 71–72

Mole, 255
    Cocoa, Chile, and Bourbon Mole, 133–34
Moli. See Salsas
Muffins, chile cornmeal, 23
Mushrooms
    Kale Canelones with Country Ham and
        Mushrooms, 185–86
    Mushroom and Leek Empanaditas, 64–65
    Pickled Mushrooms, 67

Nachos, 151
New Southern-Latino Cornbread Dressing, 186–87
    New Southern-Latino Turkey paired with, 129, 186
New Southern-Latino Lime Pie, 239–40
New Southern-Latino Turkey with Bourbon Gravy,
        129–31
    New Southern-Latino Cornbread Dressing
        paired with, 129, 186–87
New World Chocolate Cake, 240–41
New Year's black-eyed pea and rice tradition, 217
New Year's Collard Green Empanadas, 66
    Black-Eyed Pea Salad paired with, 84
Nixtamalization, 45, 103, 104, 254, 255
Nuevo Red Beans and Rice with Chiltepín
        Gremolata, 157

Okra
    Fried Okra with Chipotle-Lime Mayonnaise, 210–11
    history/uses of, 158, 162, 217
    Shrimp and Okra Asopao, 158
Onions. *See* Vidalia onions
Oranges, 239
    Collard Greens, Oranges, and Pepita Salad with
        Buttermilk Dressing, 83
    as pibil pork barbecue seasoning, 62, 63
    Romaine, Orange, Avocado, and Pepita Salad
        with Creamy Serrano Vinaigrette, 99
    in whipped cream, 237

Palmitos (hearts of palm), 184
Palta reina (avocado filled with creamy salad), 150
Paltas. See Avocados

Pandebono (Colombian bun), 18
Panela (unrefined sugar), 29, 237, 251, 255
Panes con frijol (black bean sandwiches), 255
Papalinas (fried potato chips), 76
Papas a la Huancaína (Peruvian salad), 196, 211
Parchment paper, 78
    fish fillets wrapped in, 139–40
Parmentier, Antoine August, 93
Parsley, cilantro vs., 121
Pasapalos. See Appetizers
Pasilla pepper, 11, 255
Pasta, 212
    squares as crepes substitute, 186
Pastel de choclo (Chilean casserole), 182, 255
Pastry
    for cobbler, 237–38, 251–52
    for empanadas, 61, 64, 65, 234
    making by hand, 173
    making with food processor, 170, 224, 251
    pre-chilling ingredients, 173
    re-rolling method, 234
Peaches
    Crab Cakes Salad with Peaches and Tamarind
        Vinaigrette, 88–89
    Mango, Peach, and Tequila Cobbler, 237–38
    Peach and Bourbon Tres Leches Cake, 241–42
    Peach Salsa, 33
        Spice-Crusted Tuna and Yuca Fries with, 136–37
    selection/peeling of, 33
Peanut and Guava Sauce, 112–13
Pebre (Chilean spicy tomato sauce), 134
Pecan Milanesas with Corn and Blueberry Salsa,
        131–32
Pecan Rum Cake with Figs, 243–44
Pectin, 116, 117, 122, 151
Pellagra, 104
Pepitas (pumpkin seeds), 255
    Broccoli Salad with Pepitas and Tamarind-
        Buttermilk Dressing, 85
    Green Mango Salad with Pepita and Benne-
        Dusted Shrimp, 91–92
    grinding of, 92

Pumpkin Seed Brittle, 244
Romaine, Orange, and Pepita Salad with
    Creamy Serrano Vinaigrette, 99
spiced, 75
toasting of, 85
Peppers
    chiltepín, 12, 24, 98, 254
    handling caution, 24
    piquillo, 53–54, 255
    planted in salsa garden, 179
    see also Chiles; Jalapeños
Persian limes, 239
Peruvian cuisine, 196
    ají amarillo, 12, 88, 98, 211
    causas (layered potato salad), 81, 94
    ceviche, 72
    Chinese influences, 198, 201
    papas a la Huancaína (salad), 196, 211
    potatoes, 81, 93, 94
    sillao (soy sauce), 86
Pibil barbecue sandwiches, 62–64
Picadillos, 58, 182–83
Pickled foods
    Carrot Escabeche, 50
    Pickled Chiles, 97
    Pickled Mushrooms, 67
    pickled pig's feet, 107
    Pickled Shrimp, 68
    technique for, 67, 68
Pickles and relishes, 97
Picnic roast. *See* Pork
Pico de Gallo, 34, 250, 255
    Cucumber Pico de Gallo Salad, 89–90
    Hamburger Sliders with Latin Pimiento Cheese
        and Pico de Gallo, 58
Pies, 221
    Apple Pie with Rum-Soaked Cherries, 224–25
    Bacon, Vidalia, and Chayote Pie, 170–71
    New Southern-Latino Lime Pie, 239–40
Piloncillo (unrefined sugar). *See* Panela
Pimiento and Cheese Chilaquiles, 187–88
Pimiento Cheese. *See* Classic Pimiento Cheese;
    Latin Pimiento Cheese

Pimiento Sauce, 36, 187–88
Pino and Grits Casserole, 182–83
Pinto beans, 144
Piononos (savory rolled cakes), 69
Piquillo peppers, 255
    in Cocktail Chiles Rellenos with Latin Pimiento
        Cheese, 53–54
Pizarro, Francisco, 93, 245
Plantains
    Maduros (Fried Sweet Plantains), 213
    peeling tip, 73
    ripeness stages of, 195, 213
    ripening tip, 191, 213
    Shrimp Ceviche with Plataninas, 72–73
    Sweet Potato and Plantain Casserole, 191
Plataninas. *See* Plantains
Poblanos, 21
    Confetti Corn and Poblano Toss, 204–5
    in Green Rice and Corn Casserole, 181
    heat level index of, 98
    mole, 133, 229
    Potatoes and Poblano Bake, 215
    roasting method, 116
    in Squash Casserole Enchiladas, 189–90
    Vidalia, Poblano, and Asparagus Soup, 164
    see also Ancho chile
Pollo encebollado. See Caramelized Chicken
Ponche (holiday drink), 74
Pork
    baby back ribs in Nuevo Red Beans and Rice
        with Chiltepín Gremolata, 157
    Bacon-Wrapped Tenderloin with Guava and
        Peanut Sauce, 112–13
    Buttermilk and Pork Rind Biscuits, 18–19
    Cajun tasso, 186
    in Creole Black Bean Soup with Rum, 155–56
    Garlic-Studded Pork, 123–24
    Herb-Encrusted Pork Tenderloin, 124–25
    history in the Americas, 106–7, 126–27
    Mini Pibil Barbecue Sandwiches, 62–64
    in New Southern-Latino Cornbread Dressing, 186
    Pork Tenderloin with Cocoa, Chile, and Bourbon
        Mole, 133–34

in Sweet Potato Posole, 160, 161
temperature/cooking time, 125
Whiskey and Tamarind–Glazed Baby Back
    Ribs, 138
see also Ham; Sausage
Pork rinds, 107
    method for making, 18–19
Potatoes, 81, 93
    Best Potato Casserole, 171–72
    Creamy Potato-Leek Soup with Chimichurri
        and Country Ham, 154–55
    in Ensalada Rusa (Russian Salad), 90–91
    history of, 81, 90, 93
    Huancaína-Style Potatoes, 211
    Layered Potato and Egg Salad, 94–95
    Potato and Poblano Bake, 215
    Potato and Yuca Cakes with Chile Honey, 214
    Two-Potato Cakes with Green Butter, 77
Potluck dinners, 166–69, 221. *See also* Casseroles
Poultry, 107–8, 113. *See also* Chicken; Turkey
Pralines, 174
    Butternut Squash Canelones with Coconut Sauce
        and Praline Powder, 174–75
    Hot Praline Sauce, 247, 248
Preheating oven, 13
Preserved chiles, 12, 116
Pumpkins (*calabazas*), 194
Pumpkin seeds. *See* Pepitas
Pupusa (El Salvadoran flatbread), 45

Queso fresco, 256
    in Brazilian-Style Pimiento Buns, 18
Queso seco, 21, 256
Quinoa
    Tomatoes Stuffed with Quinoa Salad, 101

Raised biscuits. *See* Biscuits
Red peppers, 53–54, 255
Relishes, 30, 110–11. *See also* Salsas
Rendered fat, 18–19, 111
Rib Eyes with Pimiento Cheese Butter and
    Chimichurri, 134–35
    Potato and Poblano Bake paired with, 215

Torta de Acelga (Swiss Chard Frittata) paired
    with, 218
Ribs
    Beef Short Ribs with Roasted Tomato and
        Molasses Gravy, 145
    Whiskey and Tamarind–Glazed Baby Back
        Ribs, 138
Rice, 200–201
    and beans combination, 157, 200
    and black-eyed peas combination, 217
    Carolina Fried Rice, 198
    Carolina Mexican Rice, 199
    Chorizo Dirty Rice, 200–201
    Coconut Rice, 202
    fried, Chinese-style, 198, 201
    Croquetas de Arroz (Rice Fritters), 205–6
    Green Rice and Corn Casserole, 181–82
    Hearts of Palm and Rice Casserole, 184
    history of, 199, 200–201
    Nuevo Red Beans and Rice with Chiltepín
        Gremolata, 157
    sautéed in achiote oil, 14
    testing seasoning of, 182
Rocotó, 256
    in Bacon, Vidalia, and Chayote Pie, 170
    heat level index of, 98
Rolled Ham Salad Cake (Pionono), 69–70
Romaine, Orange, Avocado, and Pepita Salad with
    Creamy Serrano Vinaigrette, 99
Rompope (Latin eggnog), 74
Rum
    Anise and Rum Strawberry Shortcakes, 223
    Apple Pie with Rum-Soaked Cherries, 224–25
    Creole Black Bean Soup with Rum, 155–56
    Pecan Rum Cake with Figs, 243
    preferred brands of, 224
Russian Salad (Ensalada Rusa), 90–91

Sage, 11
Salad dressings
    lemon juice, cider vinegar, honey, 101
    lime juice, chipotle chile, cumin, 92
    mayonnaise–sour cream, 91

for Mod-Mex Caesar Salad, 96
soy sauce, molasses, and mayonnaise, 86
Tamarind-Buttermilk Dressing, 85
see also Vinaigrettes
Salads, 80–103
    Avocado and Pimiento Cheese Terrine, 47–48
    Black-Eyed Pea Salad, 84
    Broccoli Salad with Pepitas and Tamarind-
        Buttermilk Dressing, 85
    Carrot Escabeche, 50–51
    Christmas Wreath Salad, 86–87
    Coleslaw, 27
    Collard Greens, Oranges, and Pepita Salad with
        Buttermilk Dressing, 87
    Crab Cakes Salad with Peaches and Tamarind
        Vinaigrette, 88–89
    Cucumber Pico de Gallo Salad, 89–90
    Ensalada Rusa (Russian Salad), 90–91
    Green Mango Salad with Pepita and Benne-
        Dusted Shrimp, 91–92
    Ham Salad, 70
    Layered Potato and Egg Salad (Causa
        Vegetariana), 94–95
    Mod-Mex Caesar Salad with Pecans, 95–96
    Pickled Chiles, 97
    Rolled Ham Cake (Pionono), 69–70
    Romaine, Orange, Avocado, and Pepita Salad
        with Creamy Serrano Vinaigrette, 99
    Russian (Ensalada Rusa), 90–91
    Shrimp and Cilantro Mousse, 71–72
    Shrimp Ceviche with Plataninas, 72–73
    Tomato and Vidalia Salad with Mint
        Vinaigrette, 100
    Tomatoes Stuffed with Quinoa Salad, 101
    Two-Corn Summer Salad, 103
Salpicones (main course salads), 82
Salsa Blanca. See Béchamel Sauce
Salsa garden, 179
Salsas
    Chiltepín Gremolata, 24
    Corn and Blueberry Salsa, 131, 132
    Mango Salsa, 32, 118–19
    Peach Salsa, 33, 136–37

Pico de Gallo, 34, 250
Vidalia Onion and Herb Salsa, 113–14
Sandra's Ultimate Guacamole, 37
Sandwiches
    leftover fried green tomatoes and Latin
        pimiento cheese, 60
    Mini Pibil Barbecue Sandwiches, 62–64
    tomato and mayonnaise, 250
Sauces
    Béchamel Sauce (Salsa Blanca), 16–17
    caramel, 231, 233
    dulce de leche and bourbon sauce,
    Chimichurri, 26, 135
    chocolate, 249
    Cocoa, Chile, and Bourbon Mole, 133–34
    Coconut Sauce, 174, 175
    guajillo chile sauce for Squash Casserole
        Enchiladas, 189
    Guava and Peanut Sauce, 112–13
    Hot Praline Sauce, 247, 248
    Latin Tartar Sauce, 31, 55
    Mojo (citrus and garlic), 119, 138
    Mole, 133
    pectin thickening of, 117, 122, 151
    Pimiento Sauce, 36
    Tomatillo Sauce, 176
    see also Gravy; Salsas
Sausage
    in Albóndigas with Sweet Fire-Roasted
        Tomato Chutney, 110–11
    in Creole Black Bean Soup with Rum, 155, 156
    in Nuevo Red Beans and Rice, 157
Savannah red rice, 199
Scoville, Wilbur, 98
Scuppernong grapes, 122
Seafood, 108
    Catfish Soft Tacos with Mango Salsa, 118–19
    ceviches, 72, 254
    chowders, 143
    Crab Cakes Salad with Peaches and Tamarind
        Vinaigrette, 88–89
    Crab Croquetas with Latin Tartar Sauce, 55
    Crab Dip, 56

Crab Salad Nacho, 150, 151

Crab Soup with Artichoke Fritters, 153–54

Green Mango Salad with Pepita and Benne-Dusted Shrimp, 91–92

Pickled Shrimp, 68

Shrimp and Cilantro Mousse, 71–72

Shrimp and Okra Asopao, 158–59

Shrimp Ceviche with Plataninas, 72–73

Shrimp 'n' Grits, 135–36

Spice-Crusted Tuna with Peach Salsa and Yuca Fries, 136–37

Yucatán Fish Cartuchos with Maque Choux, 139–40

Seasoned butters. *See* Compound Butters

Seasoning

    of cold foods, 84

    rice testing method, 182

    spice adjustment, 211

Serranos

    heat level index of, 98

    vinaigrette, 99

    See also Chiles

Sesame seeds. *See* Benne seeds

Shortbread, 51–52

Shrimp

    Green Mango Salad with Pepita and Benne-Dusted Shrimp, 91–92

    Pickled Shrimp, 68

    Shrimp and Cilantro Mousse, 71–72

    Shrimp and Okra Asopao, 158–59

    Shrimp Ceviche with Plataninas, 72–73

    Shrimp 'n' Grits, 135–36

    stock, 68

Side dishes, 193–218

    Bacon and Squash Toss, 197

    Carolina Fried Rice, 198

    Carolina Mexican Rice, 199

    Chorizo Dirty Rice, 200–201

    Coconut Rice, 202

    Collard Green Tamales with Pimiento Sauce, 203–4

    Confetti Corn and Poblano Toss, 204–5

    Croquetas de Arroz (Rice Fritters), 205–6

    Fresh Corn Tamales, 208–9

    Fried Okra with Chipotle-Lime Mayonnaise, 210–11

    Huancaína-Style Potatoes, 211

    Macaroni con Queso, 212

    Maduros (Fried Sweet Plantains), 213

    Potato and Yuca Cakes with Chile Honey, 214

    Potatoes and Poblano Bake, 215

    Three-Cheese Grits with Loroco, 216–17

    Torta de Acelga (Swiss Chard Frittata), 218

Sillao (soy sauce), 86, 198

Skillets, recommended sizes, 13

Slave food traditions. *See* African cuisine

Smith, Bill, 58

Soda Shop (Davidson, N.C.), 76

Sofrito, 36, 117, 135, 256

Soft tacos. *See* Tortillas

Sopa seca (Mexican rice or pasta dish), 199, 212

Soto, Hernando de, 106, 127

Soups, 142–43

    Butternut Squash Soup with Chipotle and Bacon, 147

    Chilled Avocado-Buttermilk with Crab Salad Nacho, 150–51

    Crab Soup with Artichoke Fritters, 153–54

    Creamy Potato-Leek Soup with Chimichurri and Country Ham, 154–55

    Creole Black Bean Soup with Rum, 155–56

    garnishes for, 143, 153, 154

    Shrimp and Okra Asopao, 158–59

    Sweet Corn Soup with Cinnamon Hushpuppies, 159–60

    Sweet Potato Soup, 163

    Vidalia, Poblano, and Asparagus Soup, 164

Southern Biscuits, 20, 226–27

Soy sauce, 86, 198

Spanish *conquistadores*, 102

    anise seed, 223

    cattle, 58, 134

    chiles, 98

    churros, 248

    citrus fruits, 239

    corn, 104

escabeche, 30, 50, 67
lentils, 146
pickled vegetables, 67
pigs, 106, 107, 126–27, 129
potatoes, 93
rice, 200, 201
sugar, 245
tamales, 207
tamarind, 138
tomatoes, 250
turkeys, 129
Spice-Crusted Tuna with Peach Salsa and
    Yuca Fries, 136–37
Spiced Pepitas, 75
Spices, 11
    adjusting to taste, 211
    grinding method, 137
Spicy Honey, 76
Squash, 174, 194
    Bacon and Squash Toss, 197
    Bacon, Vidalia, and Chayote Pie, 170–71
    Squash Casserole Enchiladas, 189–90
Steak, 107
    Barbacoa de Carne with Vidalia Onion and
        Herb Salsa, 113–14
    Country Fried Steak with Cilantro-Lime Gravy,
        119–20
    Rib Eyes with Pimiento Cheese Butter and
        Chimichurri, 134–35
    steam roasting, 129
Stews, 143–44, 217, 250
    Braised Lentils, 146
    Chicken and Dumplings, 148–49
    Drunken Chicken with Muscadine Grapes and
        White Wine, 122–23
    Nuevo Red Beans and Rice with Chiltepín
        Gremolata, 157
    Shrimp 'n' Grits, 135–36
    Sweet Potato Posole, 160–61
Stone-ground flour, 12
Strawberries
    Anise and Rum Strawberry Shortcakes, 223

Stuffing
    dressing vs., 186
    New Southern-Latino Cornbread Dressing,
        186–87
Sugar
    history of, 245
    see also Panela
Sweet Corn Ice Cream with Hot Praline Sauce,
    247–48
Sweet Corn Soup with Cinnamon Hushpuppies,
    159–60
Sweet potatoes
    culinary uses of, 162
    history of, 191
    Potato and Poblano Bake, 215
    Sweet Potato and Plantain Casserole, 191
    Sweet Potato Chips with Smoky Honey, 76
    Sweet Potato Churros, 248–49
    Sweet Potato Posole, 160–61
    Sweet Potato Soup, 163
    Two-Potato Cakes with Green Butter, 77
Sweet Tomato Cobbler, 251–52
Sweet Vidalia Pies (Empanadas de Viento),
    233–34
Swiss Chard Frittata (Torta de Acelga), 218

Tabasco, heat level index of, 98
Tacos
    Beef Carnitas Soft Tacos, 114–15
    Catfish Soft Tacos with Mango Sauce, 118–19
Tahini
    in Chimichurri-Benne Mayonnaise, 49, 50
Tainos, 113
Tallarines con crema (noodles and cream), 212
Tamales, 168–69, 207, 256
    Collard Green Tamales with Pimiento Sauce,
        203–4
    freezing of, 203, 209
    Fresh Corn Tamales, 208–9
    Grits and Pino Casserole, 182–83
    history/varieties of, 196, 207
    reheating of, 209

Tamarind
    Broccoli Salad with Pepitas and Tamarind-
        Buttermilk Dressing, 85
    Crab Salad with Peaches and Tamarind
        Vinaigrette, 88–89
    history/uses of, 88
    Whiskey and Tamarind–Glazed Baby Back
        Ribs, 138
Tartar Sauce. *See* Latin Tartar Sauce
Tasso, Cajun, 186, 256
Thermometer, instant-read, 12
    for frying oil, 25
Thomas grapes, 122
Three-Cheese Grits with Loroco, 216–17
Tilapia
    Yucatán Fish Cartuchos with Maque Choux, 139–40
Tomatillo Sauce, 176
Tomatoes, 250
    Beef Short Ribs with Fire-Roasted Tomato and
        Molasses Gravy, 145
    blanching method, 100
    culinary uses of, 250
    Green Tomato Chutney, 30
    history of, 250
    Masa-Encrusted Fried Green Tomatoes with
        Cilantro Crema, 60
    peeling method, 100
    Pico de Gallo, 34, 250
    planted in gardens, 179
    sliced as salad, 81
    stuffed, 82, 101
    Sweet Fire-Roasted Tomato Chutney, 110–11
    Sweet Tomato Cobbler, 251–52
    Tomato and Vidalia Salad with Mint
        Vinaigrette, 100
    Tomatoes Stuffed with Quinoa Salad, 101
    Tomato Salsa, 34, 250
Torta de Acelga (Swiss Chard Frittata), 218
Tortas de carne (meat patties), 58
Tortillas
    Beef Carnitas Soft Tacos, 114–15
    Catfish Soft Tacos with Mango Salsa, 118–19
    Chicken Enchiladas with Tomatillo Sauce, 176–77
    chips, 187, 188
    corn vs. flour, 45
    frying technique, 151
    heating method, 115
    nachos, 151
    national varieties of, 45
    Pimiento and Cheese Chilaquiles, 187–88
    Squash Casserole Enchiladas, 189–90
    strips in Christmas Wreath Salad, 86, 87
    Sweet Potato Posole with, 161
Tuna
    Spice-Crusted Tuna with Peach Salsa and
        Yucca Fries, 136–37
Turkey, 108
    New Southern-Latino Turkey with Bourbon
        Gravy, 129–31
Turnovers. *See* Empanadas
Turrón (meringue), 241, 242
Two-Corn Summer Salad, 103
Two-Potato Cakes with Green Butter, 77

Vatinet, Lionel, 20
Vegetable garden, 179
Vegetable oil, 12
Vegetables, 162, 194–96
    charring of, 145
    chutneys, 30
    escabeches, 30, 50–51
    pickled, 67, 82
    see also Salads; *specific types*
Venezuelan cuisine
    arepa (flatbread), 253
    guasacaca (avocado paste), 134
Vidalia onions
    Bacon, Vidalia, and Chayote Pie, 170–71
    Empanadas de Viento (Sweet Vidalia Pies),
        233–34
    Tomato and Vidalia Salad with Mint Vinaigrette,
        100
    Vidalia Onion and Herb Salsa, 113–14
    Vidalia, Poblano, and Asparagus Soup, 164

Vinaigrettes, 83
  for Carrot Escabeche, 50, 51
  citrus, 81
  Creamy Serrano Vinaigrette, 99
  Mint Vinaigrette, 100
  in Pickled Mushrooms, 67
  in Pickled Shrimp, 68
  Tamarind Vinaigrette, 89

Warm Pimiento Cheese Logs, 78
Whipped cream, 13
  on lime pie, 239
  orange, 237
Whiskey and Tamarind-Glazed Baby Back
    Ribs, 138
  Braised Lentils paired with, 146
White cornmeal, 12
Wiener schnitzel, 131

Yellow cornmeal, 12
Yellow squash. *See* Squash
Yuca
  Brazilian-Style Cheese and Pimiento
    Buns, 17
  Chicken and Dumplings, 148–49
  Yuca and Potato Cakes with Chile
    Honey, 214
  Yuca flour, 12, 18, 45
  Yuca Fries, 136, 137
Yucatán Fish Cartuchos with Maque
    Choux, 139–40

Zapallo (butternut squash), 174, 246